CHARLIE SMITH
A MAN AFTER GOD'S OWN HEART

JIM USHER

PRESS

VISION is dissatisfaction with what is,
and a clear grasp of what could be.
It begins in certain instances with indignation over the status quo
and grows in an earnest quest for an alternative.
~Charlie Smith

This Book Is Dedicated To
Visionaries,
who, like Charlie Smith,
endure much in pursuit of the dreams
God places in their hearts,

and to

Their Spouses, Families and Friends,
who both suffer and celebrate along with them.

CONTENTS

RECOMMENDATIONS

Because Charlie loved the poor so much, it seems appropriate to allow their humble voices to be the ones to recommend these stories of his life:

"Charlie was like a father to me. If it were not for him I would still be working in the fields. Charlie loved the poor of Honduras so much because God put His heart in him, and that is how he loved–with the heart of God."
~**Victor**, first truck driver for Heart to Honduras

"For me, he was very special. He never came with his hands empty. He always had things to give." ~**Paola,** Charlie's caretaker during his last days

"Charlie loved me and our community, especially our widows: [my mother] Mercedes, and Magdalena and Rosa. My mother had a lot of gods made of wood. Charlie gave her doctrine and it helped her remove them from her house."
~**Pastor Mario** of Chagüitillos

"Charlie loved us with a true love. Every time he came to our community, we knew it would be another party." ~**Oscar**, campesino

"Charlie gave his best blanket to my mother. He provided clothes for our children and he brought me a guitar." ~**Chilano**, leading village elder

"Charlie was humble and simple and a true Christian. Few men lived like Charlie. He was like a saint. He loved Christians from whatever church and he loved the little children. He is the best person I ever knew. He was my *amigo*."
~**Antonio**, former persecutor of the evangelical church in his village

"I remember Charlie because he would eat with us and walk with us. For me, Charlie did not die. He is in paradise waiting for me. "
~**Suyapa**, simple mother in a village church

"When I was a little boy, Charlie touched my head and gave me a hug. He would feed the children, and that made us healthier. He gave us food but always gave us the word of God. He would bring Christian videos to show us. I still remember a movie with a puppet named Bobo. These movies helped me later when I became a pastor." ~**Joel**, pastor of a church in Colmenas, Honduras

It begins with a character, usually, and once he stands up on his feet and begins to move, all I can do is trot along behind him with a paper and pencil trying to keep up long enough to put down what he says and does.
~William Faulkner

PREFACE

Kentucky thoroughbreds grazed on dew-covered bluegrass as I drove my light green VW alongside their white-fenced pastures that September morning in 1969. I was a seminarian at Asbury in Wilmore, and had accepted an invitation to conduct the morning and evening services at the First Church of God in Lexington. Little did I expect this day to be different from any other. But it turned out to be a day that changed my life forever.

It was the day I first met Charlie Smith.

By noon I had preached the message, prayed the benediction, announced the content of the evening service and begun walking down the aisle to leave the church. Walking toward me with his family was a man who introduced himself as Charlie Smith.

The first thing I sensed about this man was presence. Casually dressed and socially engaging, he was full of life but relaxed. His voice was pleasant, his smile inviting, and his manner exuded confidence. Charlie's round face, accentuated by his emerging baldness, reflected a maturing seriousness about life, but there was a sparkle in his eyes. As we parted, I thought to myself, "This is a person I would like to know better."

That evening I shared a slide program which highlighted my summer sociology assignment ministering at the Salvation Army day camp in Spanish Harlem, and my frequent street encounters with New York's heroin addicts and homeless. It had been a very stretching summer for this Mississippi boy, and my hope was to awaken others to the need for missions that reached beyond the confines of what had previously been my very comfortable, but narrow, world.

After the service, Charlie approached me and offered to share his Peace Corps slides with me, and a lifelong friendship was launched. Our casual friendship deepened as Charlie frequently phoned me, seeking to engage my participation in his latest vision. Two decades later, when I finally acquiesced and joined his work in Honduras, I made a discovery: visionaries have few friends who understand them. They are seeing things that others do not see, thinking thoughts that others cannot think, and as such, they need a supportive friend. A golfer needs a caddie. A dentist needs an assistant. David needed Jonathan. And I realized that I was to fill that role for Charlie for a season.

i

Writing this book was a humbling experience. The project pursued me. It haunted me. It arrested me. Only after a series of events beyond my control did I contemplate its possibility. It was a six-year process, and I often had to remind myself of Charlie's words: "Trust the process."

Charlie was instrumental in birthing two dynamic visions–H.E.A.R.T. and Heart to Honduras. Through the former, people all over the world have been taught how to maintain sustainable lifestyles. Through the latter, hundreds of Central American leaders have been trained to lift others out of their misery and thousands of ordinary North American citizens have been changed by seeing suffering through the lens of poverty. These people and others who will follow need to know the heart and soul of the prime mover of these two visions.

Few people were as gentle and simple as this man. When he first arrived in the rural mountains of Honduras, he came as an American. When he drew his last breath 14 years later, he was a Honduran. He had power and privilege at his disposal, but he gave it away by incarnating himself among the poor. He did this by eating their tortillas, drinking their coffee, playing with their children, and feeling their pain.

His genius was his ability to vision. His visions had staying power. They were people-centered. They were like seeds. Once planted in good soil, they brought forth much fruit.

The more I was around Charlie, the more I was amazed at his ability to vision. Charlie could look at a pig walking inside a dirt-floored, stick-walled house and envision every home in the village with a concrete floor. He could see a tangle of undergrowth and perceive hundreds of homes dotting the hillside, their clay tile roofs resembling miniature Red Roof Inns. He could look into a 12-gallon stainless steel pot and picture it full of rice for a village fiesta. He could envision a medical clinic built where others saw only a hopeless patch of weeds. He could perceive a discipleship school flourishing beneath mango trees when others could only see a steep bank falling away to a tumbling mountain stream.

Even though I was called to undergird him as a supportive friend, it was not within my abilities to understand him. His thoughts were too deep for me, his visions too great. His concepts were too complex, his theories too unconventional. His dreams were in Technicolor–full of imaginative notions, grand designs and a montage of creative plans so large in scope that they left lesser visionaries to dream only in black and white. Many people remained deaf to Charlie's admonitions, but they could not remain callous to his presence.

This remarkable visionary was often as misunderstood as an Old Testament prophet. Visionaries and prophets both live in a world of strange ideas. They are counter-culture and express concepts that threaten the status quo. They are strangers in the night and oddities in the day. Charlie fit the words G.K. Chesterton used to describe one medieval saint: "He was sane. He always hung on to reason by one invisible and indestructible hair. He was not a mere eccentric, because he was always turning toward the center and the heart of the maze; he took the queerest and most zigzag short cuts through the wood, but he was always going home."

In writing this biography, I have chosen to use first person in the chapters that deal with occurrences for which I was present, mostly those in the final third of his life. Charlie and I were very close friends in those years, and though it is a challenge, I have tried to stay objective. I did not want to be guilty of hagiography like writers in the early Middle Ages who wrote the biographies of "saints" with undue reverence, exaggerating their good points and omitting their faults. It is true that the Hondurans saw Charlie as their hero or deliverer, even a "savior" astride a white horse when he came to their villages. This is understandable, for he treated them with dignity and sought to lift them out of their poverty. Yet, I have purposed to include the times when Charlie dismounted and revealed his weaknesses. His daughter Anne-Marie said:

> All I ask is that you not simplify Daddy. He was a complex and deep man.... Please don't make it appear that the organized church, etc., was altogether okay with him. Please don't pretend he didn't enjoy wine and chewing tobacco.... Remember, he was a Democrat. You can show the people who read your work that Christian is not synonymous with Republican.

Charlie launched many projects in his lifetime, but when he died, he had many more spelled out in numerous folders. In fact, there were so many folders in the file cabinets in his storage shed that when his daughter Felicia was going through them after his death, she exclaimed, "If I find another folder labeled 'VISION,' I'm going to scream!"

One "vision" that was unfinished at the time of his passing was the writing of a book he had hoped would include the applied principles of anthropology encapsulated in all the teachings of Jesus. Though I am not capable of writing as he would have written it, I hope this book will in a small way carry out Charlie's dream of setting forth some of the basic principles and values that guided his life.

One day near the end of his life, he and I discussed the possibility of a book about his life, and I asked him what he would call it.

Charlie reflected on the love he had for the little burro, the beast of burden for many Hondurans as well as the animal of choice of Jesus when He humbly rode into Jerusalem on Palm Sunday. Charlie thought about his goal to be a humble burro, carrying the love of Jesus wherever he went. He remembered a saying that he had had printed on a Heart to Honduras ministry T-shirt that contained a bit of unconventional language to startle people out of their conventionalities. Finally, he responded to my question about a title for his autobiography. "I would call it 'I'm an Ass for Jesus. Whose Ass Are You?'" based on Jesus' words in the King James Version of John 12:15.

I hope Charlie will forgive me for not using his preferred title, and I hope the reader will be inspired by Charlie's life story to answer God's call to whatever conventional–or unconventional–ministry He has for you.

JIM USHER
2013

The inscription on the back of this photo reads:
"Charles Smith's Philosophy of Life:
'Get out in the current and hang on to the vine (Jesus)'
Be a branch. Produce fruit.
February 11, 1994"

iv

When you enter a town and it welcomes you, eat whatever is set before you.
~Jesus in Luke 10:8 NLT

Muy Sabroso
Very Delicious

Antonio and his family

Crunch! Charlie Smith was enjoying a bowl of rice and chicken soup with his friend Antonio Rivera in the tiny mountain village of Chagüitillos. But a loud crunch seemed out of place when one was eating soup.

Charlie had become acquainted with Antonio through some development work he was doing in the remote areas of Honduras in Central America. Antonio was a leader in his community and also served as one of the leaders in the local Catholic church. He knew that Charlie was a Protestant, and although Antonio had persecuted the local Protestant church, he had become friends with Charlie and invited him to dinner.

The headquarters of the organization through which these men had met was located several hours from Antonio's home, so accepting this invitation for a meal meant that Charlie and his driver/translator had had to travel all morning. Antonio's simple adobe house was a welcome sight to the men who had to hike the last 15 minutes of the trip and had arrived hungry and thirsty. Antonio's home was surrounded by shade trees and colorful flowers that demonstrated his love of nature and softened the harsh edges of the ever-present poverty.

As the men approached, a smile emerged on Antonio's face that reflected gratitude that Charlie was a guest in his house. Often he would say, "Charlie *es*

v

mi amigo!" The plastic chairs on the porch were soon occupied and a lively conversation ensued. Antonio had a vivacious spirit and an animated personality that was well-matched by Charlie's gregariousness and his translator's enthusiasm. Tied under one of Antonio's trees, the family donkey stood aloof to this noisy interruption of his peace and quiet. A cat positioned herself near Charlie's feet in anticipation of any crumbs that might fall during the ensuing meal. Soon Antonio's wife served bowls of rice and chicken soup that, for Charlie, produced the ominous crunching sound.

Thinking–actually hoping–it might be a small chicken bone, Charlie discreetly reached into his mouth, mindful that neither Antonio nor his wife were looking his way, and pulled out the object. It was a cockroach.

Expressing neither shock nor creating an embarrassing scene, Charlie quietly laid the cockroach on the floor in front of the cat, which quickly and gratefully consumed it. Charlie turned again to his bowl of soup and continued the flow of conversation. He was thankful for his own blessings. He knew this was a special occasion for the Riveras. He realized this chicken was a sacrifice for them to give and that he was an honored guest. How could he not team up with the cat to overcome a difficult social predicament and at the same time show appreciation for the hospitality he was being shown?

Following the meal, Charlie stood up, and as he was leaving, said to his host and hostess, "*Muy sabroso*"–very delicious.

Charlie always modeled the grace of Christ regardless of his audience. Because of his humble spirit and simple lifestyle, the rich and the poor were drawn to him. He was gentle, warm, kind, accepting and forgiving. He was constant–ever displaying a *muy sabroso* attitude.

But a *muy sabroso* attitude defined more than an attitude of gratitude to a poor campesino woman who fed by mistake a cockroach to her honored guest. It defined who he was as a person. It defined how he embraced a simple lifestyle. It defined the way he loved, the grace he extended to the powerless, and his unconditional acceptance of others who were different. It defined his servant-leadership, his values. It defined the ministry of Heart to Honduras.

A *muy sabroso* attitude endeared Charlie to the needy Honduran people. It was how Charlie incarnated himself among them. Because of this Christ-like example fleshed out before them, they followed him as he followed Christ. And many became followers of Christ because Charlie loved them with a *muy sabroso* love.

What shaped this man into one who could remove a cockroach from his mouth without embarrassing his hosts? And what was the fruit of a life lived with such sensitivity to the poor? We begin with the story of the personalities and experiences that formed him and follow with the absorbing journey of his life.

vi

PART ONE

1840 – 1940

Roots

The lines are fallen unto me in pleasant places;
Yea, I have a goodly heritage.
~Psalm 16:6 KJV

1

The Acorn Falls Close to the Tree

THE SMITHS

It's not surprising that Charles Robert Smith became a visionary who wasn't afraid to stand against the status quo. Among Charlie's ancestors were people who exhibited creativity, stood up for justice, and walked out their beliefs in decisive action. There were grandparents who lived close to the earth and others who walked the halls of academia. There were those who challenged human rules and those who discovered the benefits of following God's principles. So many threads of who Charlie became can be traced to the unique DNA of his family tree.

For creativity, we can look at an incident that occurred on the Smith side of the family, when Charlie's great-great-grandparents, John C. and Cynthia Ann Lee Smith, were moving their family across the lower Mississippi River.

Four generations of Smiths:
Frellsen Smith holding son Charlie,
Dr. Charles Wilson Smith,
John Franklin Smith

In 1840, no bridges had yet been built, so John and Cynthia loaded their belongings onto a ferry, which accommodated everything but their cows. The plan was for the cattle to swim over, but, frightened by the rapid current, they resisted entering the water.

Cynthia came up with a creative idea. As the ferry slowly pulled away from shore, Cynthia positioned herself at the edge of the ferry, waving ears of corn before the hungry cattle. The cattle took the bait, waded into the Mississippi and swam across, eyeballing the corn all the way.

With their cattle and other belongings, all of which made it safely across, the family homesteaded in Winn Parish, Louisiana. One hundred years later, Charlie was born in this county, where food cooked either Southern or Cajun style was the centerpiece of gatherings. Throughout his life, he incorporated the concept of food as a drawing card for people, and his cooking always reflected his Louisiana roots.

John Franklin & Lucretia Smith, 1926 with their granddaughter Florine

Out of the union of this homesteading couple was born Charlie's great-grandfather, John Franklin Smith. When John Franklin was a teenager, he fought on the side of the Union in the Civil War, and when the war ended, he married Lucretia Hatten, a girl whose parents owned sixteen slaves and presumably supported the Confederacy. It would appear that this couple had to stand strong, both in fighting for their convictions during the war and later for a marriage across differing points of view. It's easy to see Charlie in the actions of these two ancestors, for he often found himself standing against the tide of public opinion.

Another bit of Charlie can be seen in the actions of the children of John and Lucretia—one of whom was Charlie's grandfather, Charles Wilson Smith. It is told that the children attended a party where games were played, something strictly forbidden by their very conservative Baptist church which was opposed to all forms of worldly entertainment. John and Lucretia were turned out of the church for allowing this. Rebelling against rules, especially those that seemed man-made rather than God-ordained, was definitely a characteristic passed down to Charlie.

There are two important events in the life of Charles Wilson Smith, one of John and Lucretia's rebellious, game-playing, party-going children, which, taken together, later impacted his grandson Charlie. First, as a 4-year-old, Charles Wilson's leg was severely burned, rendering him unable to follow his father in farm work. Because of this, Charles Wilson chose to study medicine, earning his medical degree in 1906. As a compassionate doctor taking care of even those who could not pay, he spent so many hours traveling by buggy during an

4

epidemic that he frequently had to exchange exhausted horses for fresh ones to reach the next home.

But Dr. Smith was a proud man and had no time for religion. At the age of 42, he developed angina and went to the Mayo Clinic for an evaluation. His concerned doctor recommended that he return home and set his affairs in order. This pronouncement forced him to reevaluate the direction of his life. By searching the Bible he came to faith, was healed, and his

Charlie's father Frellsen as a toddler in Dr. C.W. Smith's doctoring buggy

career path changed again–this time to planting churches for the Church of God.[1] A willingness to live sacrificially came to Charlie through this grandfather, and his affiliation with the Church of God, Anderson, is directly traceable to the theology Dr. C.W. Smith developed through his personal Bible study. Even the many hours Charlie spent reading and studying the words of Jesus are a part of the heritage passed down from this grandfather.

Clara, Frellsen, and Dr. C.W. Smith before daughter Florine was born

Dr. Smith and his wife Clara had two children, a boy and a girl, born 14 years apart. The son, Frellsen, became Charlie's father. Frellsen was a dedicated scholar and received university degrees in music and English. He had the privilege of spending one year of post-graduate study at Harvard University, where he studied Shakespeare and Old English. These degrees led him to a teaching position at Northeast Junior College in Monroe, Louisiana, and then to a professorship at Louisiana Tech University, where he remained until he retired.

---

[1] More details are given on the life of Dr. C. W. Smith in Chapter 41, United In Community, on Charlie's theology of the church.

5

THE CARVERS

The Carver side of the family gave Charlie a somewhat different set of DNA. Here is Charlie's description of his mother's pioneering relatives:

The Carvers were people of the earth.... They cleared the land with cross-cut saws and blasted stumps out of the ground with dynamite. They plowed the fields with horses and mules and planted the ground expecting a harvest.... I recall the men rocked back in cane bottom chairs in a semi-circle around the open fire, telling stories, talking about the events of importance. The Carvers were smokers, chewers and dippers. With the fire burning bright, the men would from time to time spit tobacco juice in the fire, often hitting the hot cast iron log holders with a sizzling blast–any evidence of moisture was quickly gone. Even the women had their tobacco vices. Ma Carver dipped snuff. Great-grandmother Morrison smoked a stone pipe.

In 1885, a covered wagon transported the belongings of the first Carver family to homestead in Louisiana. One of the boys bouncing his way to a new life in that rugged wagon was ten-year-old George Robert (Bob) Carver, who became Charlie's grandfather and from whom he received his middle name.

"Patsy" & Bob (Ma & Pa) Carver

Bob apparently grew up to be a responsible young man, evidenced by the fact that by 1899, at the age of 24, he was employed to oversee the farm of a Mr. Morrison. Soon he found himself courting Martha Ann "Patsy" Morrison, the daughter of his employer.

Throughout his marriage to Patsy, Bob Carver was active in the community, the schools, the churches and the Democratic Party. He farmed, bored water wells, owned and operated a sawmill and lumber company, had a road-building operation, and operated two general merchandise stores.

Reading Charlie's maternal aunt Beulah's description of her father's store gives us a glimpse of his personality, and a peek into a gene that was passed down to Charlie:

6

"Mr. Bob" was a favorite among the children. He always had a smile and a kind word for them…and they were sure to leave [his general store] with a bit of candy. He always rewarded their school accomplishments, helped arrange for movies to be shown on weekends in a tent erected on vacant space behind the store [and] occasionally [allowed] the traveling circus to pitch its big top there.

Grandpa Bob Carver was a very generous man, extending credit to needy families who often failed to reimburse him. Pastors who visited his store often left with a cash gift or a basket of groceries, regardless of their denomination. He often volunteered his faithful Mercury to transport rural people to town, the 4-H club to their events, or the cheerleaders to games in surrounding towns. This non-discriminatory blessing of others also became a trademark of his grandson Charlie.

Charlie loved entertaining children (here with co-worker Miguel's Shelly and Charlito), a trait he had in common with his Pa Carver.

The fifth born of Bob and Patsy Carver's 13 children was Myrtle, who became Charlie's mother. Myrtle was one of those 4-H students her dad transported, and he observed with pride and joy her emerging leadership skills. Following in her father's footsteps of community involvement, Myrtle became the secretary of the state 4-H organization, won first place in the canning contest, was selected as the best all–around 4-H girl in the state in 1927, and as best potential in leadership in the state in 1928. This enabled her to win free trips to the Dallas Fair and to Chicago and Massachusetts for national leadership training. Myrtle not only repeated the 4-H pledge hundreds of times, but she developed into a compassionate leader who lived out the pledge in her everyday life: "*I pledge my head to clearer thinking, my heart to greater loyalty, my hands to larger service and my health to better living, for my club, my community, my country, and my world.*"

Myrtle's leadership skills so impacted her dad that he discussed with his wife

7

Patsy the need for Myrtle to further her education. He remembered the time when a Dr. Charles W. Smith of Ruston had held a revival in their town. Bob Carver had been deeply impressed with Dr. Smith's preaching, character and overall Christian commitment. So Pa Carver told his daughter Myrtle that he would mortgage the farm so that she could attend college at Louisiana Tech in Ruston. Ma Carver sternly added, "Myrtle, you can go on one condition: Dr. Smith and his wife must be willing to let you stay with them. We will pay them for your room and board."

And so it was that Myrtle Carver, college student, came to board in the home of Frellsen Smith, who was still living with his parents while he pursued his education. Over the next six years Myrtle's initial opinion of Frellsen ("Oh, that ugly thing!") changed to a long, drawn-out courtship.

Frellsen delayed marriage because he knew that the chance of completing his education would be slim if he married before his university course work was completed. By the time Myrtle began to be impatient with the delay, he had a master's degree and had spent a year at Harvard. He had been given a teaching position, and the time had come to settle down.

With $100 in his pocket, he borrowed his dad's Model A Ford and he and Myrtle drove 25 miles directly north of Ruston to a little town called Bernice. He pulled up to a parsonage and asked the preacher to marry them. The preacher wanted them to come into his house for the wedding, but Frellsen refused. So without getting out of the car, the young couple was married in one of Henry Ford's famous 40 horsepower, $385 cars. With the minister's wife and a neighbor serving as witnesses, Frellsen said "I do!" and, it would be supposed, kissed his beautiful young bride. He slipped a generous 10 dollar bill into the preacher's hand, shifted the three-speed transmission into first, revved up the engine and drove straight to Hot Springs, Arkansas. This site was not chosen for their honeymoon because of its relaxing hot springs, but because it was the location of a two-week religious camp meeting–an indication of their value system from the very beginning of their marriage.

Frellsen and Myrtle Smith's wedding photo 1934

These newlyweds had received, from their varied ancestors, traits they would soon be passing to Charlie and his siblings. Some traits would come through DNA; many would come through example. Their legacy of creativity, leadership, compassion, humor, and a love for God's Word, His church and His people, would, through Charlie, impact the world.

8

Before you were born I set you apart;
I appointed you as a prophet to the nations.
~Jeremiah 1:5 NIV

2
Birth of a Non-Conformist
1938

The black phone on the wall rang in a little frame house in Ruston, Louisiana. It was Tuesday, July 26, 1938. Teenager Florine Smith answered and heard her brother on the line, with news the family had been waiting anxiously to hear.

"Florine, it's Frellsen. I just want to let you know that all is going well with Myrtle. And little Marie is just doing great."

Florine answered, "Oh, you had a little girl?"
"Yes, and we also have little Charles."
Florine gasped, "What?"
"We had twins."

Marie was hale and hearty. She took greedily to the milk, but not jaundiced little Charles. As his aunt Florine recalled, "You would have to shake him, or he would go to sleep without taking his milk. He would suckle a little bit, nod his head and go off to sleep. He did not fill out and gain weight like Marie did. He was the weaker one. But he outgrew it."

The twins with Myrtle at three months show that Charlie [left] had caught up with Marie.

When Frellsen and Myrtle Carver Smith's first child Anita was born in 1937, Frellsen took one look at this precious new life and declared, "She is so beautiful. She makes me want to have five." Within 32 months his wish was well on its way to being granted. The twins were born in 1938 and Lorna in 1939. The fifth came much later, with Alvin's birth in 1950.

Myrtle chose to give up her career track and focus all of her attention on the children. Frellsen wrote of this chaotic but delightful time in their marriage: "One of the most exciting times was when she was able to take our four babies back to

9

church. Once they were all in church together, they never missed a service except during an illness, and that was rare."

As she dedicated her talents to her children in their formative years, Myrtle taught Charlie a song that resulted in one oft-told memory from the year after Pearl Harbor. Charlie was only 4 years old that Christmas season when the family walked to downtown Ruston to see a nativity display in one of the store windows. His younger sister Lorna recalled the incident in an essay written many years later:

In the center of the observers stood a young couple with four small children–three girls and a little boy. Little Charles walked up to the display and pressed his hands against the glass, seemingly mesmerized by the scene in the window. With his eyes focused on the Christ child, he began to sing a simple tune his mother had sung many times. His sweet, childish voice – clear and beautiful – rose uninhibited, loud enough to silence the chatter.

Charlie with [top to bottom] Anita, Marie, Myrtle, and Lorna in 1940

The dear little Jesus once lay in the hay.
He slept and He smiled and He grew day by day.
Until He could run and could play and could be
A help to His mother, like you and like me.

The simple message of the song brought back the meaning of the celebration so easy to forget, with the hustle and bustle of holiday preparations added to the concerns of a world at war. The crowd, hushed by the sweet sounds of the child, seemed to feel at peace as they dispersed and went on their way.

When it was time to start going to school, Charlie, his siblings, and some of his friends received a first-rate elementary education from the A.E. Phillips Laboratory School. This was a model school set up by Louisiana Tech for their education majors to have a place to do their observations and practice teaching.

10

Charlie was accepted because his dad was a professor at Louisiana Tech. This is where he met his close friend, Wiley Hilburn, who was admitted because his dad had attended that school. Wiley looked back on his time at the school: "They offered the finest education possible in the state between first and eighth grade. It was a wonderful school.... They only had teachers with advanced degrees.... They taught art, and music was compulsory."

During his early years at A.E. Phillips, Charlie revealed a rebellious side that would characterize him for the rest of his life. At this young age, he was bold and had the brazen effrontery to defy his teachers. According to Marie:

> It was obvious in the third grade that he did not want to be boxed in by anybody. He had this attitude, "Don't tell me what to do." I remember the teacher being so red-faced. We were just eight years old. Charles had taken off his shirt and I remember she picked him up and threw him down in that chair for not having his shirt on. He was not one who could just sit in class. He resisted correction and wanted to be free to do his own thing.

But there was also something about Charlie even at this young age that caused people to warm up to him. Marie loved her brother and Charlie loved her. They were so close that in their teen years Marie was an honorary member of Charlie's boys-only gang.

Lorna. Charlie. Marie. Anita

11

Teach [the commandments of God] to your children.
Talk about them wherever you are,
sitting at home or walking in the street;
talk about them from the time you get up in the morning
until you fall into bed at night.
~Deuteronomy 11:19 MSG

3
Taught by Godly Example
1938–1951

Despite four pre-schoolers competing for their attention, Frellsen and Myrtle still found time to be active outside their home. With their strong faith in God, they lived an exemplary life before their children and their community. Every week, Myrtle drove seven miles to teach Sunday School in the women's ward of a tuberculosis hospital before returning home to attend church with the family, where she taught another Sunday School class.

Charlie's daughter Felicia recounted another act of compassion that she felt influenced her father:

> My grandmother was always reaching out to the poor. On Sunday morning, she and my grandfather would go and pick up children on the other side of the tracks. Sometimes it would be Daddy's turn to go with him and see that part of town. It made a deep impression on Daddy, and I know those sights, smells and sounds impacted his life and embedded in him things that changed the course of his life.[2]

Frellsen modeled servant leadership when he took his children with him on Saturday evenings to clean the church. Charlie recalled "going with my father on the weekends to sweep the floor of the church building. My father used special oil on the rag to dust the seats. I can almost smell it as I type." His siblings remembered turning up the theater seats to scrape off the gum. Nothing was too

---

[2] Three generations of some of those same families who were brought to the church by this early form of a bus ministry continued attending the church for many years.

12

menial for Frellsen. It was the Lord's house, and he wanted it clean.[3]

The seed for Charlie's involvement in the desegregation movement was sown through Myrtle's involvement in the Girl Scout program. In Louisiana, where racism was deeply embedded, Myrtle became the interracial chairman for the Girl Scouts program in Ruston. She spoke on behalf of Girl Scouting at most of the black churches in Ruston and helped organize the Negro Girl Scouts programs in Grambling and Ruston.

When Myrtle was not Girl Scouting, she was Cub Scouting as Den Mother for Charlie and his friends. She had a way with the boys, who respected her even when she suggested they pause for prayer before venturing out into the neighborhood.

Myrtle was also good at teaching relational skills. Once there was a conflict with a contentious neighbor, a Mr. Norris. A large hedge connected the two back yards. One day, Myrtle was hanging up laundry when Mr. Norris came over and said, "Mrs. Smith, your hedge is on my property and you are going to

Thornton Street house during a rare Louisiana snow

have to move it." Myrtle responded, "Well, I tell you what Mr. Norris, I am going to give you that hedge. That hedge is yours. It is not mine, anymore." Charlie's sister Lorna reflected: "I remember that old hedge, but I remember most the lesson mother taught me by giving that hedge away. No longer did she have to trim it. Mr. Norris had to trim it."

Encouraging self-reliance and calmness in emergencies, Myrtle handled childhood adventures with aplomb. At age 3, Charlie climbed up their sweet gum tree and called to his mother, "Come see where I am!" His mother finally located him high in the tree, as high as the tip of the roof of the house. As she retold the incident later, she admitted to having been so frightened that she nearly fainted, but she maintained her calmness and said to her little boy, "Now Charles, you were man enough to get up there. Let's see if you are man enough to climb down." And she prayed as he stretched his short legs to each limb until he was down and safe in her big hug.

---

[3] Dr. C.W. Smith had planted this church and built the theater seats for it.

When Charlie and his younger brother Alvin had rather dramatic accidents, Myrtle demonstrated a practical life of faith. The first occurred when young Charlie and his buddies were playing around with firecrackers. One blew up in Charlie's face, severely injuring his eyes. Others were afraid he would lose his sight, but Myrtle's response was, "This is in God's hands!" She simply rested in God, and Charlie's eyes were completely restored.

The most serious incident exhibiting Myrtle's strong faith in God occurred on a Sunday morning after the family had moved to Nelson Street. Alvin was just learning to walk. Myrtle thought the older children had Alvin in the car with them; they thought he was still in the house with their mother. In actuality, he had toddled out the door unseen, and when Frellsen backed the car out of the carport and down the driveway, everyone felt a bump as the car hit Alvin and he rolled under the car between the tires. Marie jumped out first and grabbed Alvin as everyone screamed and neighbors poured out of their houses to investigate the commotion. Myrtle came out, took Alvin from Marie, marched everyone into the house and said, "You children stop that screaming right now. This is God's baby. We are in God's hands. We are going to the pastor's house for prayer."

After the prayer with the pastor, they took him to the emergency room, where he was declared fine except for a few bumps and bruises. The family returned to the church, where Myrtle proceeded to teach her Sunday School class with Alvin on her lap. Neighbor Patrick Garrett wrote in his book *Harps*

Alvin stands in front of Charlie for this family photo taken a couple of years after the car incident.

14

Upon the Willows, "Though we all questioned the delay in going to the hospital, nobody ever questioned the truth of Alvin's deliverance from harm and death."

Many nights on Thornton Street, Frellsen would seat himself in a rocking chair beneath the light bulb in the closet that connected the only two bedrooms in the house, open *Egermeier's Bible Story Book* and read to his children before they went to sleep. Snuggled in the little bedroom where the girls shared the double beds and Charlie had the single bed to himself, the children were given a strong foundation in the Bible as their dad read exciting stories about Abraham and Isaac, Joseph the Dreamer, Daniel in the Lion's Den, and David and Goliath. He was planting spiritual seeds in their tender minds that would hold them steady in the years ahead.

Charlie remembered: "Smelling breakfast cooking, Daddy reading the Word and praying before the meal, conversation around the table that taught us about life and relationships—it was a wonderful life! I cannot imagine anyone having a better childhood."

With the birth of Alvin and the maturing of the older children, Frellsen decided to build a larger home around the corner on Nelson Street.

If you were old enough to ride a bike, the place to ride to in Ruston was

The neighborhood children enjoy a birthday party for Marie (left)
and Charlie (right) in the Smiths' backyard.
Grandmother Smith (back left), their mother, Myrtle (back right)

15

Frellsen and Myrtle's house. It was not a mansion, but it was a home, and with four active children serving as social magnets, as well as Myrtle's gift of joyful hospitality, the neighborhood children were attracted to the Smiths' yard. She often said the Smith House was like Grand Central Station with such a large family and so many neighbor kids congregating in the yard and running in and out the back door. But she was accustomed to this lifestyle; in her childhood home, with 15 mouths needing to be fed, Myrtle grew up with an understanding of how to prepare food for a crowd, a skill her son would emulate in his later ministries.

There in the backyard, pudgy Raymond "Round Man" Edwards, Ronnie and Flora Jean Linder, and the four Smith children carved out some unforgettable memories. The Tech campus just one block away served as an extended

playground that gave this little band of elementary Rustonians greater freedom and room to key on their skates[4], ride their bikes, and aim their BB guns at tin cans.

One day Charlie and the gang killed a red breasted robin with a BB gun. However, they learned a rule of hunting when Ronnie's dad taught them that a hunter eats whatever he kills. Ronnie's dad made them pluck the feathers, gut the robin, boil it–and then eat it. It may have been the first time Charlie ate something strange, but it was nothing compared to some of the foods he encountered in Malaysia and Honduras in later years, including the *muy sabroso* cockroach that day in Chagüitillos.

When Charlie's mother headed up his Cub Scout troop, the neighborhood children learned to skin goats in their grassless back yard to make drums. This skill came in handy in his missionary training work later in life, as did learning to catch crawdads in a nearby creek.

Charlie on his bike

Of these days of play in a yard where too many feet made it impossible for the grass to grow, Charlie wrote: "I have no doubt that creative play stimulated the creativity in me that has characterized my life."

---

[4] Roller skates were a metal platform which fastened to shoes with adjustable foot and toe clamps. Children wore a "key" around their necks to make the adjustments.

PART TWO

1950s

Wings

I remember Mom was the one so anguished over Charles.
She came up with a prayer that she said over and over and over again:
"I have confidence in the Lord concerning Charles."
That was her total prayer and it got her through some very difficult times.
~Alvin Smith

4

Painting the Town Red

1952-1956

As childhood friendships turned to high school buddies, Charlie found himself a member of a group that called themselves *The Blue Jersey Gang* or *The Marauders*. The names were far more fearsome than the boys or their escapades. You most likely would find these Southern boys, wearing the blue jerseys they bought at Penney's, spitting tobacco juice onto the burning embers left from cooking their hot dogs, rather than engaged in back alley gang activity.

The Marauders lived for Friday afternoons. No sound brought more delight to their ears than the ringing of the last period school bell. Robert Barham's Buick, parked on the school's asphalt parking lot, was their ticket to freedom. With the gang piled in the car, clouds of dust spiraled from behind Robert's 364 V-8 and those back roads were, in member Wiley's words, "like a green tunnel in the road that would never end. None of us could fight. We just put on our blue jerseys and every Friday night we would get in Robert's car and we would think, *We've got the whole weekend to ourselves!*"

Out of the eight members (plus honorary member Marie), the five regulars in that weekend gang were Charlie, Billy, Peter, Robert and Wiley. Their unpredictable behavior and foolish pranks celebrated with a few beers in a circle of friendship at Robert's lakeside cabin gave them unforgettable highs. Here they shared their secrets, puffed on cigarettes and smoked Havana wooden-tipped cigars, as well as told lies about personal conquests made on dates with innocent girls wearing polka dot skirts over lace-trimmed petticoats.

Even though Robert was crippled from a bout with polio and would ordinarily have been rejected by his peers, he had the status of being the son of the lieutenant governor of Louisiana. Robert had several more things the other gang members lacked: money, a cabin with a pond in Piney Woods, and most importantly, a car. At first it was a Chevy, then later a brand-new 1956 Buick, and the following year a 1957. Buicks were gutsy and spirited with that sweeping

19

chrome strip that ran from the front bumper to the rear wheelhouse. Cruising town in Robert's '57 gave the Marauders a bit of sophistication and respect.

According to an article by his friend Wiley, they could often be found "...pulling on the last rung [of the Louisiana Tech water tower] until it gave a good two inches in rusty protest, dangling [us] off the edge into the darkness.... [We] dropped tiny torpedoes off the T.L. James Building, chug-a-lugged a quart of Falstaff at Hood's drive-in, pushed [Robert's] Buick to the 120 mph peg in chicken runs...and [back in school] dared the geometry teachers to nail [us] for cheating." The boys would call local radio station KRUS and say "This is the Marauders–Ruston's phantom outlaws..." and then they would request *Don't Be Cruel,* or *Peggy Sue.*

Frequently the activities that Charlie engaged in with the gang–or alone–must have torn at his father's heart. Lorna said that their father "...could be very stern with him, telling him as did Mother, how much he loved him and how Charlie knew right from wrong, that they believed in him and expected him to make good choices."

Myrtle's greatest disciplinary influence was intercessory prayer, saying, "I have confidence in the Lord concerning Charles." Charlie once said:

> Many nights I would tip-toe through the house, thinking I had arrived in my room without being revealed, only to find my mother in my own bed praying for my wayward soul. My parents gave me sufficient slack to hang myself, and I about did that on several occasions.... We had a lot of fun doing some very stupid things during the days of our youth.... We drank our fair share of booze and smoked enough cigarettes to kill a giant.[5] But we were not cruel and always returned home to come under the influence of our parents.

The site of one of their more brazen stunts was the old Dixie Theater on Vienna Street, where one could see the current flick with the purchase of a 10-cent ticket. Built in 1928, the theater had a massive chandelier hanging from its ceiling, and, in the prejudice of Southern

---

[5] On many occasions Charlie requested that Robert stop the car so he could retrieve his hidden cigarettes. Charlie, being half Carver, loved his tobacco. (Some believe he would chew tobacco, deceiving his friends by using a coffee cup as a spittoon.)

customs of the day, a balcony for blacks only. In the fifties, this theater was a place where some of the Marauders took their dates in hopes of getting a romantic kiss during a love scene. However, on this particular Friday night, dates were not a part of Charlie's, Wiley's, Robert's and Billy's plan. Sitting in Robert's car, the tension built as they rehearsed their strategy, which involved the screen on the theater's stage. This screen created a silhouette of shadows whenever someone walked behind it, and conveniently for their stunt, there were building exits on either side of the stage. Just before the show was to begin, the Marauders stripped off their clothes and streaked behind the screen to the shrieks and laughter of a totally surprised audience of teens and Tech students who had just received a bonus attraction for their 10-cent ticket. The guys high-tailed it out the exit and over to the filling station where Robert's getaway car was waiting. There was a buzz around town the next day, but the Marauders refused to brag openly about the risqué escapade. Though proud of pulling off their daring exploit, Charlie and his friends were protective of the Smith family's reputation in the town.

The Marauders liked to play around with the forbidden, as also evidenced by their visits to *The Cheniere Inn*–the French name everyone mispronounced as "Shinny." Their joke about their visits to this liquor establishment, which was about 28 miles out of Ruston, was "Shinny Inn and Stagger Out." It was actually a takeout place, but the Marauders would go inside and just talk and purchase a few beers. They did not need a discounted "Happy Hour," as they created their own.

Whiskey became the catalyst for one of the most foolish stunts in which these "outlaws" were involved. Louisiana Tech had an away game in Monroe. Charlie and Billy Harp drove to the game while Wiley and his date went separately. On the way, Charlie and Billy both drank a half pint of "something strong." After the game, they followed their friend and his date to a nightclub where there was dancing and downed the liquor Wiley bought. As Charlie remembered it later, when he and Billy left the nightclub:

> We were worse than three sheets to the wind. Billy was too drunk to drive, so I, like an idiot, drove east–instead of west to Ruston. I finally stopped at what I thought was a gas station. It was a state weigh station, and as I asked the state trooper directions to Ruston, proceeded to spit tobacco juice on his shoe.

Billy and Charlie were put in jail that night, charged with a driving under the influence and given a large fine. It was a long night for Charlie. His biggest concern was not being able to go back home for church the next morning. It was

21

also a long Saturday night for his parents. Late the next morning, Billy dropped Charlie off at his house, where he waited for his family to return from Sunday morning services. He wrote:

> I knew I was in big trouble....As soon as they arrived I confessed fully to my parents, and after also confessing to the pastor, he prayed that I would be strong to resist the temptations of the flesh, which were great.

The DUI charge was dropped at the pleadings of Charlie's parents and a family friend. If word had gotten out, it would have brought great embarrassment to Frellsen in his position as college professor. Even Frellsen's sister Florine and Charlie's little brother Alvin were never told of the incident.

Charlie's reputation was broader than what he gained from his stunts with the gang. He was voted Most Handsome by his high school peers, and he was a starting member of the basketball team. At just under six feet, he was a steady player of some renown. In fact, he played all four quarters on March 14, 1956, the first state basketball championship of the Ruston Bearcats, a game that was so close throughout, the coach never put in any substitutes.

The excitement of this championship game, which ended in a 52-49 score from a last-second shot, reinforced Charlie's goal to someday teach physical education and coach basketball.

In reflecting on the relationship of this varsity basketball player to his non-basketball-playing buddies, one of the Marauders said:

Charlie was voted
Most Handsome
in his senior class

> Charlie was not a star, but when you win a state championship that is something you remember the rest of your life. We did not particularly like jocks...but Charlie never put on airs. He was still our friend. He did not even hang out with these players ...and the funny thing is, he never talked about basketball when he was with the Marauders.

22

Years later, gang member Wiley[6] wrote a piece in the local paper about the end of these high school days and the escapades of this special group of friends:

Weren't those sinful Friday and Saturday nights in Robert's car something special? They were special and, yes, they were sinful. Yet, even The Book Charlie loved so dearly states, "...there is pleasure in sin for a season." Not long after Charlie was arrested, the whole landscape of the Marauders' colorful exploits that held Ruston spellbound for a season came to a screeching halt. Military service, marriage, budding careers and graduation began to redirect the emotional bond that held the Marauders together like a blood covenant. On graduation day, the Marauders sat in maroon and white colors awaiting their diplomas. As they walked across the stage, it was bittersweet. They knew they were saying goodbye to something more special than being valedictorian, winning the State Championship or a new Roadmaster Buick. They were saying goodbye to precious memories never to be duplicated, emotional attachments that would fade with time, innocence that would be tainted by wrong choices, feelings that were warm and the loss of togetherness on Friday and Saturday nights near the "Shinny" Inn. And this is why following high school graduation they formed a circle of love...and prayed together about the tomorrow that would be their future.

**The Ruston Bearcats 1956 Championship Basketball Team.
Charlie Smith is wearing #25.**

[6] Charlie's friend, Wiley Hilburn, became a columnist for the Ruston newspaper and often wrote about high school days, the relationships that formed then and continued.

As a young man, I tried the ways of the world, especially during the Navy. I got drunk once, landed in jail, but eventually that life proved to be shallow... if not empty of significant meaning and purpose. Though I knew what I was doing was wrong, and my conscience bothered me, I did not let that stop me. ~Charlie Smith

5
Don't Fence Me In
1952-1956

From his elementary days through his teenage years, Charlie demonstrated that he did not want to fit into any particular mold. He spoke with regret of those years of wandering from his parents' instruction:

I saw their example and experienced the power of love, but had to go my own way–a way contrary to the life my parents wanted for me. I never stopped going to church and I always respected my parents, but I had to try life out in its many dimensions, including the life that is lived without God.

His twin sister Marie always envied Charlie's freedom:

Charlie had a lot more fun than we girls did. I am not sure why, but it was either because he pushed our parents more than we did or they just were more lenient with him. Charlie went to high school dances, but we girls never went to the dances–not one. And Charlie and Anita were able to express themselves, but Lorna and I were not given that freedom. If Charlie wanted something or wanted to go somewhere, he just got up and went.

24

By going to the high school dances, Charlie was crossing a forbidden line in both Frellsen's and Myrtle's value systems. They did not believe high school rock and roll dances were appropriate–these dances where teens gyrated to the powerful beat of "Tweedle Dee" and guys held their girls tight while dancing to "Mr. Sandman" and "Earth Angel."

Twins Charlie and Marie graduate together in 1956

Lorna believed Frellsen was convinced God's hand was upon Charlie's life, and God would discipline him, take care of him, and use him in the right season of his life.

Anita, on the other hand, thought Frellsen consented to a lot of Charlie's antics because her father was incapable of coming out of his conservative, traditional box and wished he could be more like his son. She felt her father internally admired Charlie for his spontaneous lifestyle and unconventional behavior, such as the way he dressed, his horsing around, and his uncanny knack of filling up the house with his vibrant personality.

The youngest sibling, Alvin, who was only 5 years old when Charlie was 17, recalled something from Charlie's senior year in high school:

His math teacher, Ruth Johnson, really liked Charlie, as most people did. ... But he frustrated the daylights out of her because he did not do his assignments and was failing math terribly. This was his senior year and graduation was just around the corner. Charlie failed the class but Miss Ruth gave him a "D", which allowed him to graduate. I don't know why she passed a failing student. Maybe...she just wanted Charlie off her hands!

As a sister who was closer in age to Charlie, Lorna stated her opinion on the incident:

Miss Ruth, and also the English teacher, Miss Lewis, passed Charlie, not because he earned a passing grade in their classes, nor because they wanted to get him off their hands, but because they wanted him to graduate with his twin sister Marie. It was a good decision.

25

There is a song that Anne-Marie remembered hearing her dad sing many times while she was growing up. A few of the words give a clue to his independent philosophy of life:

I can't look at hobbles and I can't stand fences
Don't fence me in.
No, Poppa, Don't you fence me in.

Following high school graduation, this need to be free was so dominant that even the desire to continue his love of athletics by becoming a basketball coach was not enough for Charlie to settle down and go to college. What would his professor-father recommend? Not the university. Charlie did not have the grades. Not vocational school. Charlie could barely repair his flat bicycle inner tube. It was not marriage. He did not even have a girlfriend. His dad recommended a place of discipline with the promise of travel.

26

PART THREE

1950 - 1980

Explorations

The Navy
Courtship
Peace Corps
Kentucky
Florida

Some of you set sail in big ships; you put to sea
to do business in faraway ports...
You were spun like a top, you reeled like a drunk,
you didn't know which end was up...
Then you called out to God in your desperate condition
and he led you safely back to harbor.
~Psalms 107:23 MSG

6

A Sailor in Uniform

1957-1958

After graduation, Charlie's rebellious behavior continued to bend his mother's knees every night as she lifted her strong-willed son to her heavenly Father. Many a day his father made his way with a heavy heart to his college classroom at Louisiana Tech. As he strolled toward the campus, he thought of his own role and responsibility in raising an intelligent but rebellious son with so much potential. How should he guide a son that defied tradition, bucked the system, made average grades and preferred drinking wine out of a bottle on Friday nights to taking the cup of communion on Sunday morning?

Finally, Frellsen recommended Charlie join the U.S. Navy before going to college. He believed this would give a measure of discipline and order to Charlie's haphazard life. In the fall of 1957, the entire family went with Charlie to the bus station, where he left for his three-month boot camp training at the Great Lakes Naval Training Center on the western shore of Lake Michigan.

Boot camp was a long way from those boozy nights in "wet" Monroe. It was up at 0600 for line-ups, curl-ups, sit-ups, drills, and salutes, all of which were designed to teach this nonconformist the meaning of discipline and to inculcate the Navy's fundamental values of honor, commitment, and courage.

Following his basic training alongside Lake Michigan, Charlie found himself on a military base a world away from his Louisiana roots. Treasure Island in San Francisco was built with imported fill on a sandbar coastline for the World's Fair and International Expo in 1939. During World War II, it became known as Treasure Island Naval Base and served largely as an electronics and radio communications training school and a major Navy departure point for sailors in the Pacific.

After a few weeks of being burdened with the mundane responsibilities of cooking "Navy beans," cleaning sinks, and washing pots and pans, good fortune came to Charlie. One of his naval superiors discovered that he could type 30 words per minute[7]. So, instead of peeling potatoes and washing pans, he was placed in an office cubicle with the beautiful Pacific Ocean as a backdrop. There he served two years as a typist for the U.S. Navy. He wrote of his San Francisco experience:

Here I was, an innocent little boy going off to Chicago to boot camp, then out to San Francisco, California, to that wicked city. It was wicked then, and I can assure you it is wicked now. There I was [first] assigned to be a mess cook, and [instead] for two years I typed service records. It was a good experience, but I always went to church even as a boy. And I went to the Oakland church for a while where Pastor Jack pastored, and I would lead singing and sing specials and

---

[7] When his tour of duty was over, Charlie felt he was pretty efficient at the skill he had learned back in high school. With a competitive twinkle in his eye, he visited his typing teacher, and challenged her to a typing duel. He beat her by a couple of words.

people loved me. I stayed close to the church, but I would not want to tell you of some of the experiences I had in the Navy.

Visits home were few and far between due to distance and expense. Of these occasional trips to Ruston, Charlie related one memorable one:

> I hitchhiked one time. Honestly, I hitchhiked! We had just decommissioned a ship. I wanted to go to Ruston, and it was a long way to go and this driver had left us after we had given him money to go. I went all the way from San Francisco to Ruston, Louisiana. I made it, but it took me 52 rides. I remember this one guy who picked me up was going to his brother's funeral. [The brother] had killed himself by playing Russian roulette. Hitchhiking was dangerous in those days, but nothing like it is today. I would not pick up a hitchhiker today.

His Navy experience did not completely rid him of his mischievous nature. He was still unconventional and would remain so for the rest of his life. But there was something about his white Navy uniform that gave him a sense of order and commanded respect.

Charlie served long enough to advance in rank, made 3rd Class Petty Officer, and received a raise of $1.50 per shift. But he had no interest in making the Navy a career. In his two years of service, he had not met anyone with whom he really liked to associate. In a letter home he wrote, "Everyone cusses. All I can do is feel sorry for the way they live. They really do not know that true joy and happiness." Something was changing in Charlie.

As he settled in with his family following his time in the Navy, Charlie enrolled at Louisiana Tech, but he continued to do Navy Reserves every other weekend.[8] He had purpose, but not passion. His purpose was to be a high school basketball coach, but his lack of passion to learn resulted in barely average grades for his freshman year at Louisiana Tech.

The 1959 spring semester concluded, and Charlie decided to take summer classes at Northwestern Natchitoches [*NAK-ə-təsh*] College, more for its reputation of having the most beautiful girls in the state than for any academic credit. He had no idea that this thought came as an answer to his mother's prayers.

---

[8] Reservists had to complete 180 days of weekend duty, plus work a two-week cruise, which Charlie ended up finishing just prior to his wedding in the fall of 1960.

PART THREE

1950 - 1980

Explorations

The Navy
Courtship
Peace Corps
Kentucky
Florida

Karen was the sweetest answer to all my prayers.
~Myrtle Smith

7

A Mock Suicide on Cane River Bridge
1959

On the momentous first day of the plan to check out Northwestern's girls, former Marauder and fellow summer student Robert Barham picked Charlie up and they roared down the road, top down, wind in their faces and hope in their hearts. A short while later, they parked near a popular eating place on the university campus.

As they approached a group of about eight students gathered around a lunch table, Charlie could not believe his eyes. Not in his wildest dreams had he ever expected to see again this beautiful goddess. Yet, there she was! The girl from the high school All State Chorus! Charlie recalled that initial encounter:

> I could never forget the first time my eyes looked upon Karen. It was at an All State Chorus of about 400 students from all over the state of Louisiana. I was a [junior] representative for my school and she was a [senior] representative of her school, and we performed before the teachers.
> I never knew God in all of His great abilities

Karen Stone

Yearbook photo of Karen Stone,
Class Beauty

35

could create a woman so beautiful. She was gorgeous. I knew we would only have a few days together, so I made my moves as bold as I could, being a coward when it came to relating to the opposite sex. Girls were not a part of my vocabulary, because I ran with the gang. But when I saw her, I used some of the moves I had, which were not many in those days. She did agree to ride on the bus with me to the performance in Monroe, and on the way home we held hands. How sweet it was. It was wonderful—so wonderful.

Following this meeting, Charlie and Karen, figuratively speaking, had fled separately to Shakespeare's Ardennes Forest, but neither of them "hung notes of love on a tree" to keep in touch as did Orlando and Rosalind. It seemed to be a brief emotional connection. He did not speak of it to his mother and they did not follow it up by corresponding. She had gone off to college, and he had returned to his final year in high school and then spent two years in the Navy.

But now, with Charlie's heart revving faster than Robert's Buick engine, he went up to Karen Stone and said, "I bet you do not know who I am."

"Yes, I do. You are Charles Smith."

With those words, time stood still. And that fortuitous meeting would forever change Charlie and the lives of thousands.

But if, from that moment, Charlie's heart was throbbing and fluttering with love, Karen, after first impressions of Charlie, showed little romantic inclination toward him. He was a roustabout. He smoked, drank, ran around with off-beats and had no purpose in his life. What did he have to offer someone called to the mission field while in junior high and who now was just months away from completing her nursing degree? Yet, something happened to her heart as well. Charlie wrote:

> I learned later that what impressed her most about me was not how handsome I was—but that I came from a Christian home and that my father had written a Christian tract titled, "How You Can Become a Christian." I rather doubt at that time she saw a missionary heart in me.

Karen and Charlie began to see each other more and more. They were beginning to bond, but still Karen's call to missions prevented her from committing to Charlie, which frustrated Charlie to no end.

On the weekends, Robert would drive back to Ruston and give the old gang members the scoop on Charlie's new love. He told Wiley, "Charlie has fallen in love. He has fallen in love with this girl who could be a movie star. Her name is

36

Karen, but she won't let him touch her. He wants to marry her, and she is not interested in that. She is so religious."

However, religious or not, Charlie would not be denied. He and Robert pledged that somehow and somewhere on the 35-mile stretch of the Cane River they would trick Karen into demonstrating her true feelings for Charlie.

Charlie and Robert surveyed the Cane River bridge, the height and the depth of the water, the place where Charlie would be, and the place where Robert would see that Karen was stationed. The plan was in place.

The moment came. Charlie was on a wall alongside the bridge. Robert drove Karen to a spot where she would be able to see someone in trouble in the water. No records exist of the words that passed between Robert and Karen, but suddenly Charlie splashed into the water, appearing to have jumped off the Cane River Bridge in his despair over Karen's lack of commitment to their relationship. Of course, polio-crippled Robert could do nothing to rescue his friend, so it was up to Karen. In she went! Charlie later wrote of this incident:

> Karen came in the water after me, fully dressed, pulled me out (with my help, of course), and we drove home sopping wet in each other's arms in the back seat of Robert's car. Love makes one do strange things.

Robert went back to Ruston on the weekend, and reported to Wiley:

> They are going steady! It worked! They are going steady! You have never seen anything like it. She went out and rescued Charlie. She came out of Cane River and it was like seeing Elizabeth Taylor in *Cat on a Hot Tin Roof* as she was coming out of the water. She was wearing a white dress and the water molded it against her legs. She was beautiful. It was sensual.

It was obvious, especially to Charlie, that he had won the lottery with Karen. The other members of the old gang could continue purchasing tickets, but Charlie had already cashed in.

Did you know that you are my everything
and that nobody else don't mean nothing?
(Isn't that a double negative?)
~Note from Karen to Charlie, October 10, 1959

8
The Summer of Love
1959

Louisiana summers are known to be hot and sultry, and hot and sultry certainly described the remainder of the summer of 1959 as far as Charlie was concerned, though the weather had nothing to do with it. Spending that summer with the girl who "rescued" him from the Cane River made it the most memorable of all the summers he ever lived.

Late on Wednesday, July 9, 1959, Karen wrote to Charlie after her time with him that evening:

> Dearest Charlie,
> Just floated in a little while ago after the most wonderful date with the greatest guy. Told Silvia, (still floating), "I may not be making such good grades, but I sure am having fun." She said, "Oh, yes, he is a doll." Then I told her (please don't think I am brash or bold) that you looked wonderful in a bathing suit and that your wonderful physique just couldn't be beat...Dear, do you know that was our twenty-second date plus the two that we had in high school?
> Must close, sweet dearest. I miss you, Karen

They spent hours together, never tiring of each other's company in this season that Charlie termed "the summer of love." But because it was heavy on love and weak on learning, it was a bittersweet time. Charlie alluded to some of its consequences:

> Academically, the "summer of love" was nearly disastrous for us both. We "studied" together just to be together, and our grades reflected exactly what we were NOT doing–studying. Karen was a graduating senior and had earned good grades

until "the summer of love" when she came close to failing philosophy and had to petition for a higher grade so she could graduate with the rest of her class. As for my summer, it was great, for the mystery of love had invaded my total being. Classes? Grades? Who cared? My grades reflected what I did that summer–Two "F's" and one "D"–two of those in physical education classes, my major!

Surprisingly, Charlie's mother was not too disappointed: "Mother said that last summer was bad in view of my grades, but she said that the best thing that ever happened to me was finding you there. I said, 'Yes I found my life's partner there this summer. My bride to be.'"

In the fall, Karen enrolled in Central Bible Institute in Springfield, Missouri, where she was following her call to mission work. Charlie returned to classes at Tech, where he was studying to be a coach. Time together was limited to occasional weekend visits. Charlie would borrow his dad's car and drive the 424 miles to Springfield to visit Karen, or Karen would catch a ride home with her roommate who had a car. These short visits also meant time with each other's birth families. When Charlie visited Karen's home he found that church was as much a priority for the Stones as for the Smiths.

Of course, as in any relationship, there were some differences to work through. One that Charlie and Karen faced involved the very different styles of worship to which they were accustomed. Charlie grew up in the Church of God, Anderson, which held to a strong anti-Pentecostal position regarding certain gifts of the Spirit such as speaking in tongues and animated forms of worship: running in the sanctuary, lifting both hands in worship, and slaying in the Spirit. Karen grew up in the Assembly of God, which often worships in that demonstrative, Pentecostal way. In a letter to Charlie, Karen pleaded with him to be open and not fearful of her church, and pledged to afford him the same courtesy. Through this early conflict they were able to sort out the fundamentals of their faith and came to accept the validity of Christians who worshipped under a variety of denominational names.

The change in Charlie's behavior through Karen's influence was gradual but profound. One of the first things she did was to insist that Charlie quit smoking. She knew a smoking missionary would not be a good witness on the mission field. His friend Wiley said:

> There was just this sea of change in Charlie all because of Karen. But what was so great about it was that he did not become this pious saint...he did not quit drinking immediately and he still smoked occasionally after he met Karen. He would smoke just one or two and then he would take mints so that Karen would not know he was still smoking.

One of the most vivid examples of a turnaround in Charlie's way of living manifested itself when he decided to go to a movie at the Dixie Theater with the old gang. He wrote to Karen:

> I went out with dear old Robert Barham and was so embarrassed when I found out they had all been drinking and we all went to the show together. Well, honey, there I was, walking into the show with three boys that smelled like a bottle of beer. I just stood back and let them go get seated and I waited till the lights were off and went and sat down by them. Was I wrong? I just did not want everyone thinking I was drinking. Wish I could find some friend who didn't drink. I really felt sorry for them.

Some very good news arrived by way of Western Union that December 9. Evidently Karen's Bible classes in Missouri and her frequent letters to Charlie did not interfere with studying to pass the state boards to become a registered nurse. The Western Union Telegram read: Dearest Charles. Passed State Board. Thanks for your prayers and encouragement. All my love Karen

40

I remember weeping uncontrollably as our pastor was preaching—about what I cannot remember. I felt God was asking me to be a missionary for him.
~Letter from Karen to Charlie

9
Here Am I, Send Me
1949 and 1959

On December 7, 1949, a sweet 12-year-old girl was weeping in a church pew in Louisiana. That was the day Karen Stone realized that God was calling her to be a missionary, and her later choice of nursing as a career was based on her tearful commitment to the call that day. Now, 10 years later, that calling was being tested, as she found herself in love with a man named Charlie Smith, who wanted to be a coach in a gym, not a missionary in a jungle.

Karen's parents, Dean and Ruth Stone

The Christian training that Karen received as a child was not corrupted by a rebellious and independent spirit like Charlie possessed. Karen had eagerly received the mentoring of her maternal grandmother, Ethel Andress, who had a ministry to boat people on the Mississippi River during Karen's formative years, and of her parents, Dean and Ruth Stone, who loved the church and always taught Karen the importance of putting God first in her life. In light of the conflict in career choices that could jeopardize this commitment, Karen's parents were also experiencing doubts about Charlie as the "perfect mate" for their daughter.

In November of 1959, Charlie and Karen talked about being with one another over the Christmas holidays that year. Charlie had urged Karen to have Christmas with his family at the Nelson Street house, but she politely but firmly explained to him that Christmas was a strong tradition in her family as well. It

41

appears she had some discussion with her family on this issue over the Thanksgiving holidays, evidenced by a letter she received at school the following week. Her father wrote with a tenderness characteristic of this man who had not allowed the harshness of his experience as a tank commander in World War II to harden his heart:

Dear Karen:

I hope you had a safe trip back to school. I am afraid your vacation was unpleasant for you. I could sense that you were evidently disturbed and that Ruth[9] was also. You must make allowances for Ruth's outlook. I do not think that she has objections to your friendship with Charlie like you think she does. I believe she just cannot see how he can be worked in with your plans for mission work and to the career he is preparing for. I know the Lord will work it out for you and that you will be happy with His solution. When you were quite small we dedicated you to the Lord and all your life have seen His hand upon you. Because of that I feel completely relaxed and at ease at the situation and trust Him to direct you. I want you to know that I have no objections to Charlie and want you to know that the sole responsibility of choosing someone must be yours. Just do not be blinded by emotions of the moment. Analyze the possibilities of a happy future and lean upon the Lord for guidance and accept that guidance with joy remembering that "...all things work together for good." I hope that when I see you in three weeks that you will be relaxed, happy and the tensions gone. I am not an irrational person but I can recognize tensions in others. Most world shattering, uncontrollable, soul-possessing, personal problems go away when ignored. Just relax, seek God's guidance and when you come Christmas you will not have a care...I love you. Dean.

---

[9] It appears that at times Karen called her parents by their first names.

42

*Some people, no matter how old they get, never lose their beauty—
they merely move it from their faces to their hearts.
~Martin Buxbaum*

10
Chantilly Lace and a Pretty Face
1960

Family and friends were seeing a different Charlie. One friend said, "He was all of a sudden a leader. He had ideas and began to talk about politics. He wanted to do something for people who needed help. He got all of that from Karen."

For the Smiths, Karen's arrival was the long-awaited spring sunshine, inspiring growth in the field Charlie's parents had cultivated so well. Myrtle shared her feelings about Karen in a letter to her future daughter-in-law:

> I want to thank you for being you! To me you are one of the very best, most admirable girls in the whole world! I love you very much, and I have loved you since that first weekend you came home with Charlie. You are 'tops' to me and I pray daily that all of your dreams and aspirations may come to pass!

By the end of Karen's year of Bible study in Missouri, the wedding date was set. They would marry in September. Karen moved to Ruston and lived with Charlie's grandmother for the summer of 1960. She found work as a pediatric nurse in a local clinic while Charlie pursued his physical education degree at Louisiana Tech and chipped away at his required 180 days in the naval reserves.

Charlie and Karen chose Thursday evening, September 1, 1960, to walk down a sacred aisle at Life Tabernacle Church on Grand Avenue in Shreveport, Louisiana and consecrate their marriage before God.

Following their honeymoon in New Orleans, they returned to Ruston, where Charlie resumed his studies at Louisiana Polytechnic Institute and Karen continued her employment as a nurse. Though they had their differences, they adjusted well.

As they adapted to life as a married couple, Karen continued to model Christ's love before her husband. As had Charlie's parents in the past, Karen

43

reached out to the downtrodden through her life, her words and her call to the mission field. She was the lamb that tamed the lion.

Three and a half years after their wedding, Charlie graduated from Louisiana Tech with a master's degree in education. During this time, Karen's life purpose had woven itself into Charlie's heart, and he had yielded to the call of God. Charlie and Karen united with a singleness of purpose. Service beyond the sleepy southern town of Ruston now beckoned.

In the early 1960s, they contacted various mission boards seeking an open door to serve, including the national headquarters of the denominations of their childhood churches: the Assembly of God in Springfield, Missouri, and the national headquarters of the Church of God in Anderson, Indiana. They wrote letters. They made phone calls. They made visits.

When Charlie and Karen got in touch with the mission board in Anderson, they were very hopeful, due to Charlie's family's historical affiliation with the Church of God. They believed that because Karen was a registered nurse and Charlie had a master's degree in education, there would surely be a place of service for them somewhere in the world through this agency. Their hopes were dashed. Charlie later wrote: "We asked the [Church of God] mission board if they had any openings for us. We were disappointed to find that all doors were closed."

Charlie Smith, with his beautiful bride Karen dressed in her gown of ivory taffeta and Chantilly lace

PART THREE

1950 - 1980

Explorations

The Navy
Courtship
Peace Corps
Kentucky
Florida

Charles has been a marvelous camper...
He is the life of the party and has kept everybody's spirits up.
~Karen Smith, Hawaii, 1964

11
The Jungle Gentleman in Waipio Valley
Spring 1964

The glow of staffers' watches in the darkness surrounding the Detroit airport indicated it was 2 a.m., Oct. 14, 1960. The long day for the Kennedy presidential campaign had included a debate with Republican candidate Richard Nixon. Everyone in the Kennedy party, from reporters to aides to JFK himself, was looking forward to some sleep in Ann Arbor before the next day's grueling whistle-stop tour across Michigan. But when the motorcade reached town they were surprised to learn there was a crowd of several thousand University of Michigan students waiting to greet the senator. He could have waved and gone to bed, but instead, Senator Kennedy made his way through the enthusiastic crowd to the Student Union Building.

Positioning himself on the steps, he spoke extemporaneously to the students, asking how many of them were studying to be doctors, engineers, and teachers. Then he asked how many of them were willing to devote one, two or 10 years of their lives in peace-promoting service in countries like Ghana, Malaysia, and Chile. And finally he said, ". . . on your willingness to contribute part of your life to this country, I think, will depend the answer whether we as a free society can compete. I think we can, and I think Americans are willing to contribute, but the effort must be far greater than we have made in the past."

With those words spoken on the steps of the Student Union Building at the University of Michigan, the seed for the Peace Corps was planted. Three weeks later, Kennedy was elected President of the United States, and by 1962, this seed of an idea had grown into an organization that would eventually affect the lives of many American youth and impact people in countries around the world.

It wasn't long before Charlie and Karen heard about this visionary program. Here was an opportunity to serve with their skills as a nurse and a teacher in an overseas assignment. Recognizing that no doors had opened at the Assembly of God headquarters in Springfield, Missouri, nor at the Church of God Missionary Board in Anderson, Indiana, Charlie's father encouraged their decision to

47

respond to this initiative from the Foreign Service Office of the new Kennedy administration. They applied to join the U. S. Peace Corps.

On November 22, 1963, Charlie and Karen were watching the soap opera *As the World Turns* while they ate lunch. Ten minutes into the program, Walter Cronkite broke in saying that President Kennedy had been shot. A few minutes later, the postman arrived with a letter from the Peace Corps announcing their acceptance for service in Malaysia. How strange to have received both the news of the assassination of the visionary of the Peace Corps and their acceptance into his greatest legacy in the same hour.

It was an honor for Charlie and Karen to be chosen out of thousands of applicants as potential Peace Corps volunteers. Charlie and Karen were told to report to the Southeast Asia Center for International Relations at the University of Northern Illinois in DeKalb. Along with a group of other Peace Corps volunteers, they participated in cross-cultural training sessions for primitive living. The *DeKalb Daily Chronicle* printed a picture of Charlie and other volunteers learning to cut trees at Camp Rotary Mac Queen near the University. With hands in his pockets, Charlie is dressed in leather boots, a sweater and jeans, observing a tree-cutting demonstration.

On April 18, 1964, a Peace Corps commencement dinner was given in the Ballroom Center of the University. President Leslie Holmes addressed the volunteers: "All of us at Northern Illinois University wish you success as you leave the campus to begin the final step of your preparation of service as a volunteer." As Charlie and Karen left the commencement exercise, they carried in their hearts a prayer written on the back of the banquet program, "May the kindly and almighty Providence guide your steps now and in the years to come." But they also carried an uncertainty. Would they be among those chosen to take the next training step?

Charlie and Karen sang in the closing program in Chicago.

They returned home depressed. The training had been so hard. Doubtful of their future with the Corps, Charlie began job hunting and secured a position as a driver's education teacher. But he never got the chance to start. They were surprised to learn that they had been accepted into the next preparation stage.

On May 13, 1964, they arrived in Hilo, Hawaii and were immediately taken into meetings on the grounds of the old army hospital just below Rainbow Falls. Charlie and Karen were stunned by the beauty of the waterfall that poured over a natural lava cave into a ginger-encircled, turquoise pool, but their enjoyment of the setting was tempered by jet-lagged bodies.

The next day, they were interviewed by two psychologists and evaluated for flexibility, courage, stamina, culture shock, and motivation. Following the interviews, Charlie and Karen went to Hilo to purchase supplies they would need in the Waipio Valley of Hawaii, the first model training center selected by President Kennedy for Peace Corps volunteers.

Returning to the army hospital with camping gear, food, survival kits, and other supplies, they packed their bedrolls, stuffed their canvas duffle bags, and boarded a bus that carried them to their primitive training area.

Peace Corps volunteer and registered nurse Toni Lawrie sat near Charlie and Karen. Remembering those days, she wrote: "My first impression of them was 'what a handsome couple.' Both of them were very genteel, and had the nicest southern drawl...and not a deceitful bone in either body. Charlie was Karen's Superman (and  she was his Lois Lane). Charlie's strengths were his natural leadership and his sense of purpose. They were very loving and sincere."

Approaching a treacherous precipice, the bus stopped and all the volunteers had to disembark and continue their journey on foot. The guide warned the group that on every journey down into the valley, some volunteer falls on the hazardous trail. Karen wrote to her parents of how she was part of the fulfillment of his prophecy: "The driver let us off at the top of the valley and we climbed down the steep rocky road. I fell once–only abrasions to the knee. After two miles of this, we arrived to the camp site."

The camp held five primitive grass huts: two were Thai, two were Filipino, and a Borneo type *long house* was being built. All were on stilts. The floors were wood. There was no electricity. Water came from a nearby stream and had to be boiled. The toilet was behind jungle foliage with only banana leaves or bushes for privacy. They did all their cooking on a kerosene stove beneath the 14'x15' grass hut they were assigned.

With his body aching from several hours on a wooden slab, Charlie wrote, "The first night we did not sleep well at all. In fact, my hips are still sore. However, I feel that we are adjusting as well as could be expected." The

49

primordial environment of pristine waterfalls, multi-colored orchids, and exotic birds and trees aided their adjustment.

Charlie described it to his parents: "Waipio Valley is a tremendous valley. It is seven miles deep and has walls up to 1,800 feet.... It is the most beautiful place I have ever seen.... Words or pictures could never describe the beauty. My eyes could hardly contain the sight. Everything is so green. It is a real refreshing sight after being in Chicago so long."

After three days, Charlie became uncharacteristically angry during a training exercise. He was upset because of the approach the Peace Corps was using with prospective candidates. He had flashbacks to his Navy boot camp, when his First Class Petty Officer would look down upon his Seaman Apprentice position and scream orders at him. He wrote home, "They yelled at us, tried to make us walk down the hill faster, and took us through waist-high water and thick undergrowth. They pushed and pushed and pushed. At first I got mad. Now I think I can see the reason why.... They wanted to see if we could take it, for they realized that 'lemons' overseas can do much damage. However, I don't agree with many of their approaches." This dissatisfaction would inspire a very different approach to training in Charlie's own programs to come.

Charlie's and Karen's grass hut in Hawaii

Along with physically exhausting exercises, Charlie also resented the psychological pressure. He and Karen felt they were being screened by undercover agents for every word and step they made. After a few days of this, they began to wonder if the FBI and the Peace Corps were colluding to select the most patriotic volunteer! In a letter home, Karen wondered if they were suspected of some kind of conspiracy when she wrote, "Last night two psychologists led discussions on our day's activities. There is a psychologist behind every tree here. They hide outside the windows when we are having group meetings. We feel like monkeys in cages."

In another letter to her parents, Karen said they were assigned to mend fences, feed the animals, build pens and cages, and plant and harvest crops. She noted how Charlie was beginning to be a real farmer, as there were chickens, ducks, rabbits, dogs and other animals to feed. "Charlie is in charge of the pigs and trash dumping. He's a real outdoor man–and even a gentleman in the jungle. Don't guess I would make it over here if it weren't for him.... We have killed, dressed and cut up chickens (the Moslem way). We have made jam, learned to pickle *foons* (Chinese noodles), dry, cure and smoke meat. We are going to make bread and build with bamboo."

On May 28, she wrote: "Charles has been a marvelous camper – wonderful 'jungle gentleman.' He's the life of the party and has been keeping everybody's spirits up."

Another Peace Corps volunteer gave additional details of the experience: "Throughout training, the group studied Pasar (bazaar) Malay intensively, learned something of the history of Malaysia, completed practice teaching assignments in Hilo's schools, and went through a regimen of physical exams and psychological tests."

They were inventive in both work and play. Karen joined a team of ladies to fix a screen for the outside toilet and was involved in nurses training in Hilo. Karen's friend Toni Lawrie recalled: "We nurses brought sand from the beach to put in a volleyball court. Karen and I also fashioned a washboard out of bamboo for another project and left it down by the creek where we bathed and did our laundry."

The pressure was very great on the Peace Corps volunteers to prove they could handle an overseas assignment, for they would be representing the United States as de facto ambassadors. The reputation of the United States was still on the line in this second year of the Peace Corps experiment. A trainee named Guy Breyman wrote the following reflection of his 1965 experience in Waipio Valley:

> Occasionally, trainees would disappear overnight, having been "deselected" and sent back to their homes.... Those of us who remained in training resented the speed and secrecy of the de-selections, but in hindsight, there was probably no better way to accomplish the separations.

On May 28, 1964, Charlie wrote home to his parents, "This is just to let you know that we passed our final Selection Board. We feel fortunate that we are still in because eight were selected out." Karen wrote less modestly to her mother Ruth:

> I understand that 300 people have been consulted concerning us. Charlie had the highest rating of anybody on his peer rating (which we all did on each other). We are proud to be selected in, but we know that we have to do nothing less than our best to be successful. At this point, we feel very humble and know that we need God's help more than ever before.

Following a successful orientation and training experience, Charlie and Karen said their goodbyes and joined 16 other Peace Corps friends bound for

51

the Orient. They would be representing the United States in a foreign culture full of strange customs, ambiguous dialects, and unfamiliar territory. But for both Charlie and Karen, the joy stemming from being obedient to God's call on their lives far outweighed the risk of venturing into the unknown.

I want to warn anyone who sees the Peace Corps as an alternative to the draft that life may well be easier at Fort Dix or at a post in Germany than it will be with us.
~Sergeant Shriver

12
On the Train to Kangar
June 1964

The moment Charlie and Karen stepped onto the tarmac in Kuala Lumpur, Malaysia in June of 1964, they were anxious to delve into their assignments. But before these Peace Corps volunteers could proceed to their final destination, there was a required orientation conference. "I really didn't particularly care for the brief three-day program that was held for us," Charlie wrote. "My primary thoughts were on reaching our assignment." This attitude was typical of Charlie: he was not one to be bound by institutional polices, bureaucratic budgets or slow-moving legislation.

Like so many idealistic Peace Corps volunteers, Charlie felt, especially with Karen at his side, that he could tackle almost any assignment given him. But this thinking was about to change.

Following the conference, Charlie and Karen boarded a train bound for Kangar in northwest Malaysia. As rubber trees and flooded rice paddies flashed by, Charlie's exuberance began to fade as a "...foul smell coming from somewhere on the train made my stomach repel food. To me, it smelled something like the skin of a goat that had been soaking in stagnant water for several weeks."

Finally, his hunger pains and his curiosity about the source of the smell overcame his repulsion. Hoping to come across a wholesome Malay buffet, he carefully made his way back toward the diner car. With every step, the stench grew stronger. He discovered that the smell was emanating from the coconut cooking oil. Malaysians use this as their primary oil for cooking, even though it is prone to spoil quickly. Charlie had just encountered his first major culture shock.

"I decided to eat, even though that smell was so repulsive. And eat I did! A huge plate of fried rice....This was my first mistake [and it] caused me several days of misery with the worst case of G.I. upset that I have ever had."

Lawri, who had also been assigned to Malaysia, agreed with attributing his sickness in the train diner car to the coconut oil, though there was another possibility: "I thought it might have been his first encounter with durian, a fruit described by the locals as tasting much like 'eating custard in an outhouse.'"

As the train clattered down the tracks, their window view revealed incredible amounts of filth, rotting carrion, and worse scattered throughout the countryside. The gutters and ditches were full of trash. The homes were filthy. The people were unclean. Charlie wrote, "They wore T-shirts that looked like something my mother would have used for a dust rag." He was starting to see humanity in a different light, and perceived that "...each culture has its own set of living conditions...."

Charlie and Karen experienced the inevitable frustration of two languages clashing as they traveled closer to their assignment. It was difficult to order something as simple as a cup of tea. Blank faces stared at them when they used English. With the bit of Malay they had learned in their training, they would start a sentence, trip over a word or two, back up and start again. Charlie said, "I was beginning to discover that 200 hours of language instruction didn't guarantee a mastery of the language."

When the conductor stopped at the Kangar terminal, Charlie and Karen disembarked only to enter another disheartening ordeal. They had no adequate transportation. This was unexpected and put them in a grave situation. Charlie later wrote: "We were anxious to find a place to live, but we had no way to get about except by local taxi, which was a trishaw [three-wheeled rickshaw]. These slow-moving vehicles made me come down to earth rapidly."

They were told that the housing shortage was intense, the possibility of finding housing in Aura, where they were assigned as teachers, was very slim, and there was no government housing available. It seemed that problems were increasing exponentially.

Fortunately, for the first few days they were able to stay in a hostel, where they developed a friendship with an individual who owned a car. This gave them greater mobility in seeking permanent housing in Kangar. Eventually, they found a house to rent that, in Charlie's opinion, was ready to fall. It was built on stilts, and large cracks in the floor exposed the ground below.

He wrote his twin sister Marie, "We have bugs, spiders, mice and lizards in our house. They find our grass roof makes a wonderful breeding ground. We hear and see them moving around. The people accept this as a necessity."

Another cultural trial occurred when Charlie and Karen visited homes of the parents of his students, where they were served tea or coffee and something to eat. The experience was made more difficult with his severe intestinal problems brought on by eating the rice on the train. This was Charlie's lowest point to date:

I began to get sick of these cakes and horrible coffee. My G.I. upset was also getting worse, yet I managed to force the

54

food down with a simulated smile. That night, I thought that I had reached the end of the line. Nothing was working out as I had planned. I went back to the rest house and cried. I thought I was too old for such things, but not being able to see any bright lights for the future was too much for me. The Peace Corps thoroughly trained us in what our instructors called "Culture Shock". They related how one volunteer returned to America after being in Thailand for 48 hours. I could not understand how this could happen, but now, after being here a month, I understand. Yet I knew that things would work out if I gave them time. I even told my wife this, but I couldn't possibly see how they could ever work out.

Karen nurtured and loved Charlie through this depressing cultural ordeal, in spite of her own difficulty with the new Malay diet, which was causing her to lose weight. Charlie was deeply grateful for her support. He began to have compassion for the other Peace Corps volunteers who ventured to a foreign country without a supporting partner to discuss and share trials and sufferings. He was grateful to be married to Karen to discuss events and felt for those who did not have this blessed privilege. He thought about how difficult it must be not to have someone to communicate with in the English language.

By early October, Charlie and Karen both began to improve, mentally and physically. He wrote his sister Marie, "Karen is doing much better with her eating. She's not gaining weight (still 97 lbs.) but she is eating well. You ought to see her put away that rice. It does me good to see her eat well. Don't worry about us. We're all right!!! Life is great here. Wouldn't trade it for the world." Karen agreed with Charlie that life was good in the rice paddies: "We're thrilled with our assignment to Kangar, here in Malaya. People here are just great–so hospitable– as hospitable as Southerners are. In fact, they could probably teach us a few lessons."

Getting adjusted to the new culture was both scary and rewarding. Karen wrote a letter to her old medical friends–Dr. Brown and several nurses–back in Ruston:

> Tell Glenda and Lerline that I have not seen any snakes hanging from trees, but Charlie encountered a cobra in the middle of the road.... Although this experience was rather unusual, it served to make us more cautious.... Charlie says we're not in any more danger than in Louisiana because of the many snakes there.

Karen mentioned her frustration at the lack of security fences around the medical compound where she was assigned to use her nursing skills during her second year of service. She complained that in one ward of the hospital, she had trouble keeping the goats and cats out, as animals roamed freely everywhere. But on one particular day at her house, the lack of a fence turned out to be a blessing. "When we first came, a chicken flew in my house and laid an egg on the kitchen table. How's that for service?"

For two years, Charlie and Karen lived in this little house supported by stilts. It would forever change their way of thinking about material things, money, food, clothing, and living conditions, including limited and primitive medical facilities and resources. As Karen wrote, "I am learning here that I took many of the medical supplies at home for granted. We make Q-tips here by using a stick from a dried palm branch, glue, and cotton. We cut and fold our gauze squares from gauze material and make our own cotton balls."

Another cultural experience that they often found amusing had to do with "honey."

Charlie and Karen paid their landlord a few *ringgits* rent each month and became accustomed to life in the little house on stilts. They adjusted to their "neighbors" in the thatch over their heads. They even discovered life wasn't so bad living with a "honey bucket." In a speech chronicling his Peace Corps days for some students at the University of Kentucky, Charlie referred to the latrine in

56

back of a Malaysian house. "Now I don't want to get too detailed at this part, but a little explanation is in order–a bucket latrine is a raised platform with a hole in the floor above a bucket and once a week the honey bucket man, as he was called, would come by and empty that bucket in a larger one that he carried on his shoulder–awful job!"

It was next to this honey bucket that Karen and Charlie found strength to love each other, pray for God's guidance, plan the day's activities and envision their future. As simple as it was, the experience laid a foundation for all they would become as they incarnated the love of Christ among the world's poor.

CHRISTMAS GREETINGS FROM OUR HOME TO YOURS

CHARLES & KAREN SMITH

57

When Karen and I served in the Peace Corps...
we learned a Malay proverb:
'Huntang emas, boleh di bayar; Huntang buti, bawaw de mati.'
Translated it means,
'When you owe someone gold, you can repay them.
When you owe them kindnesses, you will carry it to your grave.
~Charlie Smith

13
Sama, Sama
1964-1966

Evidently the Smiths rode a motorcycle at times!

Charlie and Karen had a built-in alarm clock. At the 6:15 sound of yard roosters and ducks, they would slip out from under their mosquito nets to begin their daily routine. There was one faucet in the back of the house with enough pressure in the evening to fill up a 45 gallon tank for showers and washing clothes. Most of the time they found that sufficient water had accumulated in the tank overnight to meet their morning needs. Breakfast usually consisted of coffee and milo, a type of grain sorghum made into a cereal or couscous, to go with either biscuits or French toast.

Around 7:20, they hopped on two Peace Corps bicycles[10] stationed underneath the stilt house and rode to the bus stop. After a 15 minute bus ride, Charlie and Karen[11] entered the secondary school in the village of Arau along with 25 other teachers and 600 students. It was the only secondary school in the state of Perlis. English was the language of instruction. As Charlie entered the classroom all the students would stand and in unison say, "Good morning, Mr. Smith." Charlie would respond: "Good morning, class."

Grateful for pictures of everyday life in America which his sister Marie had made for him, Charlie wrote to her: "Thanks so much for taking the slides for us. We can hardly wait till we receive them. Like Wiley said in his newspaper article, we are flooded with questions about America, and the pictures will help us to explain what America is really like."

The class session was usually 50 minutes of comprehensive oral lessons as Charlie drilled the students and explained the many nuances and complexities of the English language. When the ringing of the school bell brought closure to the class, Charlie would gather his class notes and books. As he stood, the students would all stand and in unison say, "Thank you, Mr. Smith." Charlie responded with, "*Sama, Sama*," meaning, "You are welcome."

After the 1:30 closing bell, Charlie would put his teaching materials in his briefcase, rendezvous with Karen, and they would ride the bus to Kangar. By 2:00, they would straddle their bikes and ride the rest of the way to their thatched hut. Charlie would spend the

The Smiths relax in their Malaysian home, their coolie hats decorating the walls.

---

[10] "Transportation was good if you had a scooter—we had a 50cc Honda—and I think Charlie and Karen stuck to bikes for most of their time. We also took taxis for long distance travel—there was a taxi station in almost every town of any size, and then there was always that train that ran on a narrow rail that rocked you to sleep if you got a bunk for the night."   ~Toni Lawrie, fellow Peace Corps nurse

[11] Karen was first assigned to the school. Later she used her nursing skills in a clinic.

59

afternoon preparing English lessons for the next day and taking care of his chickens.

Following a meal of the customary rice and curry, both would spend their free time reading books brought over from the States. Books were priceless commodities. "Books have become our friends and companions," wrote Charlie, "and we are discovering a world of information that we feel will help us to be better Americans when we return home."

These two Peace Corps volunteers from northern Louisiana usually ended the day with a cold shower before crawling underneath a priceless mosquito net that served as a protective canopy over their bed. They were a long way from Ruston, but together they were as contented as newlyweds in a bridal suite. The pest-infested thatch roof above and five-gallon honey bucket on the ground below in no way lessened their love for each other.

Casting sanitary toilets out of concrete molds was a project initiated by Charlie. He drew a design of an inexpensive toilet on a letter written to the States. It shows a pipe connected under the seat of the toilet, bent upward and then bent again toward the outer wall for the flushed water to drain. This provided huge health benefits for the people where large families shared outdoor privies and had to have their waste carried away in buckets.

Charlie and Karen also started clubs for the students. Charlie's goal was to help the boys improve their sanitary conditions at home, learn how to raise chickens and use improved methods of rice production. It was a slow process. Charlie wrote of his frustration, "Perhaps I should add here that much of the work done is very slow. It is impossible to move into a situation expecting to change the way people have lived for centuries.... It takes many hours of convincing to

Karen next to Charlie, center in dark shirt, with students in Arau, Malaysia

inspire someone to take a small step."

His desire was to create an atmosphere of openness to change in the minds of the young boys. He wrote, "If we can work with the young, flexible minds then there is hope that they can help the older rigid minds that are found in their homes....These boys will, in all probability, take over their parents' places, so perhaps this experience will produce some long range results."

Charlie with neighborhood children in Malaysia

Karen taught homemaking and was able to locate a hand-driven sewing machine donated by CARE International. She taught the girls how to make dresses and used her culinary skills to teach them how to make American-style cakes.

"Our days are really full," Charlie typed in their second year, reflecting a major change in their daily schedule. "We usually stay at school nearly 12 hours a day and then there is always work to do at home when we return. It is now 11 p.m. and I am getting tired but still have a lot to do before I retire for the night," adding, "It always seems to me as if we have slept only a few minutes when the chickens are awakening us again to begin another day."

Living in Malaysia for two years during the early years of their marriage impacted Charlie and Karen in a powerful way. The little city of Ruston no longer captured their hearts. They missed Myrtle's cooking. They missed the family. They longed to visit with friends. However, Malaysia cut the nostalgic umbilical cord to such an extent that Ruston was becoming a place not to live permanently but to visit occasionally. Louisiana represented the past; Kuala Lumpur the present, and the radical change in their cultural worldview, the future. As Charlie wrote his twin, "Marie, we won't be the same people that we were before we left Ruston..."

Responding to a tape from his parents, he wrote,

> Yes, we do get homesick once in a while, especially when we are sick and are glad to know that you think of us and, like you said, worry about us. ...I used to feel sorry for missionaries, but now I know that they wouldn't want to be anywhere else....

61

In a journal entry reflecting on this period of his life, Charlie wrote of the joy he and Karen shared together. "We had few of this world's possessions, but we were supremely happy.... There we learned that happiness is not dependent on possessions but rather on the purpose for which you are living and the quality of relationships."

When their two-year term of service was up, they took a very roundabout way of getting home, visiting 25 countries on a tour that had them using nearly every possible form of transportation.

Writing home from one exotic place, Charlie said: "We have been here in Cambodia for two full days now, and we have really been enjoying our stay. The ruins from the old Khmer empire are fantastic." At one point they boarded the *T.S.S. State of Madras* and sailed to India, where trains took them through the land of Gandhi. From another spot he recorded: "Greece was marvelous.... We visited Delphi, Olympus, Epidaurus, Nauplion, Mycenae, Corinth and of course Athens. We came to Salzburg, Austria by train."

In Germany they purchased a VW Bug and, ignoring the Cold War spat between the United States and Russia,[12] continued their journey through Europe. They became recreational nomads, roaming the streets of London, the castles of Germany, the museums of Paris and the cathedrals of Spain before making their way home to America by plane.[13] It would have been difficult for Charlie to travel though 15 time zones, be exposed to the world's great religions, ride his Ducati motorcycle through the streets of world capitals, and interact with cultures still locked in the Stone Age, and remain the same.

Through Karen's influence, Charlie had left those back roads of Louisiana for mountain trails in Malaysia and exchanged the sugar cane fields of Winn Parish for the rice paddies of Kuala Lumpur. This clash of cultures would form a crucible of change in Charlie's mind, producing wild ideas and improbable dreams that would someday threaten authorities, befuddle colleagues, and baffle family members, but at the same time plant seeds of hope that would bless and change the lives of thousands. One can almost hear this multitude of voices saying, "Thank you, Mr. Smith," and Charlie responding, "Sama, Sama."

---

[12] While they were traveling, an American reconnaissance plane was shot down over East Germany by the Soviet Union.
[13] They shipped the VW, which had cost $1,345 and in which they had logged 6,000 miles touring Europe, back to the States for $50.

PART THREE

1950 - 1980

Explorations

The Navy
Courtship
Peace Corps
Kentucky
Florida

Later we bought our first home in Rivals, population 13!
We were country for sure, and enjoyed the big old house
(except in the winter time when trying to heat it!)
~Charlie Smith, reflecting on their Kentucky years

14

One Mistaken Identity, Two Babies, Three Stoves
1966–1976

Making their way home from their Peace Corps service, Charlie and Karen were sightseeing near Piccadilly Square in London when a letter from his mother caught up with him, informing him of a job opportunity working with the rural poor. Under the Johnson Administration, there was an opening for a director for the Lincoln Parish Community Action Center in Ruston, Louisiana. At first Charlie wasn't interested. His heart was set on pursuing a career in the field of anthropology[14], and he was hoping to be accepted into a graduate program.

However, he knew his academic record wasn't the best, and he thought he should have some alternatives in the pipeline. The more he thought about his mother's letter regarding the Ruston Community Action Center, the better it sounded to him. He wrote to his brother-in-law, Dave Riggs, and asked him to see what doors he could open for him regarding the job. Charlie received a letter from Dave who sent him a job application for a position with a tight window of opportunity.

Charlie returned home in late June and was delighted to know that he had been accepted as director. He began working July 15, 1966, in the fiery cauldron of the Civil Rights movement. This job, which involved working primarily with blacks, appealed to Charlie because his parents had taught him that God accepted all people regardless of race, color, creed or gender.

---

[14] The seed to study anthropology was planted in Charlie's mind in Malaysia. Charlie wrote: "While working to bring about change in lives, I quickly learned that I knew very little and yearned to know more. In the Peace Corps I met a volunteer (Bill Cull) who had a degree in anthropology from the University of California. He introduced me to the discipline."

"There was never any question about [working with blacks on an equal basis]," Charlie recalled. "I had a black associate and we moved our offices to downtown Ruston, Louisiana. It was the first integrated office, and you know what the times were like. It was rough."

On May 30, 1967–halfway through the two years that Charlie worked at the Community Action Center–Charlie's and Karen's first child was born. They named her Felicia. Charlie had told Karen that he did not want to have children because of the direction the world was headed, with inner city riots, the Vietnam War, and the assassinations of the Kennedys and Martin Luther King. He later confessed that he was glad Karen convinced him otherwise.

Charlie and Karen with baby Felicia

Things went well with the Community Action work, but in 1968, the dream of becoming an anthropologist came to the forefront again. He and Karen began to think about another move, allowing him to pursue a doctorate in the field of anthropology.

Charlie applied to the University of Kentucky's graduate program in anthropology and waited hopefully for a reply. He wrote of this time:

My GRE[15] scores were not sufficiently high, so I was denied admission by the graduate school, but the chairman of the department at UK, Henry F. Dobyns, pleaded my case and they let me in on probation. He later told me that with my Peace Corps and community action background, they thought I was black and they wanted a black, in the new, applied anthropology program.

The family moved with little Felicia to Lexington, Kentucky, and in 1971 they added another little girl to their household. Anne-Marie was born on June 23 of that year, while they were living in Shawneetown–the university's married student housing. At that point, they sensed a need for relocating out of the city, both to raise their girls and to put Charlie closer to his doctoral research locale.

Felicia and her new baby sister, Anne-Marie

Taylorsville, Kentucky was a town of 900 people about 60 miles from Lexington, which served as the county seat for Spencer County. Ellen Schuhman, *Louisville Times* Staff Writer, described this small city:

> The first thing one notices in Taylorsville is the quiet. Birds sing but the air is not pierced by city noises.... At night the stars seem brighter.... Men gossip on benches in front of the red brick Spencer County Courthouse, then wander over to the Family Affair Restaurant for coffee. There aren't many stores, only a couple of gas stations, and one stoplight.

Charlie set up his research office in this peaceful, laid back community, and, a few blocks from the center of town, Charlie and Karen set up housekeeping in a cramped duplex with a small front stoop. Elsie, an elderly lady, lived next to the Smiths and often babysat the girls. It was here that the girls, especially Anne-

---

[15] A Graduate Record Exam is administered to graduates of institutions of higher learning. The scores are used as criteria for admission to master's and doctoral programs in many institutions and areas of specialization.

Marie, had their earliest memories, which included Elsie always having orange "circus peanuts" in her candy bowl. The girls delighted in these marshmallow treats because they were not allowed to have candy at their house.

Longing for open space for the children after living in Taylorsville for about two years, Charlie and Karen went house shopping. About five miles outside of Taylorsville, they drove their little VW Bug into an unincorporated rural town called Rivals, population 13. Checking out the housing possibilities in Rivals, a two-story farm house that was standing during Abraham Lincoln's presidency caught their eye. The large, white frame house had a roomy front porch. There was a tree in the front yard big enough to support a swing, and an evergreen tree grew nearby. Providing ample storage was a shed for implements and a barn with a hayloft. A gently flowing creek was near the farm and there was plenty of space for a garden. After walking over the property and thinking what a great place it would be to raise the girls, Charlie and Karen were ready to sign the dotted line.

The Smith Family's unheated "White House" in Rivals, Kentucky

Karen and Charlie were not rich in the material things of the world, but they were wealthy in relationships, purpose, meaning, imagination, creativity, vision, ideas and laughter. Throughout the rest of their lives, Charlie and Karen would never deviate from this "rich vs. wealth" value system. They chose to live simple lives–purchasing clothes at Goodwill, driving used cars, ordering a large drink with four straws at fast food restaurants, and living in simple houses. Even though it was built during the Civil War era, compared to their living space in their Peace Corps days, or the little apartment in Taylorsville, the house in Rivals was a housing upgrade for them.

This farmhouse did not have central heat. In the winter time, Karen cooked dinner in her coat and gloves. Though it was difficult for her, she held on to her sense of subtle humor. When Charlie bought three stoves in one day, Karen laughed about his inexplicable decision and told her sister, "Now we have a stove for each meal!"

68

Reflecting on those Kentucky days, Charlie wrote:

I am so thankful I took hundreds, perhaps thousands of slides of our family through [the girls'] childhood until they graduated from high school. Now Felicia and Anne-Marie can relive those wonderful days when we lived in Taylorsville, Kentucky, population 950: Hee Haw! Later we bought our first home in Rivals, population 13! Hee Haw again! How wonderful were the good times we had in that big old house, built in about 1850. As I write these words I can hear John Denver singing, "Thank God, I'm a Country Boy"– singing it at the top of his voice

Felicia and Karen trying to keep warm

(volume high) on our stereo system, and I can see the girls dancing in abandon to the music. We were country for sure, and enjoyed the big old house (except in the winter time when trying to heat it!)

Until the time Felicia was seven and Anne-Marie was four, the home in Rivals was like a perennial rural carnival: instead of carousels they had chickens, instead of roller coasters they had rabbits, and instead of bumper cars they had a barn. They spent hours playing in the creek and swinging from the great tree in front of the house. Juicy tomatoes flourished on vines, and green beans, sweet corn, okra, cabbage, yellow squash and watermelon sprouted in the garden for these former city slickers now turned "farmers." The girls romped and played with their dogs Jake, Cinnamon and True Love, while their cat Butterscotch stood sentinel at the barn door.

Anne-Marie and Felicia pose on the family car

Karen was working 25 hours a week as a rural health nurse; Charlie was working nearer the girls' school and child care. Almost daily, Charlie had to juggle school for Felicia and babysitting for Anne-Marie, all while dedicating the many hours necessary to pursuing his dream. First there was the master's degree in anthropology to earn. After that began the specialized study in applied anthropology, and just because he had been admitted under the false presumption that he was a minority student didn't mean he was given a free pass in classwork.

Six years is a long time to put everything on hold to pursue a dream. For Charlie, the years 1968 to 1974, which he spent pursuing a doctorate in anthropology, would represent 10 percent of his life. But he had grown in maturity and discipline.

After two years, Charlie had earned his second master's degree and had chosen Applied Anthropology for his doctoral studies. Charlie believed that the application of anthropological methods and theory to the problems of given cultures was far more important than teaching classroom theories without practical applications.

Meanwhile, he learned some nearby Kentuckians were being displaced due to a proposed dam whose backed-up waters would inundate their farms and houses. Red flags of injustice waved in his mind, and he turned his attention toward these people. They became his passion and the centerpiece of his dissertation:

> The most meaningful part of the academic program was the four years of research and writing I did pertaining to the socio-cultural impact of a U.S. Army Corps of Engineers dam and lake project that was being located in Spencer County, Kentucky. Four monographs [scholarly articles] came out of that study, two I authored and two others I co-authored. They were published by the U. S. Department of Interior Water Resource Research Institute who funded the research. Dr. Dobyns started the project and was my major professor.

Charlie threw himself into the research and was soon collecting mountains of data, writing monographs and progressing toward completion of his doctorate. Deep inside, he wanted this degree for his father, because his father placed such a premium on higher education, and it would have been a great way to honor him after the years of trouble and worry that Charlie had caused him. However, in the end, the doctorate was not to be his. When he thought back over his life, he recorded the following thoughts regarding that situation:

> When Dr. Dobyns left U.K. [for the vice presidency of an Arizona college], my hopes for the PhD vanished.... If Dr. Dobyns had been the chairman of my committee, he would have assured that the terminal degree would have been completed.
>
> [The new department chair] would call me from time to time to see if I wanted to make another go at it. I didn't. My pattern through life has been to "burn the bridges" of the past and to throw myself into what came next. I had no regrets leaving academia and the terminal degree. I received the best education possible, had tremendous professors and learned so much. This is what was important, not being called "doctor."
>
> Later, Henry Dobyns told the Anthropology Department they were foolish to let me go without the degree because I had done more significant research, writing and publishing than the great majority of students who earned PhD's in anthropology. He said they should have put a ribbon around my publications and given me my PhD. I agree, but if they had, my life would have surely gone in a different direction. "All things work together for the good..."

Years later he was asked, "Charlie, if you had received your PhD, would Heart to Honduras exist today?" His reply of "probably not" gives us a glimpse into how God turned what seemed a tragedy at the time into a blessing in disguise.

Even at the time, the earning of the degree was not as important to Charlie as the relationships he built and the justice he pursued through his research assignment. He stopped thinking of his work as just research and began to pour his life into the people whose lives were being turned upside down by the dam.

Having once put his hand into the ground, seeding there what he hopes will outlast him, a man has made a marriage with his place, and if he leaves it his flesh will ache to go back.
~*Wendell Berry in* Farming: A Handbook,
quoted in the Spencer County Community Report, December 1975

15
The Power of One
1975-1976

Photo by Charlie of a Spencer County farmer

Emotions were running high. Landowners were livid. Blood was boiling. Tempers were flaring. The unseen incense of rage was permeating the courthouse with justified wrath. The issue was the looming inundation of the farmlands of Spencer County. The moderator was Charlie Smith. Seated at the head table with legal papers spread in front of him, he was listening to heartbreaking stories from poor landowners who were about to be displaced from the floodplain of the Salt River.

When Charlie began his study of anthropology in 1968, he had had no idea he would end up at that volatile hearing. But there were hints along the way as he earned his master's degree and began his doctoral research in Taylorsville, Kentucky. His assigned project was to study the socio-cultural impact of the dam and lake project, but his involvement went beyond the cold research of facts and figures as he heard the stories of the lives being broken by Big Government invoking the law of eminent domain. Charlie found that he was in the middle of a major battle. It was a modern David against Goliath.

The first to speak about her experience with a U.S. Army Corps of Engineers agent was Mrs. Lilly Anzalone: "My first mistake was letting him in the front door! He wasn't kind. He wasn't considerate. I think the first time he came into my house he was [planning on] taking me to court. He finally slammed his book shut and walked out. I got so mad I got sick and had to go to the doctor. They didn't do me right."

72

At the core of the conflict in Kentucky was a flood control dam. As early as 1965, area residents had been informed of plans for this dam and an accompanying 200 to 800 acres of recreational area. But in September of 1973, the residents were shocked to learn that the government had expanded the proposal to a 17,000 acre project (13,000 of them in their county) with 4,326 of that allocated for a public park. Land acquisition was to begin immediately, and no one in the federal government had worked with the local officials to include them in the plans.

Residents had been in favor of the flood control and were fine with a small park, but this expansion without consultation was unacceptable.

That September, the head of the Environmental Resources of the Planning Divisions said it was not too late to negotiate a suitable plan for the park. County Judge Jesse Kelien, Taylorsville Mayor Charles Spears, and Virgil Snider, chairman of the planning commission, promised to take steps to guarantee that the local community would have input into those plans.

Within days, Judge Kelien and Mayor Spears set up the Spencer County Development Committee, with resident Charlie Smith joining three other citizens as members. This group set a date for the following week to meet with the Army Corps of Engineers.

There were two sides to the proposal for the Taylorsville Dam Project. In a *Louisville Times* article, Charlie stated the committee's position: "The park land acquisition is too big, the people are pressured to accept an unfair price for their land, and legal jargon is confusing to the people.... [Some] can't read and they misinterpret. The words the Corps uses are too far removed from the rural people. The land owners do not know their options." The Army Corps of Engineers asserted: "We need more land for the park for long-range planning, we are listening to the people, and we are paying a just and fair price for the land." The lines were drawn, and the road to that courthouse hearing had begun.

Once Charlie was appointed to the committee of volunteers, he became more and more involved with the lives of the farmers about to be displaced. Throughout his life, Charlie was drawn to the underdogs and made every effort to stand up for them. He began visiting farmers and hearing their stories, combining his doctoral research with real-life needs. He remembered those visits:

> The rural people of Kentucky were very friendly once you got to know them and they no longer feared you, an outsider.... When you genuinely like people, they will like you in return, and I have always liked people.

By the end of 1974, Charlie wrote of his shifting priorities:

I was more than satisfied with what I had learned [at the university.] So, I went native! The anthropologist became a part of the community. I had grown to love the people and the beauty of Kentucky, so I created a need for a position as Director of Community Development for Spencer County, Kentucky. Judge Kelien, Stuart Kelly and I went into the then governor's office in Frankfort, Wendell Ford...and he approved a grant to fund my position. For two years I worked for the county judge and the magistrates on behalf of the people being displaced by the project and on behalf of the county that would likely experience rapid change because of the lake project.

Charlie loved this photo he took of Sam, another Spencer County farmer

Changing from a volunteer on a county committee to an employee working on the same project gave Charlie an income so that Karen was not the only bread-winner, and it gave him a way to continue working with the Spencer County folk. Charlie and fellow anthropology student Dianne Smith, who was no relation to Charlie, opened a Relocation Assistance Program in the county courthouse in January 1975. Its stated purpose was to find solutions for people being relocated due to the construction of the impending reservoir whose scheduled completion had now been delayed until 1979. They wanted to ensure the government followed federal laws on land acquisition and that people displaced by the project received a fair value for their land and acquired suitable housing. They made home visits to inform the people of their rights, they provided a list of attorneys to assist anyone needing legal services, and they provided photograph packets of people's houses, outbuildings and families as mementoes of the home places they would be losing.

During his anthropology studies, Charlie had learned much under the tutelage of Dr. Art Gallaher, a professor of anthropology and deputy director of the Center for Developmental Change at the University of Kentucky. The things he learned about the importance of being an analyst had great practical application in helping the rural farmers being displaced, helping these people interpret their situation and understand what was going on.

Another of the things he had learned was to listen, so at that volatile June, 1975 meeting in the courthouse, he asked the people to talk, and talk they did.

Charlie asked the 35 landowners attending the meeting, "Do each of you believe the prices being offered are low?" All the land owners, most past middle age, nodded in agreement, and then the verbal explosion began, as Charlie opened the floor for residents to share their feelings. Anzalone stated that she had sold her 47 acres too soon and had only come to the meeting so others could benefit from her experience.

Other landowners followed, expressing their anger at the government for using scare tactics to pressure lonely widows, destitute dirt farmers, defenseless elderly and uneducated backwoodsmen. They were threatened with lawsuits if they refused to sign on the dotted line for a below-market price for their farmsteads.

"I am very distressed at stories from honest, hardworking people being pressured by representatives of the Corps to unduly sell their land," Charlie told the group. "This is deplorable. We are supposed to have a government of the people and for the people."

**One of the photos taken by Charlie of families
who were being displaced by the dam project**

Ray Goodlett, a 50-year-old landowner, angrily added, "I paid $686 an acre for land at a public auction, and the Corps is going around offering $300 and $400 per acre." Mr. and Mrs. Roy McClain agreed with Goodlett. "When we look

75

at other farms for sale outside the project areas, we find they are priced from $1,000 to $1,500 per acre."

One speaker charged that the proposed park would be nothing more than "a backyard playground" for the people of Louisville and Jefferson County. Voice after voice expressed their strong feelings about the way they and their neighbors were being treated by the government.

Charlie, seated third from left, at a UK protest over Kent State and the Viet Nam War.

Angry speech went beyond what was shared in the courthouse that day. At some point in the process, 40 angry Spencer County residents staged a protest march[16] in front of the Army Corps of Engineers office in downtown Taylorsville. A newspaper photo showed an old farmer wearing a cotton plaid shirt and holding a placard that read: "Government for the People Means Spencer Countians Too!" One of the marchers, Tom Cull, said, "I couldn't take what they offered me, so they condemned my farm. Now I don't know what to do."

Charlie's relocation work drew the attention of a young attorney, David Johnson, who was a member of a congressional committee in Washington: "I was attracted to Taylorsville by a 'relocation program' set up at the beginning of

---

[16] The Spencer County photograph does not show Charlie marching with the farmers but he had participated in public protests before. The photo above appeared in the *Lexington Herald Leader* in 1970 when University of Kentucky students staged a sit-in on the campus protesting the Kent State shootings and the Vietnam war, and the National Guard was summoned.

76

the year by Charlie Smith and Dianne Smith." He stated that this program was the first of its kind in the nation, and he knew it was financed with a $50,000 grant from the state. He came to see why there was a need for this program run by the county and funded by a state grant when the federal government had passed an act in 1971 to ensure that all federal agencies, such as the Corps, deal "fairly and equitably" with landowners uprooted for the "public good." It was his first "in-the-field" visit on behalf of his subcommittee chaired by Senator Edmund Muskie of Maine. His purpose was to observe and then report back to Congress as to the efficacy of the 1971 act.

What Johnson heard was a litany of complaints from local farmers who felt that the Corps not only offered too little money, but too little respect. "They treated me like a hound dog," said Earl Cochran, who chose to go to federal court, where he received $13,500 more than the Corps had offered.

News began to spread throughout the region of "David" doing battle with "Goliath." From about 40 miles north of Taylorsville, Tom Peterson of the *Shelbyville Sentinel-News* came down to see what kind of stones Charlie Smith was using in his humble slingshot to thwart the approaching Army Corps of Engineers. He wanted to know more clearly how Charlie was keeping Goliath from gobbling up more and more acres and paying the owners what many felt were a few "grains of chicken feed."

In the January 1, 1976 issue of the *Sentinel-News,* Peterson wrote:

> Some people call Charles Smith an idealist, a dreamer. Undaunted, he is the first to agree. This is because Charles Smith does not deny he wants to do something that hasn't been done before. Smith is the co-ordinator of the Spencer County Planning and Development Agency and as such is in charge of making sure the 3,050 acre lake now being designed by the U.S. Army Corps of Engineers for Spencer County is a recreational, educational, environmental, and socio-economic success. He laughs when he says it isn't going to be easy, but he's not trying to kid anybody. Smith is dead serious when he says the Taylorsville Lake can be either the biggest bonus or the worst disaster that the county has ever seen.... [He says that] the federal government has allocated 56 million dollars to do the job [and] to get less than the maximum mileage out of this investment is pure stupidity and laziness. The lake is designed to correct an inherent local flood problem. This was supposed to be corrected many years ago by the town flood wall. It wasn't, and Smith doesn't want to be a part of a second

inferior water project. He says to blow this project could mean both physical and economic doom for the county.

When the grant ran out and Charlie's employment there ended in 1976, Goliath—Big Government—had been forced to slow down their headlong rush to install a huge park without considering the impact on the local residents and their desires for their community. Through Charlie's efforts and the efforts of his co-worker in the Relocation Center, his partners on the Spencer County Development Committee, and the people of Spencer County, David had triumphed!

In 1976, Charlie attended the 150-year celebration of Spencer County's existence—a celebration which culminated in the burying of a time capsule on the right side of the courthouse. Charlie left his documents as both a legacy to the rural Kentuckians who were displaced, as well as a gift to his daughters. "I placed in that box copies of all of the unpublished research we did during the four years of research and writing during this pivotal time in the lives of this small county of 5,000 people. Inside those documents are written notes to my beautiful daughters. I hope that Felicia and Anne-Marie can attend the opening [of the time capsule at Spencer County's Bicentennial in 2026] and claim that publication for their own."

The park opened in 1983—a full five years later than the first plans called for. Beyond that victory, Charlie had befriended at least 25 families and helped them in the wrenching resettlement process. He had the satisfaction of knowing he had stood his ground against the mighty Corps because he believed justice was not being served. Today, the Taylorsville State Park consists of 1,650 acres—one third of that infamous 4,326 proposed in 1973. One man—one little David—had stood up for the underdogs, encouraging them to stand up for their right to be treated fairly, and Goliath—the impersonal government of the United States of America—had been forced to bow to their desires.

PART THREE

1950 - 1980

Explorations

The Navy
Courtship
Peace Corps
Kentucky
Florida

Twenty years from now you will be more disappointed by the things that you didn't do than by the ones you did do. So throw off the bowlines. Sail away from the safe harbor. Catch the trade winds in your sails. Explore. Dream. Discover.
~H. Jackson Brown

16
Land of Bugs and Sand
1976

In June 1976, an unplanned meeting in Anderson, Indiana, led to an invitation to join the faculty of Warner Southern College. Charlie was offered the position of sociology professor for the school recently founded in Florida by the Church of God. It did not take Karen long to decide how she felt about moving. She was weary after almost eight years in Kentucky. She had spent many hours alone with the girls while Charlie was off on his motorcycle campaigning against the Corps of Engineers. And she was not looking forward to another winter in the country house, cooking while wearing a winter coat and gloves. The thought of sunny Florida was very appealing. She responded immediately, "Let's go!"

Charlie was less eager. The school seemed so traditional to him that he sent out a few more résumés. But he was running out of options, and Karen was ready to make a move. He wrote:

> I was assured [within myself] that I would not touch that position with a 10-foot pole. They were so conservative and legalistic that I was repelled. But they pursued me while I continued a search for [another] job.

However, with Karen's pleas, and near-constant battles with the Corps making life difficult in Kentucky, they decided to make the move. Charlie reminisced:

> I hated the thought of...living in Florida because it was nothing but a land of sand and bugs. But we packed up a large U-Haul truck with our things, putting the VW bug we bought in Germany inside and towing the VW station wagon. The last thing

81

we loaded was a large freezer filled with vegetables and meat. [Then we] headed for this conservative Christian college called Warner Southern College that had all these codes, codes about how long your hair could be, you know, makeup, sleeves, hair. I hated those things. I rebelled against these laws.

After driving in the scorching sun for more than 700 miles, the Smith family passed through the city limits of Lake Wales and drove onto the Warner Southern campus. Crammed inside the U-Haul cab with Butterscotch the cat, the four exhausted but jovial members of the Smith family looked outside to see white sand, pine trees and a lake full of water lilies.

Little did the administration know that coming to town was not the traditional professor who would teach from faded yellow legal pads, expecting students to learn by rote. Lectures would be used, but not at the expense of discovery learning techniques and experiential activities. Objective tests were not off limits, but words such as "alternative," "progressive," "creative," and "unconventional" would be the norm. Years later, Charlie wrote:

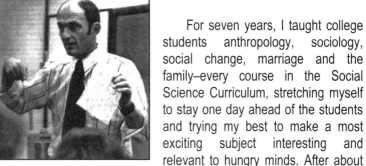

For seven years, I taught college students anthropology, sociology, social change, marriage and the family–every course in the Social Science Curriculum, stretching myself to stay one day ahead of the students and trying my best to make a most exciting subject interesting and relevant to hungry minds. After about three years of teaching, I began to love the classroom. Of course, I was an unconventional teacher, doing my best to link Christianity with my subject matter, doing my best to challenge the students to learning. From student evaluations required for each course, I found that they ranked me high as a teacher. That was personally satisfying, and I wonder today how many lives I could have impacted had I continued teaching. But again, I don't look back.

The couple would remain here for the next 21 years of their lives, raising their girls, nursing the sick, and teaching the students. Their home on "stilts" beside Crooked Lake would be the place from which Charlie would implement visions that would impact multitudes of people in North America and in a little country he had yet to visit called Honduras.

PART FOUR

1980 - 1992

Visions

Serious missionaries need serious training. H.E.A.R.T. is truly an exciting, practical approach to equipping young people to serve in Third-world[17] countries. I predict this innovative program will be a model for Christian colleges everywhere who want to responsibly prepare persons to touch and affect a hurting world.
~Gloria Gaither, Christian songwriter, member of Gospel Music Hall of Fame

17
The Great Vision: H.E.A.R.T.
1980-1981

When Charlie met Dean Flora through their common connections with the Church of God and Warner Southern College, he found he had met a man after his own heart. Both men had great love for the poor and both had little patience with institutional regulations that got in the way of ministry. Dean had served as a Church of God missionary in Panama and was now working in Florida with a ministry called Food For The Hungry.

Soon, Dean invited the Smiths to spend the 1980 summer break with Food For The Hungry at its ministry in Southeast Asia. Karen took a leave of absence from her job

Karen, Felicia, Anne-Marie and Charlie at the Equator in Kenya as part of their summer trip to Southeast Asia with Food For The Hungry.

---

[17] Third-World was the term in common usage in the 1980s and 1990s for what is now referred to as the developing world.

with Polk County Public Health, and she and Charlie took their girls, now 13 and 9, to Thailand. It was an exciting time for them to supervise 60 volunteers in an area where they had once volunteered themselves, and they enjoyed showing their daughters some of the places they had visited while working with the Peace Corps.

There were two Davids working with Charlie in Thailand that summer. One David was already a good friend of Charlie's; the other was a new acquaintance. Both men played formative roles in Charlie's life.

While in Thailand Charlie (left) and David Crippen brainstormed and produced this sketch (below) for a sustainable village.

Dave Pischel was a student volunteer that summer. He and Charlie bonded immediately and began a relationship that eventually resulted in their working together in the ministry to Honduras.

The other was David Crippen, whom Charlie had met the one year they both taught at Warner Southern College. David remembers the day in 1976 when Charlie, dressed in casual clothes, arrived late for the first meeting of new WSC faculty members. The men connected, and they, their wives, and children became close friends. The families were excited to spend time together in Thailand, and it was through Charlie's influence that David was appointed International Director for Food For The Hungry in Thailand. But the most important thing that happened between these men while they were in Thailand was a brainstorming session that resulted in David drawing a prototype Third World village that would inspire Charlie's first vision.

Back on campus that fall, Charlie went quail hunting with neighbor, friend, and fellow WSC employee, Lee Pugh, on Warner Southern's 350 unused acres of sand pine scrub. There, Charlie conceived a vision of placing the kind of simulated village he and David had discussed right on campus, providing a residential space much like the Peace Corps training

A simple quail hunt on WSC's sand pine scrub sparked a vision in Charlie

camp in Hawaii, for preparing missionaries and teaching college students ways of living simply at sustainable levels. It fit Charlie's philosophy of education–taking anthropology from the classroom to the sandbox of unused acreage on the Warner Southern campus.

Characteristically, within days of conceiving the idea, Charlie began working out the development of this vision. He presented his dream to Warner Southern missions department chair Bob Clark, college president Leroy Fulton, and academic dean Leslie Ratzlaff. With the help of Dean Flora's contacts, personnel from Food For The Hungry soon joined in, and things began to happen.

Warner Southern College leaders agreed to provide the land, teachers, curriculum, students and volunteers. Food For The Hungry personnel (Larry Ward, Ells Culver, and Dr. Ted Yamamori) agreed that their organization would provide grants and loans as well as specialists in the field of international development. The Polk County Planning and Zoning Commission was involved to approve the model project and assign county sanitary engineers and health specialists to ensure all health regulations would be met.

Charlie described the philosophy behind the project: "To invite prospective missionaries into the program, introduce them to sustainable living in family/household and community, and put them under stress to determine if they had what it took to be successful in difficult missionary assignments."

H.E.A.R.T. Steering Committee: Ted Yamamori, Dean Flora, Charlie Smith, Leslie Ratzlaff, LeRoy Fulton, Robert Clark

Food For The Hungry provided major funding to initiate the project. They employed Charlie as project director on a half-time basis for the 1980-81 academic term, with Warner Southern College employing him half time as a professor. By January 1981, several individuals had provided seed money, and a total of $18,000 was contributed in that first year to develop the program.

There was great optimism and enthusiasm during the early months. President Fulton, after having met with the Administrative Council, wrote to Charlie on February 2, 1981:

> We appoint you as the present Program Coordinator, accountable to the Academic Dean and the Chairman of the Missions Department. We temporarily designate land located in the Northwest Corner of the 320 acres owned by the college as the present site for the training program, disbursements are to be authorized by you and the Academic Dean, persons to be contacted for financial support should be approved by the President and we grant you permission to implement both gardening and small animal husbandry projects.

Charlie was deeply excited about this letter from the President and the approval to begin immediately:

For the third-quarter [spring, 1981] anthropology class, I had the students help me form a curriculum for this unique type of education and gather bibliography and other resources. Before the end of the quarter, several of the students went with me to the site to help prepare the ground for a garden and for drilling a well for water....[18]

Charlie's dedication and humility were in full force that spring. He wrote:

The day we hit water with our simple well-drilling outfit was a thrilling day. We had just about given up when someone suggested we try one more time. That was it, and there was dancing in the gushing water with joy. Small successes are often great for the confidence they give in pressing on, not quitting.

But student Phil Murphy remembers the same scene with a few extra details: "The day we got water we had actually stopped and prayed, had loaded it all in the truck and Charlie said, 'Let's try it once more.' We got it all out again, and once the pump started, water went all over the place."

Anne-Marie, Felicia and Karen Smith with Dr. & Mrs. Elmer Kardatzke enjoying the victory of striking water

---

[18] High on the list of students who helped in the first year were Mark Shaner, Phil Murphy, Summer Siehl, George and Debbie Bryant, Susan Rockett, Gerald Malzon and his wife Sherry, then Steve and Linda Coder in 1982.

With the well functioning, the students put up an old Army tent and starting making plans for building stilt houses like Charlie had experienced in the Peace Corps. Soon the sound of hammers and saws were heard, transforming the scrub pine acreage into a training area for simple living.[19] Charlie remembered those exciting, early days with fondness:

> Completing the "dining hall" and kitchen was a definite highlight. There we had countless meals together by lantern or candle light, building community while empowered by visions that would take us to distant lands to help the oppressed.

Summer Siehl thrilled at the chance to cut off this snake's head with a machete! Mark Shaner, Summer, Mark Muler, Darryl McDonald, and Phil Murphy (who remembers cooking it).

Mark Shaner came to the Warner Southern campus for pastoral studies. As a freshman, Mark quickly became part of a group of upperclassmen that was meeting from 6 to 10 p.m. every night in a makeshift building, sharing a pot of

---

[19] Louis Hartley, owner of Robin Builders, a utility shed manufacturing company, offered pressure treated wood at his expense, and Charlie's friend Deryl Johnson made the first contribution to the H.E.A.R.T. Program–$500.

beans and working out plans for a training ground that would equip missionaries and development people. He wrote:

> We divided up tasks; sanitation, gardening, buildings, animals, etc. With Charlie at the helm...we went to work, digging up cactuses, planting a garden, building buildings and buying animals. I personally worked at the H.E.A.R.T. Village for two years and lived there for nine months. When I married, I tried to get my wife, Vickie, to move to this primitive Third World village, but that was not going to happen. No running water, no electricity, enough said.
>
> I can't begin to tell the stories of Charlie's Volkswagen Bug, rattlesnakes, raccoons, bobcats...carrying water to the garden, a steady diet of tomatoes and donated orange juice, numerous missionaries [and other visitors] coming through to be eye-witness to what these college students were doing. Charlie was always dreaming the impossible that he knew could be possible.

On February 28, 1981, the Administration Council met and discussed some issues as this program was taking shape. In minutes taken by Charlie, he noted several concerns of President Fulton: that training needed to be open for "outsiders"–persons other than the Church of God; a need to establish policies and set up security for the girls, mentioning that it "scares" him that eight guys and gals are living over there; and finally, that the program was moving too fast with the college not knowing exactly where it was

Gloria Gaither, a rising star in the Gospel music world, shared watermelon with Phil Murphy (left) and Mark Shaner on a hot Florida day and declared H.E.A.R.T. a "truly exciting, practical approach to equipping young people to serve in Third-world countries."

headed. In regards to the boy/girl relationships, Ratzlaff suggested the possibility of alternate weeks for the male and female students. He expressed concern that there might not be enough work for the students to do, and hoped that no one would seek academic credit the first quarter. Another council member, who was to lead some of the programming, was concerned about moving too fast with too little planning, and wondered whether or not the students would be able to study without electricity. Would they use lanterns?

In a formal, 14 -page report to the college and Food For The Hungry written June 29, 1981, Charlie begins by stating that the name H.E.A.R.T. would replace various names which had been previously used for the program: "The Primitive Village," "The Project Across the Road Lifestyle," or "The Simple Life Village." Dr. Yamamori of Food For The Hungry had suggested that "Simple Life" has connotations that might be misleading, and that H.E.A.R.T. better described the purposes and function of what they were doing. Charlie wrote, "For all to know, H.E.A.R.T. stands for: **H** unger (spiritual and physical), **E** limination (for a few, for many), **A** ction (activities), **R** esources (persons, literature and technology), **T** raining (in the knowledge and skills of self-reliance in household and in community)." Charlie noted one objection to the definition: "Dean Ratzlaff reminded me that you *train* dogs, but *educate* people. That's perhaps true, but it would have destroyed the acronym."

One of the first assignments he completed for the administration was a 24-page research paper, which included three long-term objectives: 1) to help train 25 persons for overseas development assistant work, 2) to send two teams, one to Africa and one to Latin America, to construct and operate model H.E.A.R.T. programs, and 3) to provide basic learning experiences for 25 Warner Southern College students.

Charlie was a man of visionary faith, but the problem of unavailable funds reared its head often. He was a risk taker, and his greatest frustration was two-fold: partnering with personnel in positions of authority unwilling to take risks, and being thwarted when it came to spending funds to implement the vision. Often Charlie would take his personal credit card and purchase items, jeopardizing the finances of his own family. Charlie wanted fruit to spring up quickly so that it would be visible to potential donors. He believed that people were not attracted to needs but results. To get results, he needed finances. During this early stage, the gas tank of H.E.A.R.T. was running on fumes of faith.

Frustrated due to this lack of money, Charlie wrote a letter to President Fulton of the potential of this vision:

H.E.A.R.T. is a gold mine. It is a fundraiser's dream. Would that it would be a dream that you and others would help to realize. You can do it. I know you can. All we have to do is go out and dig the gold. It is waiting to be mined. I am convinced that if people in the know put their heads together and develop a plan for giving people an opportunity to give to H.E.A.R.T., the problem will not be due to a lack of funds but what to do with the excess that exceeds our immediate need. Do you not agree?

Even with the reassuring financial support of Food For The Hungry, by the end of the 1980-81 school year, funds were almost dried up. Reality set in as all parties began to realize that visions need cash flow, human resources, and unity as well as concepts and ideas. Charlie wrote in his 1980-81 report to the committee, "At the end of [the academic year], H.E.A.R.T. was virtually even in terms of receipts and expenditures, but the source of future funding remains uncertain. We are all aware of the realities of the situation: that for the program to continue, funds must become available."

In June of 1981, Charlie spelled out the need to require an *Agreement Contract* to be drafted and accepted by the governing boards of Warner Southern College (WSC) and Food For The Hungry International (FHI). He would regret this later, but for the present time it seemed to be the right thing to do. There were reassurances of "exclusiveness" between WSC and FHI. Warner Southern College would own the property but the program itself would be owned by both institutions in equal proportions, because as H.E.A.R.T. became well known, other institutions would want a "piece of the action." With this agreement, the involvement of any third entity would have to be with the approval of both institutions.

A five-year commitment was encouraged between the two agencies, with an annual review, so that the program would have a sense of stability, transparency and room to mature. A special administrative committee would be established to recommend a director, develop curriculum, appoint faculty, ensure financial soundness, select trainees and oversee day-to-day operations.

After considerable discussion between all parties concerned, Alternative Training Tracks were recommended in the report. They proposed summer sessions for high school graduates, credit for undergraduate and graduate students from other evangelical Christian colleges receiving training at H.E.A.R.T., training for overseas relief and development services for FHI's Hunger Corps and other relief development persons, training for missionaries on furlough to introduce holistic ministry concepts which could in turn be used and taught back on the field, consciousness raising for ministerial students to sensitize them to Third World needs, and training for Third World persons to learn self-reliance skills to take back home and teach.

In that same June report, it was noted that for the 1981-82 term, Food For The Hungry and Warner Southern College had again agreed to share equally the salary of Charlie as H.E.A.R.T. Director at $8,537.50 each, and Yamamori had authorized Dean Flora to raise funds and material for the project beginning immediately. In it, Charlie recommended that students Phil Murphy, George and

Debbie Bryant, Summer Siehl, and Mark Shaner be appointed as his staff assistants because of their donation of labor to jump-start the program, and that they be given $3,000 college scholarships. Other personnel suggested were Steve Kistner as Food Production Coordinator, Skeeter Frederick as Food Preparation and Preservation Coordinator and Karen Smith as Health Nurse and Library Resource Coordinator.

Charlie concluded his report with a partial list of needs (including "mule with rigging–plow and sled, five houses at $600 each, and dishes and eating utensils for 50 people") and the following words of encouragement: " I am gratified with the overall response to H.E.A.R.T.... The amount of work to be done is great.... I am taking one day at a time and trusting and believing that God will supply our needs on His timetable. I am ready to proceed full speed ahead if the funds, personnel and commitment are present, or I am ready to build gradually over the next year."

The extensive files that Charlie left show the many hours of work he dedicated to putting plans on paper for this vision. There are curriculum plans, purpose statements, budgets, brochures, needs lists, application forms (on which applicants sign their understanding of the rigors of living without modern conveniences), behavioral expectations of participants, and daily schedules that allowed time for academics and time for getting involved in gardening, animal husbandry or some other aspect of daily living in the developing world. The hard work resulted in the construction of living quarters, latrines, a meeting house, and plots of corn and banana plants growing beneath a water tower.

Those first two years saw a lot of development in both practical and theoretical ways, but bubbling underneath the surface excitement was a volcano of administrative lava about to threaten the whole project with destruction.

Construction of houses on stilts was done with student labor, and motivated by living in the army tent. Clockwise from upper left: Gerald Malzon hammering, Summer Siehl carrying a plank, the large army tent, Charlie Smith resting on the joists for the dining hall.

In the beginning, water had to be hauled in buckets carried on poles to the garden plot, and then carefully given to each plant, so it was with enthusiasm that the students joined in the well-drilling effort. Soon the garden was flourishing as generous amounts of water could be applied with the hose. Clockwise from lower left: Susan Rocket & Summer Siehl watering plants; Summer, Joe DeHart & Susan are the bucket brigade; Daryl McDonald driving steel casing into the well with Gerald Malzon looking on; Gerald, Phil Murphy and Susan fit PVC pipe into the well; Phil mans the hose while Gerald heads for the plants.

96

No college in the country has anything to compare with the brilliant vision of H.E.A.R.T. There is no place where students get better training for living in primitive Third World conditions.
~Tony Compolo, pastor and sociologist

18
The Great Vision Lost
1981-1982

Trouble began to brew almost immediately with Charlie's recommendation for an "Agreement Contract" between Warner Southern College and Food For The Hungry International. This agreement meant that FHI would provide funds, grants and volunteers with expertise in practical aspects of Third World living, and WSC would provide land, educational resources and students. It seemed like a perfect marriage, but strong personalities clashed, promises were broken and philosophical differences arose.

The H.E.A.R.T. vision was greater than the sum total of those who were in control and those who wanted to be in control. Charlie was not in control. He felt that if those who had the power would give him more responsibility, then his dream would come true. He believed he could change the lives of thousands through this vision.

Food For The Hungry's President, Ted Yamamori, and Charlie locked horns primarily regarding the philosophy of education that should be offered at H.E.A.R.T. Yamamori, mission strategist and author of 20 books, believed the academic side of the curriculum should be given priority; Charlie, as an applied anthropologist, believed the practical approach was the most effective.

The original plan that Charlie supported was not anti-academic. If anyone believed in academics, it was Charlie. But he wanted the hands-on experience to be primary, with academics following as supporting theory to the practical. His concern was that too many missionaries and development workers were being thrust into foreign cultures from seminaries and Bible schools with a ton of theory and an ounce of applied know-how. Charlie had been thrilled that Ells Culver of FHI advocated the applied approach and had his fingers crossed that Ells might turn things around. But when Ells left FHI and co-founded a new organization called Mercy Corps, this left a philosophical vacuum in the leadership of H.E.A.R.T., subsequently filled by Ted Yamamori.

97

The "Academic Down," or "Academics First," position espoused by Yamamori, with which it seemed the WSC personnel were in accord, combined with other issues, caused Charlie to submit his resignation as director of H.E.A.R.T. just one year into the work. President Fulton asked him to reconsider. Charlie acquiesced and withdrew his resignation, but wrote of his concerns to the president, hoping some policy changes might be forthcoming, including putting Ells Culver back in the picture. His September 2, 1982 letter said:

> You know of my frustrations concerning our relationship with Food For The Hungry International.... It is now clear to me...that we [need to] re-evaluate this linkage and pursue a new course of action.... It is my prayer that by the end of December 1982, we will be on a course that will usher the H.E.A.R.T. program into full implementation.... If by that time, however, we are unable to decide on a mutually satisfying course of action, then I will want us both to be free to pursue the leading of God's Spirit independently....
>
> I have been in contact with Ells Culver over the past several months and believe, as I have shared with you before, that he can and should play an important role in making HE.A.R.T. all that it can be. If you would initiate a contact with Ells by phone or by letter, then this would open the door for us to explore this alternative. He will be receptive to your contact.

The local newspaper pictured Charlie with H.E.A.R.T.'s water tower and flourishing garden

After pondering for months why H.E.A.R.T. was in a holding pattern, Charlie had concluded that the branch of Mercy Corps called Project Global Village[20], under the new leadership of Ells Culver, had the more appropriate vision for linkage with H.E.A.R.T. than Food For The Hungry. "Project Global Village shares the vision of H.E.A.R.T. It is concerned both with domestic and international hunger and has established a structure to address each. It has the purpose and structural foundations, as well as the motivation, for disseminating the H.E.A.R.T. approach to life, to people in need."

But a contract he himself had urged had been signed, restricting Warner Southern College from seeking a new partner. Worse, the Steering Committee placed the H.E.A.R.T. program in the Missions Department. Charlie saw the missions department as using ineffective and outdated missionary methods. He believed creative ideas emerging out of the H.E.A.R.T. program, with its social and anthropological initiatives, would be deeply hampered.

Instead, he felt H.E.A.R.T. was naturally an interdisciplinary type program. He wrote, "For H.E.A.R.T. to realize its tremendous potential, the program will need to have the capability for being creative/innovative as we diligently work to help the poor and the hungry in the world."

On December 10, 1982, the H.E.A.R.T. Steering Committee of Yamamori, Flora, Smith, Ratzlaff, Fulton and Clark met at Warner Southern College. To be fair to Yamamori, he believed in a holistic approach (academic and practical) in developing a course of study related to H.E.A.R.T. He recommended a two-year master's degree program related to H.E.A.R.T.–the first year's training on the H.E.A.R.T. campus, and the second year in overseas relief and development work. He stated, "What is emerging slowly will be a blessing to the entire missions world." But he did not want to begin the program with the applied approach.

On February 23, 1983, President Fulton, sensing discouragement over the H.E.A.R.T. program, sent a letter to the Steering Committee, seeking to rescue a ship that was beginning to take on water. He wrote, "Brethren, we have not always agreed as to schedule and process. This is unfortunate, but most unfortunate is that other persons are aware of this and the program has suffered. The time for putting this in the past is now. It is my feeling that agreement has been reached and we are ready to move ahead with the training program under the Missions department. Charles, the reports you presented were excellent and exciting."

---

[20] Project Global Village was the division that worked toward development; the other part of Mercy Corps dealt with emergency relief.

This letter was basically drawing a line in the sand between the Steering Committee and Charlie. Fulton knew full well the statement "...we are ready to move ahead with the training program under the Missions department..." would not sit well with Charlie. But leaders have to make hard decisions, and Fulton threw his weight behind Ted Yamamori.

Having read Fulton's letter, Charlie discussed it with his wife. And just as Karen encouraged Charlie to leave Kentucky, she supported him fully in his decision to leave H.E.A.R.T. She had never felt the college ever truly listened to or included Charlie in the major H.E.A.R.T. decisions. He had no official job description, and thus no authority to act. She reminded Charlie of the time noted sociologist Tony Campolo visited the campus to speak and to visit H.E.A.R.T., and how President Fulton had not included Charlie in the meetings that were held with him. On March 11, 1983, Charlie sent the following letter to President Fulton:

> Dear Brother Fulton,
> It is evident, and has been for some time, that I do not have the support from you that is necessary for leading in the implementation of the H.E.A.R.T. program as envisioned and as presently structured. It is with complete trust in God and His Divine providence, therefore, that I submit to you my resignation as co-ordinator of H.E.A.RT. I remain open to the leading of the Holy Spirit in all aspects of my life.... I have committed my life to the poor and the hungry of the world through the H.E.A.R.T. approach...and am fully trusting that doors will be opened that will enable me to continue following the Divine call on my life.... H.E.A.R.T. needs strong leadership by someone you can trust to further develop the program.... I pledge to work with you to locate and to prepare that person for this important work throughout the duration of my present contract.
> In His service, Charlie Smith 2 Corinthians 6:3-10

Five days after he submitted his resignation, Charlie went to his college mailbox and found a letter from President Fulton. As he read the president's response to his letter, he knew H.E.A.R.T. was officially a broken dream for him.

> Dear Charles,
> ...With deep feelings of regret I received your letter and accept your resignation. I am sorry that you feel you have not had my support. Had I not believed in you and wanted you in

100

the program I would have accepted your resignation last year.... With you I have dreamed of launching the H.E.A.R.T. program. I have appreciated your ability to put in writing the concepts and plans as you see them. Your enthusiasm has captured the spirit of many persons and gained their support for the program. For the past several months you have been given tremendous freedom to develop the plan and launch the program. I have asked only that you: 1) operate within the budget, 2) follow procedures which all others must follow in purchasing, 3) operate with the lines of authority which place H.E.A.R.T. under the Missions Department and the Academic program, and, 4) work in cooperation with the decision of the H.E.A.R.T. Steering Committee. While I was with Dr. Ward and Dr. Yamamori last week I requested they send Boone Sumantri to the campus for two weeks to assist you in putting together the program. Boone called Monday to state that he will arrive on March 21 and be here for two weeks. During that time we will seek to determine the present status of the program and plan for the future.

In Christ, Leroy Fulton

H.E.A.R.T. was a remarkable vision that survived Charlie's departure, going on to train nearly 800 people over the coming 25 years for service that reached 90 countries around the globe. Many people thought Charlie was foolish to throw such a vision away, among them, Jerry Grubbs, who became chairman of the board of Heart to Honduras. He wrote:

When people had conflict with Charlie over the H.E.A.R.T. program he would bristle. He was always having run ins at Warner Southern because he would not toe the academic line and be a faculty member like everybody else. So how did he handle conflict? He just walked away. Can you imagine? He just walked away from the H.E.A.R.T. program and that was his creation. That was his baby. But rather than deal with the conflict he had with the administration and at least follow some of their guidelines and get approval before he did things, instead of solving those conflicts, he just walked away from them.

But Charlie never seemed to second guess his decision to leave H.E.A.R.T. He wrote later:

Some have suggested that it is a shame that I am throwing away my dream. To the contrary, I did what I believe was necessary to free the program from my influence for those who feel so called of God to continue on with its vision. H.E.A.R.T. is God's program. It is not Charlie Smith's dream. Shame be on anyone who thinks so. I have been consistent in pointing everyone I meet to Christ Jesus–the Unifier. I was given a vision to do a task. The vision did not come at once. It evolved through much prayer, discussion, and hard work. God has been at work. I had a vision of how the program could work. I believe I could have put it together.

In some notes scribbled on a yellow note pad in May of 1983, Charlie began to put the pieces of his life back together:

It is difficult sometimes to understand why God works the way He does. I simply stand amazed at His awesome power. My separation from H.E.A.R.T. has brought me stimulation in several significant events. I have greater degree of agreement among principals involved. Ells Culver is now directly involved in my life again. Soon I will attend the dedication of the Taylorsville Lake Dam. I have an opportunity to participate in the University of Kentucky research program. I can return to my love of photography, black and white prints, and do a photo essay at the Peoples Bank. I can exhibit and display my prints at the Commonwealth of Kentucky Museum of Anthropology. Perhaps I might even finish my PhD.

I remember Charlie's "wilderness" years a little myself. He was casting about during those years, not sure of where the Lord was leading him. I remember at one time he shared with me from Psalm 77,
which spoke to him in that situation:
"Your path led through the sea, your way through the mighty waters, though your footprints were not seen." NIV
~Dave Pischel

19
The Visionary Wanders
1983-1988

PROJECT GLOBAL VILLAGE

Charlie's journal noted a pivotal invitation: "June, 1983: Thinking about visiting Honduras at the request of Ells Culver." Soon, the little country in the heart of Central America started the journey to its place in Charlie's heart.

Following that first visit, Charlie accepted a job as an applied anthropology consultant for Ells' new organization, Project Global Village. He continued living in Florida, but his job description required frequent trips to Honduras to check on the development ventures in the villages surrounding San Isidro, the small town where Project Global Village had its headquarters. One of Charlie's main duties was to raise  money for staff and various community projects. This was not Charlie's *forté*, but he had a family to feed. For him, it was a job, not a personal vision. Though he was immediately captivated by Honduras and fell in love with the people, other visions were also bubbling in the back of his mind.

With the nature of a true visionary, Charlie never lost his passion to look for the unseen in the seen, and was never content to just support another's dream. People around him could sense that some kind of plan was developing in his mind by observing his demeanor, the focus in his eyes, his countenance. Then his personality would change, as he shared in detail what he had been mulling over. Anne-Marie described her dad's behavior during this process: "My dad was always visioning with passion. Often he would wave his arms and hands in the air as he communicated his vision. It reminded me of a cockroach."

HERE'S HELP

In the second year of his work with Project Global Village, he began to test the waters for jump-starting another ministry. He wrote about a dozen friends seeking support, encouragement and advice for a new ministry he dubbed *Here's HELP*. It was to be a holistic ministry, meeting the needs of people by working through the church. He sent a three-page proposal to his friends for their input.[21] Some were supportive. Others were cautious. A few had doubts. One friend's reaction accused Charlie of being away too much from his family. He responded:

> True I am ministering in faraway places, for God is continually giving me visions that blow me away. Call me crazy, ignorant or what you will, but God has given me unique, simple, feasible answers and directions for responding to the suffering of hundreds of millions of oppressed people.... Talk is cheap. Organized religion is primarily concerned with feeding itself and only marginally concerned with the needs of the poor and the hungry. Radical Discipleship is required.

Thwarted in his attempt to start *Here's HELP* and unable to put all of his passion into his work for Project Global Village, Charlie looked around his neighborhood and began to envision ways to minister to those on his own doorstep. He started by volunteering at the South Lake Wales Church of God as a minister to college students and as community outreach director, seeking to raise missions awareness in the congregation. In addition to his work at the church, he looked for new ways to personally reach out, and he came up with some characteristically creative ideas.

DRAMA

One idea that Charlie pursued during this time was to dramatize the life of the Apostle Paul. Charlie loved the Word of God and believed in its power to change people's lives. He wrote, "I am memorizing key scriptural passages from the teaching of Jesus and of Paul, and plan to present the Word to congregations

---

[21] Charlie's draft of ideas for *Here's HELP* held many of the elements of what eventually became Heart to Honduras.

and to other groups in a unique way, [from the point of view of] a witness to these events. My beard has been growing for over a year, so I am ready for the part, save the robe and the sandals. I believe this will be a dynamic presentation and that God will bless this ministry of the Word." This vision never really got off the ground, but the great thing that came out of it was the hours upon hours of time Charlie spent memorizing the foundational teachings of Jesus and the Apostle Paul.

A bearded Charlie

Charlie's photograph of a Kentucky farmer

PHOTOGRAPHY

Having discovered that a photo had power far beyond that of the spoken word to communicate a vision, Charlie became an impressive photographer. He took innumerable slides while in the Peace Corps and hundreds more of his family, but his photographs of poor rural farmers living in the hollers[22] of Kentucky told a special story. His father wrote in *The Reminder*[23] on June 3, 1983, about photos Charlie displayed related to the Taylorsville Lake Project. "Last week Charles had an extensive exhibit of ...photographs of the old culture which disappeared with the new lake that was formed from the project..."

Often working in black and white, Charlie loved to do close ups of the human face and always admonished other photographers to keep only their best pictures and throw the rest away.[24] But his passion for photography did not meet

---

[22] "Hollers" is the regional pronunciation of "hollows" or narrow mountain valleys

[23] Frellsen Smith published a personal newsletter called *The Reminder* for many years. Charlie eventually copied this name for his ministry newsletter, in honor of his father.

[24] Many of his black and white photos are on permanent display in the offices of Heart to Honduras in Xenia, Ohio.

his need to minister to the downtrodden and mistreated peoples of the world, and rather than provide income, it was a costly undertaking. As was his next idea:

FATHER'S PLACE

During 1983, Charlie's theological understanding of food in the Bible caused a latent vision to surface for an outreach ministry with a coffeehouse setting. He wanted to provide a place for students and the community to come together in a setting that fed the dual hungers of body and soul. To accomplish this, he teamed up with a young couple from Jackson, Mississippi, Greg and Valerie Moak. Valerie explained the beginning of this vision:

Charlie saw an opportunity. He talked to one of the board members at the South Lake Wales Church about using the old vacant sanctuary kitchen and building. They agreed and when Charlie requested some of the big stock pots from the college, things really started moving. On Saturday afternoon, we would cook either at the church or his house, and transport the food for Sunday night. Charlie believed food always brought out people. It was a universal thing for him. He was always using the words, "Food is the key."

Newspaper photo of Charlie in his element - the kitchen of Father's Place

This coffeehouse was called Father's Place, a name thought up by Charlie's former H.E.A.R.T. student, Phil Murphy. It became very popular with the students, and due to widespread interest, Charlie decided to enlarge upon the concept by starting a restaurant in downtown Lake Wales. He located an abandoned nursery there, and with the financial backing of friends, Father's Place opened in January, 1985. Dave Pischel assisted in creating a logo and provided paint colors. It was a carry-out business that served international-style food that included rice, red beans, beef curry, Mexican chicken, collard greens, dumplings, jambalaya, and soul food. Charlie worked 30 to 40 hours a week on this project, but it never really got off the ground. The demand for international cuisine was not great in Lake Wales, and often Charlie's compassion and giving spirit hurt his bottom line. However, the things he learned in the food business enhanced his future visions. Charlie later wrote of lessons learned from the Father Place venture:

> It was a good concept, or so I thought, but it just could not generate the money needed to keep it going. I gave it my best shot, as did ... others who helped me from time to time. When Gary Mitkowski informed me he was leaving for Ohio, I knew I could not go it alone, so I closed it down. The faithful customer was disappointed, as was I at the time. Had I been successful, I would not be in Honduras. "All things work together for good..."

Anne-Marie also believed her dad used food to bring people together. "Dad had to do this restaurant, as he loved to cook with curry. He loved bringing people together in community. That is why he started Father's Place. He learned so much from that experience. He said, 'I have never worked so hard, learned so much and made so little.'"

Meanwhile, all of these ventures were a strain on the marriage. Karen was upset that her husband was gone so much, either to Honduras or chasing one dream after another. He often maxed out their credit cards on his schemes, and nothing he did seemed to produce income. (The cookie sales fiasco that ended with unsold boxes of cookies stacked to the ceiling of his office comes to mind.) Except for his six years of teaching at the college, Charlie never held a steady job for any length of time, so Karen was forced to be the main breadwinner.

Karen and Charlie were still on the same page, but the margins were narrowing. She shared her concerns with Charlie about their worsening relationship. His sister Marie said of this distressing time in their relationship: "Karen and Charlie had their moments. And what came out of this difficult time in their lives was that Charlie promised Karen that he would give her every

Saturday for the rest of his life. Anything she wanted. It saved their marriage." Whatever she wanted to do, he would be at her side, be it shopping at a flea market, going to the mall, painting a room, attending a concert, or going to a nursery to find roses to plant in her garden. It worked. The margins began to widen.

Charlie's consistent dedication of his Saturdays to his wife was fulfilling her needs, but his need to reach the poverty-stricken masses of the world was not being met–not by his photo essays, not by the coffee house or restaurant, not by a dramatization, not even by his volunteer community outreach work at the church, and for sure not by selling cookies. After five years of working in Honduras with Project Global Village, he continued to be restless.

Several things diminished Charlie's all-out passion regarding Project Global Village. They were great in development and had countless programs to empower and assist the needy. But Charlie looked around and did not see the church. The corn and beans were good, but Christ and the Bible give an eternal perspective that was crucial for Charlie. Charlie had ideas for helping the church take the lead in development, but no one at Project Global Village was listening. And rather than utilizing his skills as a Christian applied anthropologist, he was asked to spend his days raising funds.

These five years of wandering were discouraging in many ways, but the experiences prepared Charlie for his next step. He had lost much: his doctorate, H.E.A.R.T, Father's Place, his professorship. And he felt lost in his current job with Project Global Village. But what he had left would propel him into a fulfilling ministry and earn him respect from his previous detractors.

What was left? A special vision that would define his legacy. A vision that would take him into the rural mountains of Honduras–this time on his own.

I do believe in the not-too-distant future this vision will be realized and we can shout out to the world: "Look at this! Here is how the poor can work with their own hands to meet their own needs as members of families, hamlets and villages!"
~Charlie Smith

20
A Call from Costa Rica

In his five years of wandering, Charlie Smith may not have loved the particular work assignment he had received from Project Global Village, but he was falling in love with the land and the people of Honduras. Every flight into the country meant a view of vast acres of banana plantations bumping up against the tropical greenery covering the rib of mountains that bisects the land. Cascading mountain streams meant there was clean water ready to be piped to the people.

Though this tiny country in the very heart of Central America had a turbulent political history, in the 1980s it was relatively stable. Originally populated by sophisticated Mayan and other indigenous peoples, then discovered by Christopher Columbus in his fourth and final voyage and thus claimed by Spain, Honduras declared its independence in 1821. Since that time, it endured nearly 300 small rebellions and internal civil wars, some of which involved neighboring countries and even intervention at times by the United States. Periods of democratic governance had been interspersed with military rule.

As Charlie's interest in this area was deepening, the country had just experienced a time when it was a haven for anti-Sandinista contras that were fighting the Marxist Nicaraguan government. Though they didn't realize it, the subsistence farmers that Charlie met on his village visits were affected by government policies that kept them from having electricity, clean water in their homes, and decent roads that would give them access to health care and markets for their crops.

In rural communities, the education system extended only through the fifth grade, school buildings were in poor condition, textbooks were in short supply, and teachers were often absent from their post. For a man interested in community development, it was a wide open field of opportunity.

In this nation of extraordinary natural resources but a struggling population, a vision was forming in Charlie—the vision that would define his final years and create a legacy beyond any yet dreamed.

A pivotal phone call came to Charlie's home in Florida as the year of 1987 wound down. Miguel Pinell, a former student of Charlie's at Warner Southern College, had repeatedly turned down Charlie's pleas to come to Honduras and

see what Project Global Village was doing there. Miguel had always planned to return to the church in Costa Rica that had sent him to the States to study, but the doors of ministry had suddenly closed there. Now he was calling Charlie to see if there was a possibility of working in Honduras. Here is the way Miguel tells the story of those days:

**Charlie and Miguel,
Ministry Partners**

In 1987, I completed my studies at Warner Southern College. During my four years there, I had a wonderful anthropology teacher, Charlie Smith. He and I were molded together because I loved the way he taught the Bible. He would ask me to go to Honduras with him to do ministry. I kept responding, "No, Charlie, I don't want to go to Honduras, I don't like Honduras, I don't care for Honduras." I went that far in telling him no.

I call people [who talk like I talked] hardheaded people. Hardheaded people are those who always go against the will of God because they want to do their own will. It is not good for men to do their own will. We all must submit our will to God. There are two ways you can do the will of God: The easy way, by saying yes to God, or the hard way. Which one do you prefer? I preferred the hard way.

After I finished at Warner Southern, I went to Costa Rica. Why? My heart wanted to go to Costa Rica and be with my pastor and my family and even my girlfriend. I thought life would be so easy with all those elements in it. Yet, now I believe that in the Kingdom of God, life is not easy. You do not have to have everything in place to do the will of God, especially when you are just beginning a mission.

I remember that I preached the first service in Grecia, Costa Rica. Everyone was happy and excited because I gave that first sermon with a lot of vigor. After the service the people asked me, "Where did you learn to preach so well". And with a boasting, proud heart I said, "I went to Warner Southern College!" Right there, in that moment, I showed how proud I was.

I have found out in my own life that God delights in the humble, but like the Bible says, he opposes the proud.

A week after I preached in Costa Rica, my pastor told me he did not need me anymore. Then, the family I was working with did not want to be with me anymore. Everyone was shutting the door on my face. The last hope I had was my girlfriend. So, I went to her and asked if she loved me. She said "No, I don't. I don't want to be with you." I asked her why and she said I was too proud and she needed more time to look at other boys.

I believe that only when you are broken is when God can use you. In brokenness, there is great hope and a great future. I found myself broken and crying. I was throwing my own pity party. When those pity parties come to your life, you must get up and shake it off so you can do the will of the Father. The devil always wants to see you on the ground. The most important thing is to get up and keep going so you can fulfill your mission.

After that moment, I called upon the Lord and said I would go to Honduras. I picked up the phone and called my brother Charlie. I said, "Charlie, where is that Honduras?" Charlie said to me, "I told you not to go to Costa Rica." But I was a hardheaded man, and I still am a little bit.

Miguel remembers that after Charlie chided him, he sent him money to fly to Honduras and arranged for missionaries to pick him up and take him to Project Global Village headquarters in San Isidro. In God's providence, Miguel arrived just as organizers realized a storm in Mexico had prevented a scheduled evangelist from showing up for a week-long tent meeting. Miguel was invited to preach in his place, and the positive response of those in attendance convinced him that God's hand was in this move to Honduras. Soon Miguel took up residence in San Isidro, worked as the bookkeeper for Project Global Village, and began courting the organization's receptionist.

On Charlie's visits to Honduras in his position as consultant, he and Miguel had many opportunities to spend time together. The connection they felt as teacher and student began to deepen into a common burden for the Honduran poor. As they visited the Global Village projects, they learned that the pastors of the local churches were isolated and untrained, deserted by the various church

111

bodies that had planted them. This was disconcerting to both men. They could see the desperate need the pastors of these tiny flocks had for fellowship with each other, and for foundational teaching in the Bible and doctrine. They observed that many were meeting in inadequate facilities, often in mud-floored homes.

Miguel had a heart for meeting the spiritual needs of people. Charlie opened Miguel's eyes to the fact that the church could also be the instrument to bring aid to the physical needs of the people they both had grown to love through their work with Project Global Village.

Together they envisioned a discipleship school that would train pastors and evangelists in meeting both the spiritual and physical needs of the people. As Charlie saw it, this was a project where he could finally be *el jefe*, the chief, the director, shaping a ministry as he saw fit. This new ministry could be a living example of what he had pictured the graduates of H.E.A.R.T putting into practice once they finished the program.

The restlessness of Charlie's five years of wandering, all the things he learned in the Peace Corps and his applied anthropology studies, the visioning and practical aspects of setting up H.E.A.R.T. and lessons from his work with Project Global Village began to merge into what Charlie would refer to as a "visionary gestalt"–a whole made up of all these parts. Suddenly Charlie felt the return of that familiar passionate energy that accompanied his vision for H.E.A.R.T., a passion that had been missing in his work with Project Global Village.

The question is not what you look at, but what you see.
~Henry David Thoreau

21
Testing the Waters

In 1983, Charlie's assignment as a consultant and fundraiser with Project Global Village required visits to the villages in the mountains that surrounded San Isidro. PGV had installed water systems that brought running water either to a spigot in the yard or to an outdoor *pila* (freestanding bathroom and washing station) of the homes. Now they were planning additional home improvement projects, and Charlie was sent to work with the villagers to help that happen.

Charlie's dad, Frellsen, recorded his son's frequent trips to Honduras in his personal newsletter. He detailed a 1984 trip that took Charlie and his wife on a 12-day loop from Florida to Belize to Honduras, recording that Karen used her nursing skills to estimate medical supplies needed in the newly constructed clinic in San Isidro, and Charlie sang "Count Your Blessings" in a church service. Frellsen's paper quoted Charlie:

> [Project] Global Village is designed to help the poorest of the poor to reestablish their lives with the promise of hope through self-reliant living. Through this program we can demonstrate how people can live at basic levels and be free from hunger and poverty and all the related problems that plague so many people in the world.

Frellsen concluded that issue with these words: "This type of thing is what Charles has been wanting to do for a long time, and he is about to realize this goal....To this material advancement is added the spiritual." By the end of that year, Charlie had led six groups of North Americans to Honduras to participate in the model village vision. Twice that year there were spiritual retreats and training events.

There was progress, but Charlie felt stymied by his supervisors in Project Global Village. He was excited about the physical development projects being carried out, but he continued to feel that these things needed to be funneled through the church. He wanted to encourage more spiritual training of the local people; Project Global Village did not feel called to focus on that aspect of development.

And then it was 1987, and he suddenly had a like-minded partner in Miguel Pinell. Perhaps, together, they could launch development projects of a holistic nature. But there were practical matters to be handled, not the least of which was financial support. Salary support for both Charlie and Miguel was being sent, by their handful of donors, to the non-profit-organization status of Project Global Village. Charlie was supporting a family and Miguel was contemplating marriage, so a way needed to be found to receive tax-deductible donations for these founding staff persons. Another concern was whether or not the village pastors desired to forge a partnership.

To test the waters, Charlie did two things. He sent Miguel out to talk to the mountain pastors of the various evangelical denominations to see if they were interested in forming a pastoral association for the purpose of fellowship and receiving Biblical training. And he looked for an organization with which he could partner until he could set up his own non-profit. In both cases, the response was positive.

One of Charlie's former students, Steve Coder, was serving as president of a ministry called Hand to the Plow, which was working primarily in Haiti. Charlie approached Steve, who had been greatly influenced by Charlie's teaching and life, to request bringing a ministry in Honduras under Hand to the Plow, with the idea of naming it Hand to Honduras. As Steve had been challenged and blessed in the past by Charlie, now this was Steve's opportunity to give Charlie encouragement and assistance. Reflecting on the teacher/student partnership, Charlie wrote:

> Yes, it is a mystery how God moves us around in His Kingdom. Steve Coder says that my anthropology class and H.E.A.R.T. changed his life from climbing the corporate ladder to being a missionary. And who would want to be a millionaire when you can be a missionary, anyway? Everyone associated with Hand to the Plow received their vision for missions largely through the H.E.A.R.T. program, and that is a great source of encouragement for me to keep on being all God wants me to be in his Kingdom.

With the promise of a way to channel support funds to Miguel without going through Project Global Village, it seemed to be time for Miguel to resign his bookkeeping position with them and begin implementing what he and Charlie had been discussing regarding ministry to and through the rural churches. That done, Charlie brought Miguel to the States to formalize the relationship with

114

Hand to the Plow. Miguel met with their Board of Elders who commissioned him to begin a ministry in Honduras to encourage, equip and empower the church. The October, 1988 *Fieldnotes*, a paper published by Hand to the Plow, stated, "Exciting News! As of October 8, Miguel Pinell joined the Hand to the Plow team. His assignment in Honduras will be to coordinate spiritual development activities in the Yure River Basin—an area that includes some 30 churches."

With a covering organization in place, a bilingual field director eager to begin work, and a group of pastors expressing interest in his vision, it seemed that all lights were green. But this was no ordinary inner visionary revelation for Charlie. He was excited but cautious. The Spirit was speaking. A door of opportunity was opening. At 50, did he have what it would take to cast another vision? He began to look for a place of solitude to listen for the voice of God and to process these internal promptings of the Holy Spirit. His sister Lorna wrote of this experience:

> The call of God was so strong on his life that he knew he must do more than talk and pray. He asked Miguel to leave him at an isolated, abandoned house near [the village of] Casitas, with only the bare necessities in hand. There he fasted, read his Bible, and prayed for two weeks. When he saw Miguel drive away, he felt in the depths of despair, alone and frightened, until he turned to the Scriptures asking God's direction for his future work in Honduras. During those two weeks, Charlie surrendered to God's spirit, purposing to give up whatever would hinder God's work.

To do that it was necessary for Charlie to join Miguel and leave Project Global Village. Charlie wrote in his journal, "Making that move was difficult; especially leaving the security it provided me and my family. But I knew it had to be made." He made a phone call to Ells and resigned. It was December 18, 1988.

The country life is to be preferred, for there we see the works of God, but in the cities little else but the works of men. And the one makes a better subject for contemplation than the other.
~William Penn

22
The Ultimate Vision: Heart to Honduras
1988-1989

Meanwhile, Miguel was traveling through the rural mountains of Honduras, recruiting as many pastors as possible for a January meeting with Charlie and Hand to the Plow Elder Eddie Joyner. Miguel would visit the pastors from eight denominations in all. This emphasis on rural communities would define and enrich Charlie's holistic vision in Honduras.

From Charlie's point of view, the cities of Honduras were spiritually bankrupt, physically overcrowded, socially disoriented, emotionally depressing and politically corrupt. Thousands of poor Hondurans were taking a pathological trek to the city in search of better employment, medical services, education, entertainment, greater material options and food beyond the usual beans and tortillas. But what they found were drug cartels, unemployment and injustice. People lost the opportunity for meaningful lives as they became caught in a system where greedy money managers charged exorbitant interest rates, mirroring those Jesus cast from the temple. The city was crowded with people who had crowded God out of their lives.

Charlie envisioned a better place for the poor and landless in Honduras, similar to what essayist and journalist Alberto Masferrer championed in the early 1930s and called "the vital minimum": sufficient food, housing, health care, hygienic conditions, jobs, free time, justice and education. But Charlie wanted all of this with a Biblical perspective. He felt if people could receive this "vital minimum" in their rural villages, their dangerous migration to the cities could be stopped.

Fine tuning his vision, he wrote in his journal at his Lake Wales home, "Jesus said, 'Flee the cities and don't look back. Remember Lot's wife.' That is the message to the church for this day. Get out of the cities and the towns. Return to the countryside. Buy land outside the urban areas and build sustainable lifestyles. Cut your dependence on the world.... Learn and teach the knowledge and skills for sustainable living in household and village.'"

116

The day before Charlie resigned from Project Global Village, another momentous event occurred. On Saturday, December 17, 1988, Miguel married that receptionist he had first seen in the Project Global Village office. She was 18-year-old Nilsa Andino, a girl from a poor San Isidro family of eight children. She first met Miguel and Charlie when she was 15 and working in the Project Global Village medical clinic in San Isidro. Her family lived a pitiful existence. She once said of her childhood:

Nilsa and Miguel Pinell

We were very poor because my daddy drank too much alcohol. We lived in a house with a dirt floor with wood plank walls. We had two bedrooms and all my brothers and sisters slept together in one room–two or three people in one bed. It was head to foot sleeping. My brothers slept in hammocks and the girls in bed. We ate beans and rice and tortillas. We drank coffee as children. Then Project Global Village built a house for us. We had to pay for the house every month, so I worked in the clinic to pay for the house because my family needed to eat.

This young woman who came from such humble beginnings would soon become a powerful instrument for this new ministry with her gift of prayer and her anointed preaching.

The following month, the Yure River Basin was the site of a historic day for this budding Hand to Honduras ministry. Six pastors attended the meeting with Charlie, Miguel, and Eddie Joyner in the small village of Palmital on Sunday afternoon, January 25, 1989.[25] "A marvelous spirit of unity characterized the meeting," Charlie wrote, "as the pastors organized themselves into an

---

[25] This is counted as the first "team" to visit Honduras under Charlie's vision–just two people, Eddie Joyner and Charlie.

'Association of Congregations' and elected an executive council with the purpose of advancing the Kingdom in their rural villages."

"Long-range plans are to construct and operate a Discipleship Learning Center for the preparation of Disciples of Jesus," Charlie said regarding the need for obtaining property. The first two pieces of property were purchased in San Isidro in February 1989, giving the ministry a physical presence which until now had been merely concepts and ideas. The first large piece of land purchased was a 20-acre plot located on a hillside on the outskirts of San Isidro. A small creek ran through the property which was dotted with pine saplings, banana plants and orange trees.

The first building purchased was a small house situated on an acre lot next to the San Isidro soccer field. It was ideal for North American visitors to use as a base camp. With the small house to provide lodging, Charlie could now proclaim to the North Americans the words of the disciple Nathaniel, "Come and see." It would be the seeing that would call forth their involvement in this dynamic holistic vision and transform the landscape of the Yure River Basin.

Early visitors were housed and fed in this little blue-striped building in San Isidro.

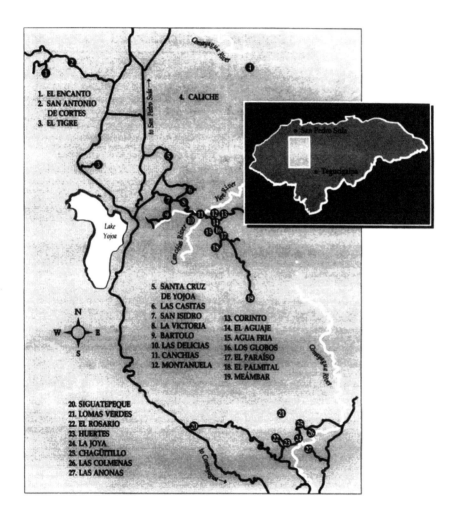

1. EL ENCANTO
2. SAN ANTONIO DE CORTES
3. EL TIGRE
4. CALICHE
5. SANTA CRUZ DE YOJOA
6. LAS CASITAS
7. SAN ISIDRO
8. LA VICTORIA
9. BARTOLO
10. LAS DELICIAS
11. CANCHIAS
12. MONTANUELA
13. CORINTO
14. EL AGUAJE
15. AGUA FRIA
16. LOS GLOBOS
17. EL PARAÍSO
18. EL PÁLMITAL
19. MEÁMBAR
20. SIGUATEPEQUE
21. LOMAS VERDES
22. EL ROSARIO
23. HUERTES
24. LA JOYA
25. CHAGÜITILLO
26. LAS COLMENAS
27. LAS ANONAS

Map taken from the Heart to Honduras
Fieldworker's Manual

119

*After spending four thousand dollars in 1992 on a trip
to the Galapagos Islands I asked myself,
"Can I justify these expenses to satisfy my personal desires?"
After spending a few days in Honduras,
I yearn to return to the Honduran countryside.*
~*Dr. Gus Jeeninga,[26]
Professor of Old Testament Studies, Anderson University*

23
A Trickle Before A Flood
1989-1990

Pastor Terry Collier and Dr. Rick Cherry saw something in Charlie's vision that they liked, and in April of 1989, they traveled from Florida to Honduras with him. Terry held a pastoral retreat, preaching a series of six sermons on "Thy Kingdom Come," and Rick provided medical care. This two-person team (three if you count Charlie) was the second team, and the first with a medical component, to visit Honduras under Charlie's vision.

Little did Charlie know that this was the trickling start of a flood of such teams, who would become the lifeline of the ministry. In the decades to come, they would provide the resources of finances, prayer, counsel, encouragement, personnel, staff, vehicles, doctors, engineers, nurses, dentists, masons, teachers, carpenters, farmers and more.

In 1989, I was a pastor in Alabama and had spent several years working for another missions organization. The friendship Charlie and I had formed in our post-graduate days in Kentucky had strengthened, mostly through his frequent phone calls inviting me to come and see his work in Honduras with Project Global Village. A couple of times a year I would find myself driving through Florida on my way to lead a short term missions team to Central America. I would spend the night at Charlie's house on the way to the airport, and our conversations over good food and laughter always included his perennial, "Come and see."

---

[26] Dr. Jeeninga was retired from his professorship when he decided to learn Spanish–his seventh language–and volunteer as a translator for medical teams.

Nearly twenty years after our first meeting, and countless invitations later, I had capitulated. It was August of 1989, and I was on a plane with Charlie, headed for Honduras. Joined by Steve Coder of Hand to the Plow, we became the third team to make a trip under Charlie's new vision.

I still recall buckling my seatbelt on an American Airlines flight out of Orlando and Charlie throwing a 40-page document on my lap. When I asked what it was, Charlie replied, "Jim, this is a working document for Miguel." It was the rough draft of *The State of the Ministry and Decision Making* and contained Charlie's original vision for the ministry. Charlie's role was visionary commander-in-chief; Miguel was the boots on the ground. As the years unfolded, my role would be to serve as Charlie's armor bearer, confidante and sounding board.

Casitas

On this 1989 trip, Charlie and Miguel initiated Steve and me by taking us to visit a different church every night. The living conditions were very primitive and the roads were so riddled with potholes that we were told tires had to be changed on the vehicle every three to six months. I remember that the church in Casitas was extremely poor. As we entered, the only light came from a small pile of pine sticks flickering on the dirt floor. No electricity. Not even a lantern. Yet there was great joy in the believers as they worshipped. And after the service, they sacrificed some of their meager supply of corn to serve us tamales.

Palmital

The church in Palmital was full of superstition, with some habits that were foreign to us. During the service, both the men and women would spit on the dirt floor of the church. Stranger still, they would endure the suffocating fumes from oil lamps, because they believed evil spirits were outside and closed windows would keep those evil spirits at bay.

Montañuela

The shade of banana trees provided respite on a hot Friday morning in the village of Montañuela, as we met with a dozen pastors for the second Pastors Fellowship. We sensed great unity among the group. Having chosen an executive council at their earlier meeting, they elected officers at this one in keeping

Jim Usher preaching in the dirt-floored church of Montañuela, 1989

121

with the ministry design of self-government.

When we met with this group for worship, I was chosen to give the message. How well I remember when I stepped in a "deposit" left by the dogs which were wandering in and out. This was humbling, but the meal at the pastor's house afterwards was even more so. The kitchen where the pastor's wife was preparing the meal was constructed of sticks separated by wide gaps, so that we could see what was happening inside from our position outside. Expecting a full meal, we were surprised when all she served were small pieces of boiled ears of corn with some salt to dip our fingers in and rub on them. She parceled these out to her guests and her children, and eventually the pastor gave some also to the neighbors' children who were gathered to see these strange-looking visitors. Extreme poverty contrasted with rich generosity, as the poor pastor fed the poor at his door.

Chagüitillos

The next day, we drove to the village of Chagüitillos[27] at the invitation of Chilano Rivera, who had worked with Charlie and Miguel at Project Global Village. We travelled three hours and arrived in the town of El Rosario at high noon. Chilano, his brother Antonio (of *Muy Sabrosa* fame) and Pastor Mario met us with four horses. It was hot, and the road to the village looked as if army tanks traversed it daily, digging ruts that made the choice of horses over even a 4x4 a wise one.

After a long hour's horseback ride, we arrived at the home of Chilano. He proudly showed us his 15-day-old son, wrapped in swaddling clothes and swaying in a hammock, reminding the team of the birth of Jesus. Chilano had named the baby Carlos Miguel after Charlie and Miguel.

Board of Advisors

A week after this trip, in a letter dated August 28, 1989, Charlie wrote his sister Lorna, sharing his excitement and asking her to consider being on the board he was forming. "We have just returned from Honduras safely and are encouraged with what we experienced…. We are doing the work God called us to do and that provides a great source of satisfaction. The part you are playing in this work is key to its success. How thankful I am for your commitment to the oppressed…. It is our prayer that you will make a commitment to serve on our board of advisors." Lorna would agree, serving on that board with others who

---

[27] For over 20 years we thought the people were saying "Chagüitillo." The lack of a city limits sign with the name, and the Castilian-accented Spanish of the local people that drops the final "s" combined to keep us ignorant of the fact that it is "Chagüitillos."

122

eventually were invited to join the ministry in that capacity: Steve Birch, Terry Collier, Jerry Grubbs, and Gordon Garrett. (It should be noted that Charlie's time with Project Global Village served him well in his Heart to Honduras vision. Jerry, Steve, Terry and Gordon all made their first trips to Honduras with Charlie through PGV. Jerry served as chairman of the HTH board from its inception; Gordon became president of Heart to Honduras in 1999.)

Now a steady stream of teams began to pour into Honduras through the Hand to Honduras ministry. Word was getting out that Charlie was up to something big. Excitement was in the air. Many began to feel this vision was going to have more promise and potential than his former ones. Charlie was even more confident. He had a spring in his step and a song in his heart that often spilled out through his harmonica.

The first construction team to go to Honduras was a month after our trip. In September of 1989, Phil Germany and Walter Williams from the Lakeland (Florida) First Church of God, Buck Brazell from Columbia, South Carolina, and Mary Jean Daniels from Collinsville, Mississippi, visited Honduras. They helped the church in Las Delicias put on a new roof and the church in Montañuela pour a concrete floor.

Churches as well as individuals began to commit to Charlie's vision. In December of 1989, the Parkview Church of God of Meridian, Mississippi, composed of Robin Bauer, Rose Lang, Evelyn Shumate and Mark Martin visited. This team was visibly touched by seeing a blind boy named Marcos. They became burdened for the children of Honduras and purchased a building in San Isidro to be used to feed and educate them. Called TLC (The Little Children), this ministry was launched the following February, and Miguel's wife Nilsa was appointed director.

1990

The pioneer teams of the first few years were made up of just a handful of people, but they were seeds of encouragement to Charlie, who had set his hand to the plow in a new field, broken ground and planted. Now the seeds were sprouting, even flourishing and bearing fruit.

During 1990, Charlie and Miguel began sharing the vision with pastors and church leaders in the United States, using a nine-minute video called *The Honduras Experience*, produced by Pastor J.D. Woods of Indiana.

The two men visited New Castle, Pennsylvania, where former Warner Southern student Keith Wilkins pastored. Pastor Keith recruited about a dozen pastors and churches in western Pennsylvania to visit Honduras in the ensuing years, his enthusiasm fired by his trip to Honduras. Keith had just taken a dozen people with him to minister through building a church facility in Bartolo, holding daily mobile medical clinics, and on one memorable night, using a generator to

123

show the *Jesus* film to over 200 people who had never before seen a movie. This resulted in several of the attendees giving their lives to Christ.

Petrona, in head wrap

But for the Pennsylvanians, the most memorable visit of all occurred in Casitas when the medical team was confronted with 19-year-old Petrona, who was moaning in pain. Her mother reported that Petrona had had seizures since she was 3, and six months ago had begun having such severe pain in her head that all she did all day was moan. Doctors had been unable to do anything for her, and the doctor with this team was no different. He said it was most likely a brain tumor, about which he could do nothing. The team gathered around Petrona and began praying to the God whose power is just the same today as it was in Bible times. Pastor Keith's team stated their belief that relieving Petrona of her suffering would be a witness to the people in this village. After an hour of praying, the team left with the sounds of her moaning still echoing in their ears. Several days later, Charlie brought another team to visit and discovered a completely healed Petrona, and a father who had given his life to the Lord because of what he had seen happen to his daughter through the power of prayer. No wonder this Pennsylvania pastor was inspired to encourage more people to "come and see."

On that 1990 trip around the eastern half of the United States, Charlie and Miguel also visited the Austinville Church of God in Decatur, Alabama, which was under the pastoral leadership of Harold Coomer. This church would eventually give over a quarter million dollars to the ministry, primarily supported by the income from a local AM radio station.

Another stop was at the Eastland Church of God. Steve Birch, who had known Charlie when he was pastoring in Florida, was now pastoring this church in Lexington, Kentucky. Steve had accepted Charlie's invitation to visit Honduras when he was still working for Project Global Village, and now he was ready to encourage his new congregation to participate in a mission trip there. This team became a significant one over the years, due to its large size and repeated visits. Steve galvanized his church to raise funds for a 4x4 Toyota extended cab truck which provided much-needed transportation over the rutted roads.

In January 1990, a group of Mennonite farmers from Ohio visited Honduras and brought two kinds of seeds: a 16 mm projector sponsored by Child Evangelism, and new crop seeds along with fertilizer for the farmers. In February, architect Doug Warman of Vancouver, Washington came and prepared plans for the new Discipleship Center which at the time was proposed to be built on the 20 acres in San Isidro. And in December, the Parkview Church of God from Mississippi returned for their second trip.

Though Charlie was reaching out to other denominations, the vast majority of people in his personal network of acquaintances were in the Church of God, Anderson, resulting in a high participation of that group in his ministry. For the 1990 annual convention of the Church of God, convened in Anderson, Indiana every June, Charlie held a reunion of those who had gone to Honduras in the past couple of years, knowing that many of them would be present for the convention. He reserved a meeting space in Park Place Church of God, cooked a huge pot of beans and another of rice, and invited all who were interested in this ministry to come. It turned out to be a great opportunity for sharing what was happening in Honduras. There were testimonies from his sister Lorna and others who had been to Honduras, and

Charlie's sister Lorna Kardatzke sharing at the first HTH reunion at Park Place Church of God.

there was a showing of the video *The Honduras Experience*. Charlie displayed photos of the Honduran people and spoke with great enthusiasm to a fellowship hall full of people enjoying his Honduran meal and eagerly receiving the information on how to get on board. This was a time when short-term missions trips were gaining in popularity, and people were excited about the opportunity to participate.[28] The evening was such a success it became an almost annual event for the next two decades.

---

[28] The short-term missions movement began in the late 1950s with Operation Mobilization (OM) and Youth With a Mission (YWAM) taking young people for a week or two, or even a year—as opposed to the traditional adult career missionaries. In 1963, OM took more than 2,000 people overseas. In 1989, OM took 7,000 but the total from all sending groups had grown to 120,000. By 1998, there were 450,000 participants.

Start by doing what's necessary; then do what's possible;
and suddenly you are doing the impossible!
~Saint Francis of Assisi

24
A Pivotal Year
1991

Miguel rests beside Canchias River

Miguel was on a little donkey (or ass, as Charlie preferred to call it) when the plans to locate a discipleship training center in San Isidro were changed.

Having ridden to visit the village of Palmital, Miguel was on his way back home and stopped at the Canchias River to cool off. An elderly *campesino* was near the river, and Miguel asked him where the owner of this land was. Cundo responded by saying he himself was the owner.

Cundo Velasquez had come over to Canchias from El Salvador to work with his cousin cutting mahogany trees. When the logging companies left, he stayed behind. Now, his wife was very sick and his only son was lazy and refused to work and support the family. Cundo's one good fortune was owning 10 acres of land situated on a slanted hill dotted by a few mango trees.

Off to one side of the property was Cundo's thatched-roof house. Inside the house was a wooden table, a few farming implements, a hammock and some clothes. Plastic bags, cooking utensils and a few pots and pans rounded out most of his belongings. Hanging from the ceiling was a small gunny sack dangling from a fiber string holding about a dozen ears of corn.

That day by the river, Miguel asked Cundo if he could buy five acres of his 10 acre tract. Because this was only half of the land, Cundo agreed to sell his land for $500 to the ministry. Later, Charlie and Miguel approached Cundo about selling his other five acres. By that time, Cundo had decided he wanted to relocate to the city, so he agreed to sell the remaining acres for another $500.

This fledgling ministry was now highly favored of the Lord to possess 10 picturesque acres facing the cascading waters of the Canchias River. By 1991, the ministry center was moved out of San Isidro,[29] and Charlie began implementing his holistic dream.

The Canchias River tumbles alongside ministry property

And in May of that year, a special group came that would impact Heart to Honduras as no other team.

May Medical Team

The story of that May team has roots as far back as Charlie's childhood in Louisiana. In those days, he came to know Jerry Grubbs, who was also being raised in a Louisiana congregation of the Church of God, Anderson. The two were not close friends as young people, but they were aware of the career paths each had taken. When their paths began to converge again, Jerry was a professor at Anderson College in Indiana. He was one of those who responded

---

[29] The office space and vehicle maintenance center remained in San Isidro, but housing for North American teams and facilities for the School of Discipleship were built in Canchias, less than five miles, but a back-breaking 45-minute trip, away.

by bringing a team of college students to Charlie's Project Global Village work. So, in February 1991, when Jerry was a speaker at the annual missions convention at the Meadow Park Church of God in Columbus, Ohio, he mentioned Charlie's work in Honduras. This prompted a physician, Dr. Girardi, to say, "Jerry, let me know if there is any way I can be of help to the ministry in Honduras." Without missing a beat, Jerry responded, "You can bring a medical team to Honduras."

A scant four months later, what eventually became an annual team known as the May Medical Team made its first trip to Honduras with Jerry Grubbs [dark glasses in photo above] as its leader and Doctor Jerry Girardi [mustache, right] and Doctor Larry Lilly [back] as lead physicians. Many significant things came out of this trip: it birthed the HTH medical ministry; Charlie asked Jerry Grubbs to become a board member; Dr. Larry Lilly began doing surgeries and spearheaded a drive to erect HTH's first medical facility; hundreds of medical personnel with skills and resources eventually committed to the ministry through this contact, and because the medical personnel were from different denominations, contacts made first through recruiting at a Columbus, Ohio hospital resulted in adding a large Lutheran and Presbyterian component; and it later birthed two teams that each had far-reaching impact on the ministry.

But a man from Bartolo, who was the beneficiary of the first hernia surgery performed by this medical team, did not look at the things that would come later. He was just grateful that, very soon, he would be able to work again. He could not stop saying, "Gracias."

Partnerships with Churches and other Organizations Formed with Heart to Honduras between 1989 and 2006

Heart to Honduras Partners
CHURCHES
168 Churches, 13 Denominations, 21 States, 5 Countries,
5 Universities, 17 Organizations (10 secular, 7 Christian), >4000 on mailing list,
175 Prayer Partners, 9 Sister Churches, 25 School of Discipleship sponsors (individuals and churches)

Assembly of God
Clifton Assembly of God, Clifton, CO
First Assembly of God, Lake Wales, FL

Baptist
Cornerstone, Hampton Cove, AL
Agape Baptist, Chicago, IL

Brazos Abiertos (Open Arms)
Honduras: 13 congregations
Nicaragua: 3 congregations
Costa Rica: 2 congregations

Catholic
St. Eliz. Ann Seton, Lexington, KY

Christian
Crossroad Christian, Lexington, KY
First Christian, Newton Falls, OH
So. Hghts Reformed, Kalamazoo, MI

Church of the Brethren
County Line, Harrod, OH

Church of God, Anderson
AL: Albertville, Arab, Austinville,
       Birmingham, Falkville,
       Roanoke
AZ: Scottsdale, Phoenix (Mtn.
       Park, Crosspoint, Nueva
       A'manecer)
CA: Bakersfield, Exeter
CO: Arvada, Colorado Springs,
       Denver
FL: Boca Raton, Bushnell, Daytona
       Beach, Eagle Lake, Geneva,
       Lakeland, Lake Wales (Burns
       Ave., Greater Grace),
       Orlando, Sarasota, South
       Lakeland, Tampa, Venice,
       Vero Beach, West Palm
       Beach, Winter Haven
IN: Alexandria, Anderson (North,
       Park Place), Columbia City,
       Eaton, Mooresville,
       Plainfield
KS: Augusta, Hugoton, Wichita
       (Central Community,
       Eastside)
KY: Elizabethtown, Lexington,
       Liberty, Louisville
LA: Baton Rouge
MI: Clarkston, Farmington, St. Jo
MS: Daleville, Meridian (First,
       Northpark), Piney Grove

Church of God, Anderson (cont.)
MO: Carthage, De Soto, Doniphan
NC: Drexel
OH: Clayton, Columbus,
       Dayspring, Dayton, Enon,
       Fairborn, Gallipolis, Gratis,
       Hamilton, Huber Heights,
       Kettering, Laurelville, Lima,
       London, Mansfield,
       Miamisburg, Middletown
       (Towne Blvd., Trenton 1st),
       Morrow, Mt. Vernon,
       Springfield (Maiden Lane,
       Hillside), Xenia
OK: Keyes, Oklahoma City
PA: Distant, Grove City,
       Kittanning, New Bethlehem,
       New Castle, Oil City,
       Portage, Punxsutawney
TN: Fayetteville, Kingsport
VA: Virginia Beach
WV: Beckley, Dunbar, Huntington,
       Parkersburg
WY: Casper

Full Gospel
County Lake, Huntsville, AL

Independent / Non-denominational
AHOP (A House of Prayer), Xenia, OH
Arvada Covenant Church, Denver, CO
Cherry Hills Community, Denver, CO
Christ Community, Winter Haven, FL
Christian Fellowship, Centerville, OH
Crossings Community, Lake Mary, FL
Faith, Hope &Love Gospel, Oakwood, OH
First Evangelical Free, Wichita, KS
Golden Triangle Chapel, Mt. Dora, FL
Hope Community Church,
   Mississauga, Ontario, Canada
Immanuel International, Decatur, AL
Liberty Christian Ministry, Valley, AL
Miami Valley Com., Miamisburg, OH
McDowell Mtn Com, Scottsdale, AZ
Roundtop Community, Falkville, AL
Spirit of Life Christian Ctr, Trotwood, OH
Vineyard, Columbus & Dayton, OH
Windsor Crossing, St Louis, MO
   (associated with Willow Creek)
Zion Christian Fellowship, Powell, OH

Lutheran
Southwood Lutheran, Lincoln, NE
Upper Arlington Lutheran, Columbus, OH
Women of the Elca Oh Synod, Columbus, OH

Mennonite
H'ville Mennonite, Harrisonville, MO
First Mennonite Brethren, Wichita, KS

Methodist
Aldersgate United, Tampa, FL
St. Stephen's United, Burke, VA
Southland Evangelical, Lexington, KY

Presbyterian
First Presbyterian, Harrison, OH
L. W. Presbyterian, Lake Wales, FL
Liberty Presbyterian, Dublin, OH
Pasadena Presbyterian, Sarasota, FL

United Church of Christ
Mt. Zion Church, Beavercreek, OH

INSTITUTIONS OF HIGHER LEARNING

Anderson University, Anderson, IN
Mid-America U, Oklahoma City, OK
Mt. Vernon Nazarene College. OH
University of Kentucky, Lexington, KY
Warner Southern, Lake Wales, FL

ORGANIZATIONS

Campus Crusade (Jesus film)
Chiquita Banana (container shipping)
Good Impressions Printing, Phx, AZ
Honduran Ministry of Education
Honduran Military Hospital
Joni & Friends, Xenia, OH & HN
José Reyes coffee company, HN
Legacy Ministries International, Xenia, OH
Mile-High Ministries, Denver, CO
Neighborhood Ministries, Denver, CO
Onan Corp., Huntsville, AL
Operation Christmas Child, Xenia, OH
City Council, Santa Cruz, HN
Schools for Children of the World,
   Columbus, OH &Tegucigalpa, HN
Rotary International, FL. OH & HN
U.S.A.A. Printing, Lexington, KY
Well Springs of Life, Sarasota, FL

129

Tears and Shoes

Later that year, a team from Kentucky came to finish and dedicate the church facility in Bartolo. Pastor Steve Birch wrote of the tears that flowed from the team members' eyes as they saw the women who had been up since 3 a.m. preparing 1,000 tamales and 500 sandwiches for the celebration, and as they observed 300 people cramming into the tiny building and another 200 assembled outside for the service. It was humbling to realize than 30 of them had walked four hours, crossing three rivers on foot, and would return the same way that night. But the most memorable part of the evening happened after the service when Dave, an executive with PepsiCo, walked through the mud in his socks to board the truck. The team first laughed, then cried, when they realized he had given his shoes to a man whose own shoes were totally worn out. It was true that Honduran lives were changing through Charlie's dream, but so were the lives of those who thought they had come to minister.

During this pivotal year for Charlie's ultimate vision, the first official Hand to Honduras newsletter was published with reports of the above events and more. A dozen teams visited the Yure Basin that year. Central Community Church in Wichita, Kansas, sent teams three times and helped the church in La Victoria construct a new facility on two acres of land that had cost a whopping $50. A team from Winter Haven, Florida ministered to children in four villages (La Victoria, Bartolo, Montañuela, and Chagüitillos) and also worked on building the U-shaped ministry housing facilities in San Isidro. A team from Austinville, Alabama went from village to village preaching the Word and encouraging believers. Eight common-law couples were married in the church that year, 26 pastors received support, and there were two functioning pastors' associations. A regional meeting was attended by 1,000 people as excitement built among the churches associated with Hand to Honduras.

Many good things were happening through this ministry that was still operating under the umbrella of Hand to the Plow. But the time was drawing near to become an independent organization. Charlie needed his own board and the freedom to decide how to spend the funds being generated by his contagious enthusiasm. And he told me that one man he wanted on board was the one who had ably led the May Medical Team: Jerry Grubbs.

For where your treasure is, there will your heart be also.
~Matthew 6:21 KJV

25
A Title, A Text, A Task
1991

The 1991 June reunion and informational meeting during the annual convention of the Church of God would be transformational. The gathering included the usual elements: rice and beans, testimonies from those who had traveled to Honduras in the past year, and Charlie's challenges to "come and see." But the most important event of the day occurred after this reunion.

At 8:30 p.m. on June 18, 1991, Jerry Grubbs, Charlie and I left Park Place Church and walked across the street onto the Anderson University campus. In Jerry's office in the administration building, we reviewed the events of the past couple of years, reflected on the enthusiasm of the group that had just gathered at Park Place, and thought about what God was doing. We decided it was time to set up a separate ministry. It was at this meeting that closure was brought to the name Hand to Honduras, and the name suggested by Jerry–Heart to Honduras–became the official name.

As we discussed the need for a verse of Scripture to encapsulate the essence and mission of the ministry, the question arose, "What is the real heartbeat of Heart to Honduras? What is our treasure?" We three agreed that the poor Hondurans were not only our treasure, but God's treasure as well. As we mulled over Scriptures, seeking a key verse to express this thought, Jerry recommended the words of Jesus in Matthew 6:21: "For where your treasure is, there will your heart be also." The final decision was that Heart to Honduras would focus solely on the country of Honduras so as not to spread itself too thin.[30]

After about an hour of discussion, we knelt and asked God's favor upon the ministry of Heart to Honduras. The following month–on July 15, 1991–Heart to

---

[30] In later years, when students began attending the Discipleship Center in Canchias, some came from large cities and various countries. This influx of non-Hondurans and non-rural students naturally led the ministry back toward the large cities and to neighboring countries as well.

131

Honduras was formally incorporated in the state of Florida. When Charlie received these incorporation papers, he breathed a sigh of relief.

It had been 11 years since he began to write the H.E.A.R.T. vision. But Charlie, being just a renegade in the eyes of the administration, was never given the reins to carry out that vision. With the decisions made in Jerry's office that night, he was now a leader with full authority to implement his vision with few restrictions. There was no one who had the authority to tell him how far he could ride his horse. Charlie now had free rein for the first time in his life. He did not have to worry about bureaucrats second guessing him, administrators reining him in, managers managing him or bookkeepers questioning him--because there were none. This would come later as the board began to expand, but for most of Charlie's tenure, he was given enough freedom to cast his vision without restraints.

The Heart to Honduras board has always believed its role was to set policy and hold the president (or overseer, as Charlie preferred) of Heart to Honduras accountable. But it refused to get personally involved in programs and day to day activities. It gave great freedom for the field staff to initiate programs. This is why Charlie and Miguel were able to accomplish so much in a short period of time.

That fall, the first board meeting was held in the Wichita, Kansas home of Charlie's sister Lorna and her husband Jon Kardatzke. Those in attendance on October 13 and 14, 1991 were Miguel Pinell[31] and Charlie, Lorna, Jim Usher, and Jerry Grubbs. A three-pronged mission statement was composed at this meeting:

> To enable, equip and encourage the church in Honduras to better do the work of the Kingdom of God, to inform the church in North America

Jon & Lorna Kardatzke, faithful financial partners, received a gift of beans on the vine on their visit to her brother's ministry in Honduras

---

[31] Miguel was not an official board member, as the provisionary bylaws stated a member had to be a U.S. citizen. However, the following year, Miguel was asked to serve on the board because of his vital role as the international director in Honduras and the requirement to be a U.S. citizen was struck from the bylaws. This wisely paved the way in later years for other Hondurans to serve on the board.

about the needs of the church in Honduras, and to provide opportunities for persons and churches to become involved in this ministry.

Later, Charlie composed a set of words that more succinctly expressed his desire to see that Heart to Honduras minister to the whole person. These five purposes served as a focal point for printed materials and videos that were created to publicize the work being done with the rural poor:

Food for the Hungry
Clothing for the Naked
Housing for the Homeless
Healing for the Hurting
Hope for the Hopeless

Original Board Members:
Charlie Smith, Lorna Kardatzke, Jim Usher, Jerry Grubbs

With the business side taken care of, Charlie could get back to the part he loved the most: boots-on-the-ground involvement as he led teams, contacted donors with shameless pleas for contributions, and dictated operational policies to Miguel. The momentum was exciting.

*A successful man is one who can lay a firm foundation
with the bricks others have thrown at him.*
~David Brown

26
Financial Blessings Impact Lives
1992

Exciting things began to happen in 1992, especially in the area of finances. Individual contributions totaled $80,282.58, and various churches contributed $113,450.22. In addition, a family which was very close to the ministry put up $100,000 for a matching fund program. This gift was matched and brought in $200,000 for the ministry in the coming year. Charlie was ecstatic. It would be the physical fuel to give direction to his vision.

Now Charlie had funds that he could spend on his treasure and God's treasure—the poor believers in Honduras. He proposed a budget of $275,750 for 1992. Charlie was generous and deeply concerned for the poorest of the poor in Honduras. Only the barest of essentials in the stateside office were allocated money. The bulk of the money was spent in Honduras to enable, empower and equip the poor believers to be self-sustaining, self-governing, and self-propagating so that they could move on to maturity and self-reliance. And because of this missionary philosophy of giving by Charlie, Heart to Honduras rarely had a surplus of funds in the stateside bank account. Charlie simply refused to sit on this money or place it in a conservative CD or a mutual fund. Needs were great. People were suffering. Stomachs were empty. That quarter of a million dollars could go a long way in alleviating these needs. Charlie wrote of this influx of cash in the ministry:

> The Kingdom of God is *now*, and the needs are great and pressing. This money needs to be invested in exciting projects so that it will capture the imagination of people which in turn will create greater cash flow. This money will help us to stay on target with the Discipleship Learning Center. People buy into what is true, and people will give to projects when they see it is impacting the lives of people in a dramatic way. We must not live in an "early retirement syndrome" but press on in the now, meeting the immediate needs of the poorest of the poor.

Ownership of land which excluded the poor was a major burr under Charlie's saddle, and he set out to rectify the situation in a pilot project in Montañuela. Forming a cooperative of nine landless farmers, he used ministry funds to purchase some acreage that they could farm together, sharing in the work and the harvest. As we stood among the tall corn being raised by the co-op, an old *campesino* said, "It is tremendous what God is doing on our land."

Joe Stephenson, a pastor from Alabama who had been raised on a large Indiana farm, was an interested visitor to this project. When he and I arrived by horseback at the field, he was moved to tears by the sight of the primitive lean-to that sheltered one of the co-op farmers, his pregnant wife and their toddler.

Joe's tears flowed every time he thought about the injustice of that family's plight. When he got home he became a regular contributor to a fund that provided loans for Honduran famers to purchase home grain silos. Instead of being forced to sell his grain at a low price during harvest time to a merchant who could store it in his huge silo, the farmer could store it himself and avoid the inflated cost of buying back his own grain during the "season of hunger." In small steps, justice was being served.

Charlie inspecting a home grain silo

The 1992 May Medical Team treated 3,000 Hondurans in seven days, and brought $20,000 worth of medicine. Among the team members was Cindy Penhorwood, a nursing instructor at Anderson University. This first trip led to her joining the staff of Heart to Honduras in 2004 as health care coordinator.

In July, a dental team pulled 1,100 teeth. My wife, Carol Lynne, was impressed by the stoicism of a woman who walked an hour or two to the makeshift clinic, had all her teeth pulled, and walked home again.

Later that month, Carol Lynne, an elementary teacher, worked with Nilsa Pinell in leading a Christian Education workshop for 50 Honduran Sunday School teachers. Each attendee was given teaching supplies, including stories, flannelgraph figures and chalk. Nilsa's brother Ever, who had been sent to

135

carpentry school with ministry funds, made 2-foot by 3-foot boards from plywood, which were painted with chalkboard paint on one side and had flannel attached to the other side, giving them a portable, versatile teaching tool.

The stateside staff of Heart to Honduras increased in 1992: I left the church I had been pastoring to allow more time to lead teams and do speaking, preaching, and writing for the ministry from my home in Alabama; a young lady named Kelly Prescott moved from Kansas to Florida to work as support staff; a young man named Monty Harrington, who would later become Kelly's husband, moved to Florida to use his training in video production as a way to promote the ministry. Dave Pischel's talents as a graphic artist were engaged to design brochures and produce the newsletter from his home in Oregon.

Early Staff
Back row: Nilsa & Miguel, Cristina, Estella
Front row: Wilmer, Jimmy Pinell, Charlito (Miguel's son named after Charlie), Chicas, Victor

Miguel's staff was growing, too. In addition to the partnership of his wife Nilsa, ministering to women and guiding them in ministering to children, Miguel began the year with three men working for him. Victor Fuentes, Wilmer Salazar and Felix Chicas wore several hats, including driving the ministry vehicles and giving guidance to the associations of pastors. An iron works shop was being installed and the loans to persons buying the grain silos meant both delivery and record-keeping, so there was little time for anyone to rest. By the end of the year, Miguel's brother Jimmy was helping with logistics, Victor's wife Estella was the official cook, and a young man named Pedro Huete was working with churches and teams in the area of music.

But the fruit of the hard work made it worth the effort. Three hundred people made commitments to become disciples of Christ in 1992, and among them was Antonio from Chagüitillos. Though he had been Charlie's friend from the Project Global Village days, he had been antagonistic toward the evangelical church. So antagonistic that one day he caused a hive of bees to swarm into the building where services were held, forcing all the worshippers to flee. But the night he had a vision of Jesus calling him into the Kingdom

Charlie gives Antonio a post-baptism hug

brought a change. The next day he stopped at Pastor Mario's house to ask forgiveness. What a thrill it was for Charlie to baptize his friend Antonio in the river below the village.

When a work team from Florida converted a bar into a meeting place for the church in Petrona's hometown of Las Casitas, it became one of seven new church buildings completed in 1992. Petrona's 1990 healing from an apparent brain tumor had been pivotal in the change in this community.

When we worshipped with the church from La Joya, Charlie's words of blessing gave them hope. Because this congregation had formerly had only female members, there was rejoicing that night over the six men who were recently converted.

A great spirit of joy came upon all the churches as they received encouragement from the North American team visits and investments. More than 120 North Americans visited Honduras during the year and went back with new enthusiasm to become more radical in their faith.

One day a team interacted with a woman who caught our attention because she walked on her hands and folded legs, swinging herself along with a basketful of bananas carefully balanced on her head. We learned that we could buy all 40 bananas for about 30 cents, and though we were tempted to give her five dollars, we realized the importance of staying within the culturally appropriate price. And to further demonstrate our respect for her, we allowed her to take the bananas we had bought from her and load them on our truck. It was a lesson in dignity and self-respect for each of us.

Miguel Pinell and Vic Floener from Florida had the adventure of driving two donated trucks 2,564 miles from Wichita, Kansas, to San Isidro, Honduras. They reported a lot of stress driving through Mexico and crossing the border at Guatemala, but daily saw the hand of God on their trip. The Dodge Ram and the Toyota 4x4 extended cab pickup were gifts from Kentucky and Kansas churches that blessed the ministry for several years as they hauled people and supplies over many miles of rough terrain.

The June 1992 Anderson reunion saw the addition of an art auction to the program. Several artists donated paintings of Honduras which were auctioned off, with the money going to the ministry. Becky Everitt (whose husband Chuck gave leadership to the ministry's blacksmith shop), Ruth Andress Stone (Charlie's mother-in-law), and a nurse named Judy Rentner (who was later instrumental during Charlie's illness), all contributed their artistic abilities to this endeavor, and many people went home with a lovely painting that would hang on their wall as a daily reminder of the ministry of Honduras.[32]

The year of 1992 ended with incredible excitement, the future of Heart to Honduras looked bright, and the leader was experiencing the joy of fulfilling his calling. Charlie expressed his deep gratitude for all the positive things that were happening, including the blessing of a loving wife: Karen had supported his frequent travels to Honduras throughout the 1980s while she stayed home, worked as a nurse, and kept up with their teenage girls. Now the girls were entering adulthood, the dreams he had spoken of to his wife were coming true, and, in his words, he and Karen "considered ourselves blessed at all times and thankful for each day."

He told about how Karen had given him an extra hug one day when he was on the way to run some errands and how she had reminded him of the need to be thankful for each day in light of the recent tragic death of a close family friend. After they hugged, she had said, "Charlie, life's short. There are many dangers out there on Highway 27. We don't know if you'll be back from this trip, so I just wanted you to know that it has been a great adventure living with you. I have loved you and still love you with inexpressible love." Charlie wrote, "We held each other and cried–thankful for the great blessing of being able to live up to this point."

---

[32] Another artist later associated with the ministry was Jayne Crews-Linton, who served for a time on the board of Heart to Honduras.

138

PART FIVE

Tales from Three Villages
Canchias
La Joya
Chagüitillos

Do not despise small beginnings.
~Zachariah 4:10

27

The View from Simeon's Hammock
The Village of Canchias

When Simeon Ramirez moved there as a toddler in 1943, Canchias was a tiny settlement, not even big enough to be called a village. When Simeon's father built a *choza*-a mud-and-stick, thatched-roof house-for his family, the only other dwellings housed Simeon's grandmother and aunt.

Ten years later, logging companies bushwhacked their way through the jungle-like foliage and discovered an area rich in mahogany trees and populated by a few *campesinos* living in less than a dozen *chozas*. Its location along the Yure River made it an ideal place to cut the timber and float it out of the jungle.

With the promise of good money in exchange for their hard labor, more families moved from the surrounding villages to remove the precious trees and work the sawmill. For six years the jobs lasted, but when the trees were gone, so was the logging company, leaving behind an increased population, but little else. There was no school, no church, no store, no government, no clinic.

One of the definitions of poverty is a lack of options. This was certainly a characteristic of those who had labored for the logging companies. The formerly employed

Simeon Ramirez

141

Hondurans had been left without an income and with a tough choice: move elsewhere, or stay in an area where the only advantages were a mountain stream, the familiarity of the little shack that sheltered their family, and a piece of rocky mountainside for farming. Many left. A few stayed.

Simeon was one who chose to stay. Canchias had always been home to him, and besides, by the time the loggers moved out, he had learned the skills necessary for life there: farming, making adobe blocks, and the use of the campesino's best friend: the machete. These were skills more important than the math and reading that he never had the opportunity to learn. In spite of being crippled from a bite from the venomous barba amarilla snake when he was 8 years old, he got around fine by walking on the ball of his foot, and was able to work in the fields. He had grown to manhood, taken a wife, and built a house on the main—well, the only-corner in town, and his porch hammock afforded him a commanding view of the comings and goings of a population by then increased to 100 souls.

One day an itinerant evangelist came to Canchias, and Simeon and his wife accepted Christ. The evangelist planted a church that met at Simeon's house, and soon the corner rang in the evenings with the music of homemade stringed instruments.

As a result of his position as an early settler, the location of his property on a little hill above the road which commanded a view of everyone entering and exiting the village, and his natural leadership skills, Simeon Ramirez eventually became the recognized patriarch of the village.

One person whom Simeon observed from his hammock was Isidro, known by everyone as Chilo. He was not born into one of the original families but was a relative of Simeon's wife. Chilo was born in Canchias in 1959 after his family moved to the center of the village, across from Simeon's house.

Behind their new residence was the confluence of the Canchias "River" (actually just a mountain stream) and the Yure River. One day when Chilo was 8, his father was murdered in a dispute over cows, and he and his mother

Isidro "Chilo"

142

and siblings left for a time to live with his grandmother. However, there wasn't sufficient food or space at his grandmother's house, and after seeing his 15-year-old handicapped sister beaten to death, a starving 10-year-old Chilo made his way back to the familiarity of Canchias. Simeon's wife took pity on her deceased cousin's child and took him in. Soon, Chilo was looking to Simeon as his surrogate father. In time, Chilo also became a respected leader in the community.

When Project Global Village sent Charlie to Canchias in the mid-1980s, this bearded man on a motorcycle made quite an impression on Chilo. He watched out the window of his simple adobe home as Charlie made his way down to the confluence of the Yure and Canchias rivers, taking pictures along the way. Later, Chilo observed the first meeting of two men who would develop a deep respect and love for each other, as Charlie walked over to the house on the corner, and Simeon welcomed this gringo who had a vision for assisting the village.

Over the next three years Charlie made numerous visits to Canchias. On one of those visits, and with the blessing of Simeon, Charlie stood before the entire village and said, "We would like to help you make your village better, if you would like the help. You live on dirt floors and we will assist you in making concrete floors for your houses. You live under roofs made of grass leaves. We will assist you in putting tin roofs over your head."

Neither man knew what profound changes Simeon would see from his hammock following acceptance of that simple offer of help. On that day, even the visionary in Charlie did not realize that Canchias would soon become the center of the ministry of Heart to Honduras, bringing truckloads of Central American ministerial students, local pastors seeking training, and North American mission volunteers. A medical clinic would increase the foot traffic between Simeon's and Chilo's houses, and the sound of an ice cream vendor's bell would even be heard rounding Simeon's corner!

At one time, Simeon's house was at the end of a rutted road which was seldom traversed and then only by the brave of heart. But in the years after his encounter with Charlie, Simeon would see the day when a public bus would be routed through Canchias and government officials from the capital would arrive in their big cars to check out the school across the street. As Zachariah 4:10 says, "Do not despise small beginnings."

143

"Has no one condemned you?" "No one, sir," she said.
"Then neither do I condemn you," Jesus declared.
"Go now and leave your life of sin."
~Jesus Christ in John 8:11 NIV

28

A Gift for a Prostitute
The Village of La Joya

La Joya seemed to be cursed. Poverty, poor soil and a lack of rain turned this village into a dust bowl. Heart to Honduras volunteers riding through the village on the open beds of ministry trucks were plastered with its red dust, like actors in *The Grapes of Wrath*.

But La Joya is also blessed. Tucked away on a hillside far off the beaten path in southeast Honduras, it has its own hot spring, and it overlooks the powerful Humuya River which slithers like a giant boa through mountain ravines and serves as a life support system for the village.

North American teams visiting this tiny village perched on the side of a mountain experienced culture shock as they witnessed its extreme poverty and deprivation. Someone once remarked that roosters in La Joya are so hungry they have to lean against a fence post to crow. Little children with bloated stomachs played naked in the orange-colored sand. Old men with rib cages protruding stood idle along the edge of the road. Poverty abounded because years ago, the people of La Joya sold their land to people in the surrounding villages, and now unscrupulous landlords assess high rental fees for use of a bit of ground. The helpless, hopeless, landless peasants, who toiled under the hot sun to forage for a few thin stalks of corn and a handful of red beans to keep starvation at bay, were now the poorest of the poor.

An American team from the Eastland Church of God in Lexington, Kentucky happened to be in La Joya over Thanksgiving in the early 1990s. Missing their families' celebrations back home and longing for something to ease their homesickness, they asked the local pastor if a turkey could be located. "Impossible," said the pastor. Realizing that finding a turkey in La Joya would be a miracle tantamount to Moses bringing forth water out of a rock, they resigned themselves to "feasting" on the trail mix in their backpacks.

144

A few minutes later the pastor, apparently having tapped on a rock somewhere, brought forth a miracle: two skinny, featherless chickens not much bigger than pigeons. With 20 North Americans to feed, the Thanksgiving meal hardly looked adequate, but by adding a lot of watered-down broth and some rice to the two birds, each visitor received a piece of meat the size of a slice of pepperoni. It was such a memorable experience for this team that, back home, they began holding a "Meal of Remembrance," going without food one day a month.

It was here in this village where Charlie, in his great compassion, took a can of eight Vienna sausages and cut them up with a local kitchen knife and fed 30 children on this Thanksgiving Day. La Joya was special to Charlie, and Charlie was special to the people, and to no one more than a woman named Beti.

Beti was different from the other women in La Joya. There was a natural beauty about her that caught one's eye. She had presence. Actually, she was stunning in this dusty setting of poverty and disease. One American pastor was so impressed with her beauty and potential that he remarked of her appearance, "I would like to take her to the States and have some women wash her down with lye soap and then dress her up with the latest fashion. She could represent the country as Miss Honduras in the Miss World pageant."

Beti was confident, walked with assurance and composure. Unlike the other shy Honduran women who kept their distance, she was unafraid to talk with the North Americans. Maybe she had done business with a few. But while the other women were simple and plain, she wore sparkling earrings and a necklace, carried a handbag and wore ornaments in her hair. Her red lips blended with the earth tones of her brown face, enhancing her attractiveness.

But Beti's stunning beauty came with

Beti and her son

a very high price. When Beti heard the roar of trucks signaling that men might make a stop in La Joya to wash the red dust off their sweating bodies in the Humuya River, she would position herself on the bank. As they approached the river, Beti would remove her top and dive into the water several times just to show her sensual power to tantalize the men.

It was hard to resist these shameless men, because times were hard and a few lempiras could mean the difference between life and death in the village of La Joya. Sadly for Beti, she allowed her beauty to trump her wisdom.

Charlie explaining instructions for hair dye to Beti

One would think if a poor mother with a starving baby had one request of a "gringo," it would be either powdered milk rich in calcium or some protein for her baby. But she had replied to Charlie's inquiry, "Do you need anything?" with a request for black hair dye. Hair dye applied properly would pay big dividends from some of the high rollers who lived in the big cites of Siguatepeque, Tegucigalpa and Comayagua, all just a short bus ride away.

In response to her request, Charlie had taken a step of faith and obeyed the promptings of the Holy Spirit. As the team drove through La Joya, and with translator Marilyn Aleman at his side, they stopped to give Beti a bottle of Clairol hair dye. Still vivid in the mind of everyone who was present that day, is Marilyn translating instructions read by Charlie on how to apply the dye to Beti's hair.

After giving Beti the hair dye, the team piled back onto the white Toyota truck and drove toward the hot spring alongside the Humuya River. It was a refreshing experience to bathe in water naturally warmed by steam from an underground fissure in the earth.

Stepping into the small pool of hot water was Jerry Grubbs, chairman of the Heart to Honduras board. He had not been in the soothing water long when Beti approached. When she came to the pool, the team greeted her. She smiled. And then for some reason, she walked over and knelt beside Jerry and the two of them tried to carry on a conversation as Marilyn translated. After a few minutes of broken Spanish, Beti took Jerry's bar of soap and with slight hesitation began to wash his back.

Hmm! This was going to turn out to be an interesting mission trip! But the team members were well aware that "...God's ways are not our ways and His thoughts are not our thoughts." The Holy Spirit is creative. He will not be boxed in by one's water-tight theology or rigid methods of evangelism. He can use a bar of Ivory soap to get His job done just as well as He can use the booming voice of an evangelist. I recorded the experience in my journal:

I began to sense an unusual presence of God as Beti, the village prostitute from La Joya began to gently wash Jerry's back. It was almost like a worship service, and we could not put a handle on it. There was nothing sensual or lustful to what Beti was doing. It was a mystery to us how something so unusual could seem so natural. Then, it began to dawn on us what was happening. Beti was so used to touching dirty men, that for one time in her life, she was touching godly men. It was her way of reaching out and touching God. Following Jerry's free back massage, Beti offered to give me a similar massage. I too felt the innocence and purity of what Beti was doing.

Having dried off and changed clothes, the team drove back to the village of La Joya and noticed Beti dressed in a gorgeous outfit, holding her baby. They stopped to give greetings and Beti asked Marilyn if she could ride with us to church. Maybe the Holy Spirit was using that Clairol hair dye and bar of soap after all.

While driving up the mountain, a team member asked Beti if she was a Christian. She responded, "I am going to church tonight to rededicate my life to God."

That night, Beti sat in the back of the church holding her little baby. When the invitation was given for those who wanted more of God in their lives, Beti, true to her words, came forward with the little baby. As tears flowed from her eyes, she gave her life to God.

There were many factors that brought Beti to this point. The church had been praying for her. The Holy Spirit had been wooing her. For several years, she had witnessed Christ in the life of the believers from North America. She saw men who loved her not for her body or for her beauty but simply because she was a child of God. She was not a dirty prostitute, but a beautiful woman created in the image of God. The washing of Jerry Grubbs' back in the warm pool without sensing lust from him or the other men standing near the hot spring made a deep impression on Beti. It was from this experience that she understood the affirming words of Jesus, "Go and sin no more!"

But key to winning Beti over to Christ was the example and love Charlie Smith had shown to her over the years. So often, people think of visionaries as gifted men who visualize an unseen elementary school on a barren plot of land or a community center in place of a crack house. But Charlie's visions saw potential in people as well as projects.

Charlie never judged Beti. She never left his presence feeling condemned. He never preached to her. He loved her. He accepted her. He held her little baby. And he gave her a bottle of black Clairol hair dye.

147

The Lord appeared to Abraham near the great trees of Mamre.
~Genesis 18:1 NIV

29
Beneath the Tamarind Tree
The Village of Chagüitillos

Just up the mountain road from the home of Beti in La Joya is the village of Chagüitillos. The pastor of the Protestant church there is Pastor Mario Rivera. In 1993, a small group of North Americans visiting this mountain village included Charlie and his wife Karen, their daughters, and her parents. Gathered around a table after their "missionary meal" of peanut butter and jelly sandwiches, the group sat spellbound as the gregarious pastor shared the history of the village and his commitment to preach the Gospel under adverse and trying times. Here is his story in his words:

About 200 years ago, a Franciscan priest sailed from Spain and settled in the village of Comayagua, which was the first capital of Honduras. Today it is about an hour drive from Comayagua to Chagüitillos, or a full day by horse or mule. The priest fell in love with a pretty señorita named Francesca, and eventually she became pregnant. Due to the shame of being with child by a supposedly celibate priest, Francesca moved to the mountain village of Chagüitillos and settled there. A few months later, her illegitimate daughter was born. They named her Puncha. They lived a long time by themselves in a very small, makeshift house. Her last name was Rivera.

All the families that live here have the last name of Rivera. This is how the village began as others came to settle here. All our people marry their cousins, for we are like a tribe here. We do not want any flat *narices* (*noses*). We do not want to be like the Mayans

Pastor Mario

148

or the Negroes, for we know if we intermarry we will lose control.

I was born here on August 10, 1958, and at an early age began studying to be a priest in the village of El Rosario, about an hour walk down the mountain from here. My mother was a Catholic and raised me in the Catholic Church. I learned how to pray, make the sign of the cross and say the Rosary.

When I was 16, I went to the parochial school to become a priest. I studied for four years and was mentored by a priest in Rosario named Maximillino Chilano. They saw that I was intelligent and committed. I preached for four years in the Catholic Church and served as his assistant.

During this time, it was prohibited for the local people to read the Bible. Only the priest could read the Bible. But one day, a believer named Octavio Aviala gave me a New Testament. And I began to learn things from it that were different than the Catholic Bible. I had to read it in secret. It made me upset to have to read the Bible in secret.

Octavio Aviala was a man from the nearby village of Colmenas. One day, he left the village and went to the east coast of Honduras. While he was there, he heard the Gospel for the first time and accepted Christ as his Lord and Savior. After a while, he returned to the Chagüitillos area and began holding prayer meetings in the three surrounding villages of Colmenas, La Joya and Chagüitillos. Each week, he would stay in one of the three villages and teach about this new experience in Jesus Christ. He was persecuted, because most of the people were Catholic. My brother-in-law, Oscar, whose great, great, great grandfather from Spain settled this area, brought with him the Catholic faith. But at a young age, Oscar heard the Gospel from Octavio and accepted Christ as his Savior. After Oscar became a believer, I became curious about the new message Octavio was sharing, as well. Octavio would use a 12-volt battery and speaker system to preach the Word. He would fast for a week and sleep in a cave. He heard a word from the Lord, "Go to Chagüitillos!"

Octavio said, "Do what?" And the word came again, "Go preach in Chagüitillos!" So the pastor came here and was just walking though the village waiting on God.

Oscar was sick in a hammock. He sees the man of God and says, "Oh, what are you doing here? Come, pastor, and let us talk." They talked from 9 to 5 all day.

Oscar helps carry supplies

And he said to Oscar, "You have only one choice. You have to choose the Lord." So Oscar received the Lord, October 28, 1980.

149

So while I was reading the New Testament, I began to discover the Gospel. I discovered that babies should not be baptized. I discovered that God and God alone should be worshipped, not man. I became concerned when I discovered that Mary was worshipped as much as God's Son Jesus. I heard the priest say, "Long live the Virgin." And I really got upset when the Catholic Church shipped a large statue of Mary from Spain and paraded her image through the village of Opoteca. They bowed down and worshipped this image, but I did not see this in the Bible. This statue of Mary and its influence was so great that they changed the named from Opoteca to El Rosario.[33]

I struggled with this, especially when the priest wanted to send me to Chagüitillos to be the priest. I continued to read the New Testament. I noticed in Hebrews 10 that no longer do priests offer sacrifices or eliminate sins. I realized I did not have to go through a human priest, but as Hebrews 10:21 says, "Now that we have a High Priest (Jesus), we can go right into the presence of God." We do not have to go through a human priest. When I preached this in my village, the people got very angry with me. My mother was very angry. I preached that the cross had power, not an image or a statue.

And they really got mad when I preached that Mary was not our mother. She is the earthly mother of Jesus, but not our spiritual mother. They came to me and said, "Who is your mother?" I then read to them Galatians 4:26 about Paul's illustration of the heavenly Jerusalem, "But Sarah, the free woman, represents the heavenly Jerusalem. And she is our (figurative) mother."

They told the priest what I had said. He came to me and said, "You cannot keep on preaching. You twist the word of God." So they told the village, "This young man Mario Rivera cannot preach anymore." But I found encouragement from the Word and the Lord. God put life in my mind when I opened the Bible. He said to me, "You must not depend on man but on me."

I knew God was with me. So one Sunday, Oscar and I got together. We began to talk on his patio, just the two of us. Together, we began to see more light. Then my mama saw the light. For many months, it was just the three of us. I continued to teach them. They did not know anything about the Bible, because they were not allowed to read the Bible. There had never been the Gospel in Chagüitillos.

I then began to preach with great liberty from the Holy Spirit. Now I was free to preach, and I was very active. My theme was, "*Yo tengo un Cristo viva* [I have a Christ who lives]."

---

[33] This name refers to the beads of the Rosary and is associated with a prayer that is addressed to Mary.

People in the village said, "Mario is *loco* [crazy]! He has become a Protestant. It is a scandal!" But after a while, people began to come by and listen to my sermons. From other villages, they wanted to hear the preacher in Chagüitillos. Even the priest from Comayagua came to see me. He hoped to stop me from leaving the Catholic Church, and he refused to listen to what I had learned from the Bible.

In the first year, we had 40 members commit to our little fellowship. I preached for 12 years beneath the tamarind tree over at Oscar's house. We now have over 100 members out of a village of 250 people–almost half the village. One day, a widow lady in Chagüitillos asked me if I would

Brothers Chilano, left, and Antonio, love to make music together, singing both secular and sacred songs. Chilano is a Catholic; Antonio is a Protestant

help her fix a leaky roof. I was on top of the roof of her house and I could hear footsteps of someone. I turned and looked and it was a short man and a little bit fat. I thought to myself that a visitor was coming. He asked for me, "Are you Pastor Mario?" It was Brother Miguel Pinell. It was then that our friendship began.

He had been sent here by Charlie Smith to check out the village. Charlie was friends with Chilano and Antonio Rivera who worked in San Isidro with Project Global Village. They were Catholics who were raised and born in Chagüitillos. In those years, the Catholics and Protestants did not get along. One Sunday, the Catholics came over to Oscar's house, which was our place to worship before we had a church building. One of them climbed on the roof and threw a beehive in where we were meeting. But today it is better. We have come to accept one another, and they don't persecute us anymore.

Miguel asked to talk to me. It was the first visit of an evangelical brother to this village. No one had ever asked to see the pastor. Christians came to the village, but no one ever taught the Gospel. I prayed for many years that God would bring men with commitment. We talked. Then Miguel said, "Brother Mario, do you want to work with us? You will have to visit us for one year once a month.

151

You will have to come to San Isidro." So I went for one year. I didn't have any money, so I had to walk all the way to Siguatepeque. It was 28 kilometers [17 miles] over the mountains. From there, I was able to catch a bus to San Isidro. I would leave at 5 a.m. and arrive at 2 p.m. My legs were sore when I arrived in San Isidro. I went 12 times and was there for 11 sessions. At the last meeting, Brother Miguel said, "Brother Mario, you have gone through the test. Now we will work with you in the central zone."

Charlie and Miguel flank the central zone pastors gathered for training under the leadership of Pastor Mario [standing, third from left].

Many times I would go to the mountain to pray. I felt lonely. I wanted union with my brothers in Christ. I wanted to forget the call God had placed on my life. There were times when I was persecuted for my faith. I have scars on my back to prove it. I said, "No! God has called me to ministry."

I talked with many pastors and my thought was, how can we increase the Kingdom of God in this area? The first time I heard Bro. Charlie preach, he preached from Matthew 5:6, "Blessed are the peacemakers..." I saw his tears and I knew he was a man of God. I knew Charlie would not run from the battlefield. He and Brother Jimmy were very valuable to us. But everything was through Miguel.

Our culture is so different from the States. No electricity. No water. There are a lot of other things that people have that we do not have. This is why we don't have too much evil. No pool. No television. No bar. Yet, for now, there is no corruption. We believe with time evil will grow.

Church building in Chagüitillos with 1992 Medical Team
Miguel Pinell & Jim Usher, lower left; Jerry Grubbs, left of left post; Dr. Larry
Lilly center back with glasses; Pastor Mario Rivera in cowboy hat near right
post, Jerry Girardi with mustache kneeling in center between posts.

For 12 years, we met at Oscar's house, and now we are very content with our new building which teams from the ministry of Heart to Honduras built for us. We are praying. We are happy. When the horn sounds as the ministry truck passes through La Joya, the children start running down the mountain to meet them at the water spigot. The church is very happy. God will never leave us alone. Brothers in America, fast and pray!

More than 20 years later, this pastor was still faithfully shepherding his flock in this tiny village, preaching the Gospel and reaching out to the surrounding villages to share what he had learned as he studied the Word.

PART SIX

1993

Loss

Wait for the Lord, be strong and take heart, wait for the Lord.
~Psalm 27:14 NIV

30
It's Big. Be Strong!
March 1993

Anne-Marie, Karen, Charlie, Felicia

In March, 1993, Charlie and Karen Smith were in their 32nd year of marriage. For the Smith household that year, as Charlie noted in his journal, "Life was rolling right along on the smooth lane and was treating us good. We considered ourselves blessed at all times and thankful for each day, and our love for each other was growing." This smooth lane had begun to encounter a few small bumps as December gave way to a new year. In January and February of 1993, Karen had a persistent nasal drainage and nosebleed. She was first diagnosed with a sinus infection, but when antibiotics had no effect and the nosebleeds wouldn't stop, the nurse in her knew she needed to consult a specialist. On Wednesday, March 24, morning X-rays revealed a mass in her sinuses and nasal passage.

Karen was sent straight for an MRI. Following the MRI that afternoon, the doctor approached Charlie with a solemn look on her face. Her words were few–five to be exact–and were the saddest ever to fall upon Charlie's ears. "Charlie, it's big. Be strong!" A biopsy surgery was scheduled for the next day at 3 p.m.

157

He and Karen returned home trying to process the news. Their concern centered on this awful word, mass. How widespread was the mass? Was it life-threatening? If so, how much time did she have? What about their daughters?

In those pre-cell phone, pre-Internet days, communication between the United States and the ministry in Honduras was by FAX machine–and the FAX machine was a three-hour drive away from the ministry office, at a hardware store called Difesa, in San Pedro Sula. Miguel would make this stop every week or so when he had some other reason to be in the city.

On that Friday afternoon, completely oblivious to the events that had transpired over the past couple of days with our friend in the States, I was with Miguel for the stop to check for ministry FAXes. As we drove into the city, we chatted about our upcoming trip to Guatemala and our plans to rendezvous with Charlie and Karen there in two days. Miguel was to interview a Guatemalan doctor, and then all of us were going to visit the ancient city of Antigua and check out some of its 85 language schools.

At Difesa, three FAXes were waiting for us: two from Charlie and the third from my wife, Carol Lynne. Charlie's first, which had been sent early Wednesday morning, was brief and to the point, "Dear Brothers in the Lord: Please call me as soon as possible. It is very important. Charlie."

His second FAX, sent later that morning after he and Karen had received a stronger indication of the trouble ahead, stated that an MRI was planned for that afternoon, and a biopsy for the next day–a Thursday. Charlie wrote:

> I am praying that God will perform a miracle in Karen's life. It is so hard to think of not having her at my side. This of course is a selfish prayer. She is such a paragon of strength and power. Let me hear from you soon. In His loving care, Charlie

This alarmed us, but there was still a thread of hope. The biopsy might show that all was well. Then we read the one from my wife, and our hearts dropped. At the top of the FAX, in large, bold-faced letters, we read: "DO NOT LEAVE DIFESA UNTIL YOU READ THIS. SIT DOWN IF POSSIBLE." Her FAX, which had been sent early Friday morning, continued: "Yesterday (Thurs) they did a biopsy on a mass in Karen's sinuses, and it is malignant. It has already spread to her eye and her brain. Any surgery would be extremely risky–only four surgeons in the U.S. will even try it."

Thursday, March 25, is a date that still reverberates in the hearts and minds of all the Heart to Honduras staff who were associated with the ministry at that time. As Charlie would later write of that day: "I stood out in the hall with the doctor who said, 'Charlie, it's big. Adenocarcinoma–extensive, inoperable. Think in terms of months, not years to live.'" All their plans came to a screeching halt.

Thus began an incredible three-and-a-half month journey that would shake the Smith family's faith to its core, reshape their worldview, and permanently redirect their lives, both professionally and personally.

Following the biopsy, Karen, just 55 years old, lay in bed in the Winter Haven Hospital, reflecting about the news. Felicia, Anne-Marie and Charlie gathered around her, devastated at the turn of events. Karen, sensing their hurt, brokenness, tears and fears, reached out and touched their hands, and from the poise and grace that always characterized her attitude, spoke words that encouraged both daughters and husband:

> Hey guys, we've never been here before, but let the party begin. This can be an adventure for us as a family. This is what I want you to pray for as we move into the unknown future. Pray that I will have peace and courage. Pray that everyone who comes in touch with us during this time will have their faith increased. And pray that in all things God will be glorified....Let's make a list of the things we want to do in the time we have left together and then set about doing it.

The doctor had admonished Charlie to be strong when she first broke the news, but it was Karen's strength that enabled Charlie to carry on. He later wrote, "Karen is strong, as usual. She says that she is ready to die if the Lord wants to take her now and in this way. Her faith is very strong, and she is resting in the arms of Jesus."

Some cancers move slowly through the body, attacking healthy cells. Others, like Karen's, accelerate much faster to their targeted destination. This cancer, which came on ferociously and without warning[34] displayed no favoritism as it began to metastasize to her brain, nasal cavities, and eye.

With the goal of making the best of their remaining time together, every day became like a diamond, though the sparkle of each facet was diminishing. Charlie's faith was shaken, but not shattered. The girls, who at 26 and 24 were barely into adulthood, were in a twilight zone, unsure about the future and pondering the "whys" of the present.

---

[34] For many years, Karen had worked at a medical clinic in a double-wide trailer that contained asbestos. While asbestos exposure was suspected as the cause of her illness, no definitive cause was ever pinpointed.

159

The next day, as those of us in Honduras learned the grim news, the family began to brainstorm ideas for making "this whole experience an adventure." The flights for Karen's and Charlie's planned trip to Guatemala and Honduras that weekend had been cancelled, but at Karen's request, the family agreed to make plans for all of them to travel to Honduras soon.

Second on the list of ideas was a gift for neighbor Deryl Johnson, close friend and Bible professor at Warner Southern College, who had been wounded during WWII. The family would give him a recliner that would lift him up to a standing position. Third, they decided to pay to have a house built for the poorest family Miguel could find in Honduras.

Next on the list was to watch favorite videos, look at the family albums and view the hundreds of 35 mm slides Charlie had taken over the years while celebrating Christmas in Ruston, working with the poor on the Spencer County dam project, living in Malaysia, traveling through Asia and Europe, and on the return trip to Southeast Asia with their girls. In keeping with the idea of savoring every moment, the family chose to watch the video of *Our Town* by Thornton Wilder to ponder once again Emily's thought-provoking words, "Doesn't anyone ever realize life while they live it? Every, every minute?" While a professor at Warner Southern, Charlie had played the stage manager in a college production of this play and forever etched those words of Emily into the family psyche. Along with videos, the family listed meaningful books they would read and share together.

Maria, widow supported by Karen

And finally, they would visit Maria, the elderly, fragile Honduran widow beloved by Karen. Maria lived in a house of wood slats with a dirt floor in San Isidro, just a few houses down from Miguel. She had witnessed her only son murdered with a machete near her house, and she now lived alone. Karen had been sending her $10 each month for several years to purchase corn, beans, firewood and other essentials to make life easier for her.

With this list of activities, a potential pity party had been transformed into a party with purpose.

On Saturday night, March 27, Charlie and Karen were in bed. As Charlie was holding Karen tightly in his arms, she softly shared with Charlie, "I do not think I have much longer to live." Pondering this statement by Karen, Charlie called the church phone and left a message requesting that the pastor invite Karen's Sunday school class over to the house for a time of support and fellowship the next evening. The next morning, Pastor Dave Rockness mistakenly invited the entire church of several hundred to Charlie and Karen's house for the evening.

That Sunday night, more than 100 people from the First Presbyterian Church responded to the invitation. The kitchen felt like an overcrowded elevator, and those who wouldn't fit around the bar spilled over to the screened porch and even the downstairs patio. It was the largest gathering ever in their little modular home. In addition to the church folk and the family members who had gathered, the Heart to Honduras stateside staff was also present. I had just arrived from Honduras. The evening was a time of gaiety, laughter and warm fellowship. Finger food was abundant. Charlie's bluegrass music provided the ambience. And, as always, Karen was a gracious hostess.

Just two evenings before this Sunday night gathering in Florida, more than 200 Hondurans, including many of the Heart to Honduras pastors, had gathered at the San Isidro soccer field in a special service to pray for Karen. While they were praying, Maria, the frail widow Karen supported, pushed her way through the crowd and gave a cloth (perhaps her head scarf) to the pastors to pray over on behalf of Karen's healing. Miguel had rushed it to the airport the next morning and given it to me to bring to Lake Wales. It was a very moving time when Karen was asked to sit in the middle of the crowd that Sunday evening. I still remember the sounds of nature from Crooked Lake and the gentle breeze blowing through the screens. Charlie asked me to place the cloth on Karen's head and lead a prayer. We all felt God's presence on the patio that night.

The next day, a special FAX came to the Florida office. It was from Miguel and was most encouraging to Karen.

> Dear Karen:
> Nilsa and I have shed many tears for you. I tell Jimmy at the airport that Charlie and I cry so much on the phone because we love you so much. All the churches in Honduras shed many tears for you as we pray for half an hour at our service Friday night. There were five churches and pastors at the service from San Isidro, Las Casitas, Bartolo, La Victoria and Canchias.
>
> The pastors met and they want you to know that all the needs of Karen is on the table of the clinic of God. God will do a miracle on thee. They say, "If God make a miracle, then she will be blessed of God. If God not make miracle, then Karen will be twice blessed."

161

Karen, we know that if you happen to go away from us, it will be a party. But there will be sadness in the joy. I know there will be sadness, because I have never cried so much.

Karen, Maria love you so much. I know that Jimmy will tell you about the anointed cloth and how Maria put her hand in the center to touch Jesus' garment hem for you. It was so powerful. I know the power was released and go to the States to touch you. In Jesus there is no distance, time or space.

You have a great family in Honduras that love you very much. Nilsa and I look forward to see you very much. We will take good care of you.

Sincerely in Jesus, Miguel

Arrangements had been hastily made for a trip to Honduras. If all went according to plan, the team would leave on the following Thursday, April 1. Miguel, Nilsa, and the Hondurans who had grown to love Charlie were anxiously waiting to receive Karen as she made her last trip to this place into which her husband was pouring his life.

Karen loved the color purple, and she loved Jenny Joseph's poem *The Warning* that has as its theme the freedom that comes with old age, when one can throw off society's restrictions on what is proper. Just before she left for Honduras, Karen was given a purple shirt with the names of some of her choir friends on the back, and she proudly packed her new shirt as she prepared for this final trip. This wearing of purple reminded her of the words of the poem, which reflect both her sense of humor and her determination to make the most of these last days of her life.

The Warning
by Jenny Joseph

When I am an old lady, I shall wear purple
With a red hat, which doesn't go and doesn't suit me.
And I shall spend my pension on brandy
and summer gloves,
And satin sandals, and say we have no money for butter.

I shall sit down on the pavement when I am tired
And gobble up samples in shops and press alarm bells
And run my stick along the public railings
And make up for the sobriety of my youth.
I shall go out in my slippers in the rain
And pick the flowers in other people's gardens
And learn to spit.
...

But maybe I ought to practice a little now
So people who know me are not too shocked and surprised
When suddenly I am old and start to wear purple.

We can sing when the caterpillar dies and becomes a chrysalis because we know that the beautiful butterfly will emerge from that death. And we who have put our faith in Jesus can know that life beyond the grave is a reality.
~Charlie Smith

31
You Must Be Going to a Wedding
April 1993

Weary from emotion and late-night packing, the Smith family awaited Karen's and Charlie's beloved pastor, Dave Rockness, who had graciously volunteered to drive the group the three and a half hours to Miami for their flight on TACA Airlines to Honduras. A gray cloud covered the horizon, releasing tiny, hardly-visible droplets of rain on the Smith house at 354 First Avenue in Lake Wales. Multi-colored suitcases clustered on the driveway. It was Thursday morning, April 1, 1993, one week to the day after the diagnosis. The cancer was spreading rapidly, and Karen's physical strength was already visibly fading.

Nine people–mostly family members–would be making the pilgrimage: Charlie, who was broken within but seemed composed, Karen, Felicia and her then-husband Michael, Anne-Marie and her boyfriend Scott, Karen's parents Dean and Ruth Stone, and I. Charlie wanted me to come for encouragement and support as his friend, but also to keep a written and pictorial record of the journey for the family. Gary Mitkowski, one of Charlie's early students at H.E.A.R.T. who was now a physician's assistant, had been scheduled to go to assist with any of Karen's medical needs, but a high fever forced him to stay behind.

As the drizzling rain took an unexpected break, a white 18-passenger van turned right into the driveway at Charlie's house. Pastor Rockness joined the family as they gathered in a prayer circle. There was apprehension in the air. Could Karen hold up under the strain of travel? We all sensed the finality inherent in this trip, but it was unspoken, beneath the surface.

Karen was fond of angels. For this trip, she and the girls had purchased Angel Cards. She wanted each of us to choose one at random from the stack and read it to the group. On each card was a specific word. The card with its written word would serve as an "angel" guiding and encouraging not only the individual but the entire group. We were all amazed to observe how appropriate each card was to each person, especially the ones for Charlie and Karen. The angel of *purification* was selected by Dean. Ruth chose *truth*. Michael picked *expectancy*. Scott drew *communication*. Anne-Marie chose *gratitude*. Felicia had *willingness*. Pastor Dave was given *flexibility* and I pulled out *simplicity*.

As the group heard Karen read her word—*surrender*—we pondered the marvelous way in which God was already showing us His presence. When a person has just a few months to live, all things must be surrendered. And when we heard Charlie read the word *grace*, our faith in God soared. Charlie was reminded of the Apostle Paul's words, "My grace is sufficient, for my power shows up best in weak people." (NLT) None of us could imagine at that moment how much we would each need to fall back on these "angels" throughout our trip.

Charlie needed God's grace for this trip in a special way. He had been to Honduras approximately 50 times to encourage Miguel, edify the church and strengthen Hondurans. On this trip, Charlie was the one in need of encouragement and strength. On this pilgrimage, he would question God's sovereignty. He would weep until he could weep no more. He would pray, but often his prayers would seem to go no higher than the mango trees. He would read the Word over and over but the words would fail to speak.

It was Karen who gave us the words we needed—not only through her angel cards but through the surrendered life she was living. Her faith in God was as strong as steel. And because of this assurance, it was as if God appointed Karen to be our leader.

From the first moment she was diagnosed, her trust in God seemed to increase exponentially, and she maintained her practices of putting others first and savoring the gift of each moment, even as she faced this trial. When Shari Pugh Mayfield, a childhood friend of Felicia's, came to visit, bringing a gift for Karen's rose garden, she amazed Shari with her response, just as she had amazed her when she was a little girl. Shari told this story:

> I remember the day when I was a child and I rode my bike to the Smiths' home. I asked Mrs. Smith if she would cut me a rose to give to my mom for Mother's Day. She was so amazing to me. She found a vase and walked me downstairs and out back to her rose garden and clipped me the most beautiful orange rose I had ever seen. She added water and a piece of fern and even tied a ribbon around the vase. I was in awe and I had to be the happiest little girl in the world that day.

Charlie, Felicia, Karen and Anne-Marie in Karen's rose garden

When I heard about her illness, I brought her an orange rose bush. She was in pain but she insisted on getting her trowel and planting it right then and there. She reveled in the act... feeling the dirt in her hands as she planted that bush in a very nurturing way... as if that was all that mattered in the world.

If Karen found a measure of comfort in her rose garden, her husband found comfort in another of God's gifts. During low seasons in his life, Charlie would always turn to music to bring comfort to his soul, and this day of gray clouds and misty rain was no different. About 15 miles into our trip, Charlie reached into his briefcase and pulled out song sheets for communal worship. Though death knocked at his wife's door, this trip would not be a requiem. Rather, it would be, at least on this trip to Miami, a portable church speeding down Highway 27, with music and joyous laughter. After all, Karen, our leader, had established the ground rule: this trip and beyond was to be a party.

With windshield wipers slapping time and speeding black tires humming against asphalt, Charlie took his harmonica and began playing notes with a bluegrass beat. Though some of us were a bit off tune, our spirits were lifted above the hovering clouds. We sensed God's presence invading our mobile church. Charlie led us in "Each Step I Take," "Marching to Zion" and "I'd Rather Have Jesus." There was no need for any preaching from Pastor Rockness. No

165

need for any teaching from Charlie. We all just began to sing, moving along at 70 miles per hour.

We were greeted at the Miami International Airport by Dr. Stan Kardatzke, a member of Charlie's sister's extended family, and his wife Suzonne, who gave Karen a lovely bouquet of flowers. After introductions, we made our way to *The Top of the Port* restaurant on the eighth floor. Though we were all ever-mindful of the purpose of our trip, Charlie didn't miss this opportunity to share with Dr. Stan his holistic vision for ministry, which included a new medical clinic in Canchias.

As we awaited our departure on TACA airlines, I observed Karen, her red and yellow bouquet beside her, with a tear falling down her face. Throughout the trip, many tears would fall down so many faces, but Karen's tears were different. Her tears had a mixture of softness, sadness and strength. They were stately tears. Strong tears. Courageous tears. If a string could have been threaded through her tears and made into a necklace, it would have sparkled like diamonds. This was the kind of light she was for the entire group—a light that was a shining path into the unknown.

Charlie was moving among the group, making sure luggage and boarding passes were in order. He called me aside to show me two envelopes. Inside one was a check for $5,000, given to him by Stan to pay for the team's plane tickets. Charlie had put all our tickets on his credit card believing God would provide. Inside the other was a note from Suzonne:

> In anticipating meeting you face to face today, I found myself marveling as an observer of God's Word coming to pass. Here you are saints of God–facing present adversity with courage and unflappable poise, strength, and confidence and ever...joy! You are secure in His hands and continuing with your mission to Honduras–ever trusting, ever faithful, not missing a step. What a manifestation of his grace and glory! What a testimony to believers and unbelievers! How pleased he must be with your trust in his sovereignty!
>
> Our love in Christ, Suzonne and Stan

Later that morning, we circled and landed at the Manley International Airport in Belize City. Parked near the terminal, the plane's door opened to allow passengers destined for Belize to disembark. Admiring the bouquet of flowers Karen had placed in the overhead luggage compartment, a disembarking lady said to Charlie, "You must be going to a wedding." Charlie, without missing a beat, replied, "No, but we are going to a celebration."

I prefer a meaningful life to a meaningless death.
~Charlie Smith

32
Let the Party Begin
April 1993

With Karen's red and yellow flowers visible from the open overhead compartment, the group realized that Charlie's remark came out of his desire to follow Karen's instructions to celebrate every moment that was left to them.

That afternoon, the trucks pulled into an acre plot with Miguel's office, the ministry dining hall, and the newly built, U-shaped team housing facilities. The two dormitories, parallel to each other with restrooms forming the base of the U, had a peaceful view of an adjoining property populated with 3,000 coffee plants, 800 orange trees, a field of pineapples, and a grove of plantains and banana plants. This became our personal sanctuary for the next seven days and provided Karen a refreshing and relaxing refuge. Miguel and Nilsa had used their personal living room furniture, dining table, wall pictures and floral arrangements to create a restful environment for Karen and the family to collect themselves from the emotional whirlwind of the past week–a week that felt like an eternity.

When the aroma of Estella's chicken and rice drifted over to the compound from the ministry kitchen, the family meandered over to the dining hall for the evening meal. Following the meal, Jimmy Pinell and Pedro Huete brought in a children's choir of 15 singers from the surrounding churches. When the children had sung and left, Charlie opened the floor for all Hondurans and North Americans to share their thoughts, with Miguel doing the translating. Karen was the last to speak.

Jimmy Pinell & Pedro Huete

Well, I asked God if this was cancerous, since I was ready to go, that He would just take me right on the operating table. But when I woke up in the operating room and I heard my name and my diagnosis, I knew that it was cancerous and that I was still alive. And when I got back into my room I said to my mother, "I know my diagnosis." And I know that God must have some kind of plan for me, because I prayed that I might die, and I am still here. I still do not know about the plan, but one of the wonderful things that has happened since the surgery is that I have realized the love of God's people that I never would have known had I died on the operating table. I am very humbled and grateful for the many blessings that God has allowed me to experience since that time. And I pray that you will ask God to give me peace whatever His choice is for me, and I pray that you will ask God to give peace to my family, my daughters, and particularly my husband, and my mother and father, whatever His choice is. I would appreciate your prayers.

It was a precious and tearful moment. One who wept the most that night was 22-year-old Nilsa Pinell. As Nilsa looked at both Charlie and Karen on this night of April 1, 1993, memories flooded her breaking heart. She remembered first meeting Charlie, how funny he was, and how he had a heart for the people and especially for children. She had felt blessed by his hugs and how he didn't hold himself at a distance from the people like other North Americans did. She felt that he put into practice what he had in his heart—a sensitivity and compassion for the people. It was Charlie's influence that had brought her out of miserable living conditions. She remembered how he had brought her clothes, shampoo, pots and pans, and even Pampers for their little baby, who was named Charlito in honor of Charlie. She pictured Charlie taking Charlito with him when he went walking around the village.

When Nilsa's gaze fell on Karen, she realized that she had not had an opportunity to spend much time with her, and yet her heart was deeply burdened for this wife of her friend Charlie. She knew how Karen cared so much for the widow Maria and had asked Nilsa to spend more time with her because she was sick. She had done what Karen requested—using her informal nursing training, she had been visiting Maria twice a week to clean a medical device for her.

With memories of Charlie and Karen flashing through her mind, she heard a word from the Lord: "Nilsa, do not be afraid. I want you to go and wash Karen's feet. I will be with you."

With great courage in front of all these "powerful" North Americans, she took a blue plastic bowl and filled it with water. She knelt before Karen and began to untie her tennis shoes and remove her white socks. Karen held a white tissue to her nose against the persistent dripping. Nilsa, in a blue dress with black sleeves, her long black hair resting on her back, and with the towel and basin before her, began washing Karen's feet. She looked intently at Karen with an anguished heart, and with tears of brokenness flowing, spoke. Miguel translated her words for us: "I have purposed in my heart to do this. When I was praying, I thought of my Lord as He washed His disciple's feet. I do this to show you how much He loves you and how much we love you."

She knelt and bowed her face on top of Karen's leg. Her hair fell into the water and covered Karen's feet. While Nilsa wept, Karen embraced her. In the background, Charlie could be heard praying, "Hallelujah! Glory to God! He is risen from the dead! He is Lord!"

Nilsa continued to pray with deep sobbing. "*Gracias! Gracias! Maestro!* [Teacher] *Estás aquí!* [You are here!] *Gracias, Señor! Hallelujah! Gracias, Señor! Estamos sus hijos.* [We are Your children.] *Te glorificamos!* [We glorify You], *Maestro! Gracias, Dios!*" Finishing this prayer, a still weeping Nilsa took Karen's feet and replaced the socks and shoes.

Then the tables turned. Karen stood and gave Nilsa a warm, prolonged hug, as if comforting this young woman–the age of her own daughters–who was so distressed and burdened. Then Karen moved around the circle and hugged each person in the room, beginning with her father. Once again, the one who was dying was the one who was giving comfort.

Karen's compassion was displayed daily. Throughout the entire week she was brave, gallant and gutsy. She refused to yield to her infirmity.

For instance, the following day, Manuel, a man with eight children who worked as our ministry night watchman, came to our dormitory suffering from a severe infection–the residual damage from a huge thorn which had been removed from his left eye. With Charlie at her side, the nurse in Karen quickly moved into servant's mode and administered the appropriate medication. Charlie later said, "I think Karen is laying down her life for her friends. Greater love hath no man than to lay down his life for his friends."

The Smith family visits Manuel's family, whom they blessed with a new house.

One day the family went to Canchias, so Karen and the family could see the progress in the ministry. Miguel had erected a blue and white tent on the soccer field for a worship service. In a village with a population around 200, more than 100 people gathered on the soccer field. Charlie wanted his physical family to be surrounded by the love of his Honduran family. He wanted the Honduran believers to pray for Karen.

As the excessively loud worship music came to a halt, Charlie stood before the people and shared:

> The doctor said, "There is nothing I can do. She does not have long to live." You can imagine how we felt. But I want to tell you tonight that we serve a great God. He is the great Physician. If it be God's will, we know He can heal. We are trusting God. The moment the doctor told us Karen had cancer, she said, "I have peace. Whether I live or die, I am the Lord's. My prayer is that everyone's faith will increase and that God will be glorified." We are trusting God. We know He is on the throne.

Charlie invited his wife, daughters and in-laws to come forward so he could introduce his family to the villagers and so the believers could pray and lay hands on Karen. Charlie's motive was good, but the impact of the intense crying out to God, the shaking and ardent prayers of the poor, the extreme emotional and frenzied behavior, was overwhelming. The family decided from then on to conserve Karen's energy by avoiding further protracted and intense prayer meetings that sapped her energy.

171

It was a long night for the family as they drove back to San Isidro. The mountain roads were treacherous. The service had been exhausting. Karen was not getting better, and the emotional pain refused to subside. But Charlie pressed on, clinging to what little hope he could muster. Inside his Bible, he had written thoughts on a yellow piece of paper about Karen's valiant faith and the true meaning of life:

> Few are granted the privilege to know of their imminent death. Few have the opportunity to say goodbye. Few have accepted death like Karen. Because of her faith she looked death squarely in the face knowing it had no power over her. Life is more than clothes, food, cars and vacations. Life is relationships. *Our Town* "Life you are too wonderful."

On this night in Honduras, Charlie was remembering another line from Wilder's play *Our Town.* Leading character Emily had been granted the privilege of returning from the dead to see her old town again, and now it was time to leave. She lamented that people don't realize the value of life while they are living it, "Good-by, good-by, world. Good-by, Grover's Corners...Mama and Papa. Good-by to clocks ticking, and Mama's sunflowers. And food and coffee.

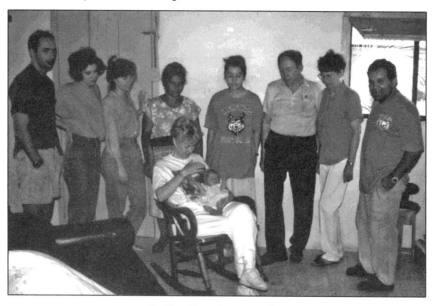

Meeting Karen's namesake:
Scott Crews, Anne-Marie, Felicia, Estella (baby's grandmother), the baby's mother, Dean & Ruth Stone, Miguel Pinell, and Karen holding baby Karen

172

And new-ironed dresses and hot baths and sleeping and waking up. Oh, earth, you are too wonderful for anybody to realize you."

Charlie knew that his wife was an exception to that rule. She was teaching all of us, especially her daughters, not only how to live but how to die. She was choosing to realize the blessings God was giving her each day, and to call the attention of everyone around her to how wonderful life was, "every, every minute."

The Smith family visited the widow, Maria,
whom Karen supported and the one
who sent the prayer cloth.

They send forth their children as a flock; their little ones dance about.
~Job 21:11 NIV

33
Dancing with the Stars
April 1993

At 10:40 a.m., April 3, 1993, the ministry's four-wheel-drive Toyota and red pickup truck arrived at the compound. The team slung their overnight suitcases in the truck bed, double-checked water supplies, medications, snacks, and cameras, and climbed aboard. Karen, Scott, Anne-Marie and I loaded into the Toyota, with Charlie behind the wheel. Felicia, Michael, Dean, and Ruth were in the red truck that Miguel was driving.

Charlie wanted the family to visit not only the village of Chagüitillos but to include stops in Colmenas and Las Anonas, all deep in the interior of the rural mountains. At one point, Miguel stopped and repaired a tire that was just minutes from losing one of its bolts. Charlie got out of the truck, stood by a mule, and passed out pretzels to the ill-clad children who gathered to stare at the North Americans. The distribution of the pretzels revealed his love for the poor. He may not have had much to give, but he was always giving, even if it was just a small pretzel from his personal supply of snacks. After we all returned to the truck, we spent some time joking about the facial features and various expressions of the mule.

Honduras is a stunningly beautiful country with majestic mountains covering 85 percent of the land. Beautiful as they are, the mountains make the drive to the village on the serpentine roads so treacherous that when one group of North Americans returned home, they designed T-shirts that declared, "I survived Chagüitillos."

As we navigated the trenches in a constant search for a smoother ride, Anne-Marie saw so many hills and peaks and mountains she began to sing the old campfire song, "The bear went over the mountain … to see what he could see. And all that he could see, …was the other side of the mountain." Though we were experiencing many tears on this trip, we joined in laughing at Anne-Marie's song, and then at Charlie's teasing answer to her question as we sped past a field of yucca plants: "I think those are pickle trees."

As our vehicles rambled along the mountain road closer and closer to Chagüitillos–and further and further from electricity–Miguel began to blow the horn of the truck signaling our approach. As the sound echoed across the valley, the little children began running down the side of the mountain to the community water source to greet us. Practically the entire village of 250 people turned out, both Protestants and Catholics. It was an incredible experience of love and encouragement. Knowing in advance that Karen would be there, they had brought their guitars to serenade her with several Spanish songs near the village's only water spigot, which was as far as the vehicles could go. The people had little to give materially, but were so full of relational riches!

The village people helped transport the team's luggage up the steep clay path. For some of us, our lodging for the night would be the ministry house located next to the church. Others would stay in the homes of church members. On the east side of the ministry house was a humble adobe room which would be Karen's and Charlie's. Miguel referred to it as the Prophet's Room. It had a clean, swept-dirt floor, a chair and a nice, comfortable bed with soft pillows. Karen would need the pillows, because she had to sleep sitting up. This humble dwelling was fitting for Charlie and Karen, echoing the simple life they had lived beginning with their stilt-house days in Malaysia.

After everyone had settled into their designated lodging facility, they began to gather at the church for evening worship. The music was fervent that Saturday evening as the people sang with the gusto typical of the village churches. The team was scattered among the 60 people in attendance—men on one side, women on the other, as was their custom. As the worship got underway, we noticed three children, two girls and a boy, slowly begin to dance to the music of guitars and a tambourine. A few minutes later, the dancing picked up pace, and the children began to leap and jump in a controlled rhythmic cadence to the music. It was not out of order. It seemed to be orchestrated from heaven. With eyes closed, they did this for the entire 30 minutes of the worship music, without stopping. The music ceased, and still they danced.

175

As the Holy Spirit continued to move during the service, Miguel went to the front of the church and lifted the large Bible off the pulpit. He placed it on the tile floor. He then asked Karen to come forward and kneel on the Bible. Without any prompting, the two girls, Cristina and Lilli, moved slowly toward Karen, still

jumping with hands at their sides. They were within inches of Karen. With eyes closed they held out their hands over her, then gently touched her hair as they wept and cried out to God on her behalf. It was as if we were beholding little child-like angels sent from heaven to favor Karen and Charlie for their love for the poor. It was an unusual gift from God, one on which a price tag could not be placed.

Cristina and Lilli after the dance

Charlie was over against the wall on his knees with his hands over his head as it touched the tile floor seeking the face of God. After about 10 minutes, the girls moved away from Karen and lay on the floor with their faces to the ground. By now they had been dancing for almost an hour. Our group was in awe of what God was doing. Without question, like Moses, we were on holy ground.

In my role as photographer and chronicler of this trip with the family, I wrote these notes during the service:

> I am presently in perhaps one of the most anointed, spirit-filled services of my life. Often I have wondered why Chagüitillos was on the grace-list of God, when so many other churches were closer to the ministry headquarters in San Isidro. I have come to believe that the grace bestowed was for us and not for them. Two small girls around ten years old are dancing in the spirit. I do not understand it. I just believe it and accept it. I have been in many services in Chagüitillos–even preached here two weeks ago and thought it was a good service and a good message, but it was peanuts compared to this service. I just asked Miguel, "What's wrong with us? What are we missing?" He whispered back, "We are tourists!"

Later that evening, Charlie said, "I have never been in a service like this. I don't understand it. But it is teaching me more and more the necessity of becoming like a little child if you are going to enter the Kingdom of God." Karen's dad was 78 years old. He was raised in the Assembly of God tradition where manifestations of the Spirit are the norm, but even he was astounded, commenting, "This might rank as the number one day of my life."

Following the evening service, Pastor Mario shared with us around the supper table. He told about the afternoon that one of the little girls, Cristina Rivera, had had a deep urge to pray. She was gathering corn for her mother in a bucket. She hastily ran to her house, placed the corn on the table and ran to the prayer meeting held daily at the church at 3 o'clock. That day the anointing of God came upon her, and she began to speak with other tongues and dance in the Spirit. Mario continued, "Many times the church will pray for an hour and leave. These two little girls will remain and pray for two more hours. Sometimes they pray for five or six hours a day."

God in His great mercy used two little children to present a precious gift to Karen and Charlie that night. It was a night etched deep, deep in the spirits of our team that will linger there for the rest of our lives.

Not everyone had been happy to come. Anne-Marie had wanted to return to San Isidro as soon as possible and had dreaded spending the night in the village, but after that service, she confessed to me, "I apologize for sticking my foot in my mouth about not wanting to come. I could stay another night."

By 11:30 p.m., every team member was either in a hammock or on a bed in one of the church members' houses. Charlie and Karen were in their little room. I closed out the night with these words in my journal: "The service tonight shows you the mystery and uniqueness of this special day. It brought me to a greater understanding of the reality of the Holy Spirit and His power in the church. How will I ever forget it... and to think I almost didn't come. "O Lord, how marvelous are your ways and how majestic is your power. The splendor of your light, the beauty of your holiness–so great and so good!"

The prophetic words Charlie spoke to the lady at the Belize airport were now being realized. God had turned this trip from a crisis to a celebration.

The next morning, Antonio's mother, the matriarch of the village, came over and gave Karen three eggs. This was all she could afford to give, and represented a tremendous sacrifice for this woman who rarely left the house due to her feet swelling when she walked. Two little girls brought our group some coffee and pancakes made of white corn.

Karen and her mother Ruth Stone ride to Colmenas.

177

Following breakfast, the family straddled horses and visited the village of Colmenas. Later, the team drove to Las Anonas to see the newest church building in the ministry. Charlie's heart was aching so much as he walked out of the Las Anonas Church that he turned to me and said, "Jimmy, why is it so hard? Where is God?" Anne-Marie looked at her mother and said, "Mom, I'm so sad!" Karen replied, "Anne-Marie, I am here today. I am alive, and I am going to live this day with you."

We decided to stay an extra night in Chagüitillos. We all sat around the supper table in the 40-year-old home of Pastor Mario. We had eaten another of the typical North American missionary meals of peanut butter and jelly sandwiches. From the ceiling, a kerosene lantern hung on a thin cord. Soon Pastor Mario held us all spellbound as he told the history of this little village and its founding by the paramour of a priest. Then he shared his personal testimony of coming to faith after reading the Bible for himself.

Back in San Isidro the next evening, the group gathered to bring the experiences of this trip to a close. Each one shared personal highs and lows of these eight days. Karen was the last to speak:

> Well, I just want you to keep praying for me that I will be healed and that I will have peace and that God will give each member of my family peace as well. I am not asking that you pray loud or an agonizing prayer, because God knows my need. I just seek your prayers that will simply say to God that I have this need and I desire His will and strength to bring it to pass, and I would like for you to do that right now.

We all gathered around Karen. Charlie prayed and thanked God for another day of life and for the faith and strength given to us. He reminded us of how God was using simplicity and not the sophisticated things of life to teach lessons. He thanked God for visiting our group through the widow Maria's simple prayer. He thanked God for the spirit of humility in Nilsa when she washed Karen's feet. He thanked God for the three eggs given to Karen by Antonio's mother in Chagüitillos, and for the two little girls dancing in the Spirit. He concluded with these words: "God, we have done all we can, even coming 2,000 miles. We abide and remain in your Word. Now the ball is in your court, and we release all to you. Amen."

It was time to fly home and wait to see what God would do next.

178

If God performs a miracle, she will be blessed of God.
If God does not perform a miracle,
then Karen will be twice blessed.
~Honduran pastors regarding praying for Karen

34
Twice Blessed
April-July 1993

The one Charlie loved so much on his wedding day in the fall of 1960, that beautiful girl whose first impression caused him to say, "...the most gorgeous woman I ever laid my eyes on," was getting progressively worse. The short time the doctors had given her to live was passing quickly. In his desperation to hear from God, Charlie did something bizarre and not at all typical of an academician. He decided to play a game of Biblical roulette.

He took his brown leather Bible, worn and torn from constant use, and pushed God to the limit. "Lord, I want to know Your will for my life regarding Karen. Please speak to me and give me Your word." He held his Bible in his hands. He flipped it open, asking God to speak to him from the first verse to make contact with his eyes. Out of the 31,102 verses in the King James Bible, Charlie's eyes fell on Ezekiel 24:15-18:

> The word of the LORD came to me: "Son of man, with one blow I am about to take away from you the delight of your eyes. Yet do not lament or weep or shed any tears. Groan quietly; do not mourn for the dead. Keep your turban fastened and your sandals on your feet; do not cover your mustache and beard or eat the customary food of mourners." So I spoke to the people in the morning, and in the evening my wife died.[35]

---

[35] The context of this verse is a prophecy through Ezekiel that God was about to punish Jerusalem for their sins, and that in that process the usual mourning practices would not be observed.

179

Charlie was stunned upon reading this verse. It seemed to perfectly fit his situation, but it did not fit his expectation. Was God actually telling him that his wife would not live? He didn't know how to interpret what he had read, but he wasn't ready to stop looking for ways to save her.

On the advice of Dr. Larry Lilly, a friend of the Heart to Honduras ministry from Columbus, Ohio, Charlie decided to contact Dr. Victor Schramm in Denver, Colorado, an otolaryngologist who specialized in nose, throat, head and face surgeries, to seek his opinion.

On April 9, Karen and Charlie called Dr. Schramm, who explained the procedure and assured them it would be successful. He stated that he could surround the tumor, remove it completely, and save the eye.

Dr. Schramm recommended coming to Denver about three days before the surgery to adjust to the altitude, and to expect to remain in Denver for a couple of weeks afterwards.

On Easter Morning, April 10, Karen wrote to her Sunday School class:

Dear Seekers:
We thank our Lord Jesus for this another day of living. This glorious day that He has made, we rejoice and are glad in it!

Our trip to Honduras was filled with the love of the sweet and gentle Honduran people. I look forward to sharing in detail with you later.

Our present plans are to fly to Denver this Wednesday and see Dr. Schramm on Thursday morning. The surgery has been scheduled for Monday morning, April 19. Radiation will be applied following the excise of the tumor, with a total expected hospital stay of 10 days.

Needless to say our spirits have rejoiced with the possibility of a feasible alternative with minor long-range consequences....We have prayed for God's intervention since the very first symptom appeared and believe we are progressing in His plan. We ask that your prayers continue for healing, support, witness to His love and power...and for sustained peace for me and my family....I have hope in Him and am sustained in His peace. Love, Karen

In Denver, Charlie, Karen, and their girls were hosted by Gordon Garrett and his wife Sandy, pastor-friends who had left Florida and were now strategically placed to offer loving care in this stressful time. [36]

The surgery and ensuing radiation went well but still caused suffering for Karen. Charlie called the Heart to Honduras staff on Thursday, April 28 and shared:

> Karen is doing great. She is now walking and all the tubes are gone. She is eating solid food. She was a little depressed Wednesday, but the nurse told her that this was normal for this kind of surgery. We are hoping to have her out of the hospital by Monday or Tuesday and then go to Breckenridge[37] for a few days of rest.

Despite the traumatic two weeks full of emotional pain, mental anguish and physical exhaustion, a tremendous sense of calm settled over the family, along with peace, assurance, joy, optimism, hope, confidence, buoyancy and relief.

But a few days later, test results showed the tumor had returned, and Dr. Schramm termed it "aggressive and ill-behaved." The family decided to return to Florida and try five days of chemotherapy at the Moffitt Cancer Center in Tampa. Remembering that painful time, Charlie wrote:

> After a week of chemotherapy that nearly killed her, and two weeks of radiation, Karen said, "Enough. Let's go and party in our own home." On the way home I was crying, so happy to have my wife with me riding down the road–such a simple thing, but so often taken for granted. I was weeping as silently as I could and Karen said, "You know, Charlie, the worst thing in life isn't dying. The worst thing is having no purpose or nurturing. We have both."

They brought Karen home to their downstairs bedroom, where she spent the remainder of May and most of June. But she suddenly decided she wanted the remodeling of the bath and upstairs bedrooms finished, a project she had started some time before all the trauma and sickness. Family friend Mary Elizabeth Story

---

[36] Gordon Garrett later served on the Board of Heart to Honduras and was selected to serve as president of the ministry in June of 1999.

[37] Family members owned a mountain cabin in Breckenridge and had made it available for the recuperation time.

was called. She moved into high gear, and with the help of some 15 people, (many of whom donated their services and goods), completed the task in record time. When the work was almost finished, Karen begged to be carried upstairs to see the progress, and she insisted on being moved into the renovated bedroom. In that room, she continually asked to be shown family slides, staying up until 3 a.m. one night to enjoy reminiscing.

The cancer began to eat away at Karen's beauty, until only the immediate family and her friend and pastor's wife Miriam were allowed in. It was so hard on the girls. But they were not passive in the ordeal. They tenderly cared for Karen during this trying time. Charlie wrote of the day of July 8, 1993:

One day toward the end of Karen's life, Anne-Marie spotted this tender scene from an upstairs window: Charlie and Karen comforting each other as they enjoyed the sunshine of their deck.

During the night I listened to Karen's labored breathing. I just held her, which is what she wanted me to do when she was hurting. In the early morning, Felicia and Anne-Marie joined me at Karen's side. We read Scriptures, sang *I'll Fly Away* and *Count Your Many Blessings*. Anne-Marie then called Miriam, friend and counselor. We sat around Karen, holding her. The girls had placed rose petals over Karen's body. We shared pictures and stories about the many good times we had with Karen. I heard her breathing change. We all gathered close to her. I asked Miriam to pray. It was a peaceful prayer. The peace of God was enfolding us in that room during that holy moment. We listened to her breathing slow down, and then she took her last breath. She was gone. The silver cord had been broken. We cried and laughed at the same time. We rejoiced at the peace that flooded the room, and that Karen had completed the race–she kept the faith. She knew her redeemer lived! God had been glorified, and Karen had been glorified. Now we knew it would be up to us to keep her wishes active. Let the Party continue. Karen has gone home. Let the saints rejoice. May the grace of the Lord Jesus Christ be with God's people. Amen.

At the time of Karen's passing, Miguel and I were in Chagüitillos with a group of North Americans. An elaborate system of CB radios had been set up in anticipation of the possibility of her passing while we were in the mountains. She died at 1:30 p.m., and the news reached us around 9 that evening. We left my wife in charge of the group and hastened down the mountain in the middle of the night, with Miguel sleeping in the pickup bed on a mattress until I got us to the main road. Then he took over, driving us to his house, where we grabbed a short night's sleep. The next morning, we caught a flight to Florida, so we could be with Charlie as he buried his wife.

The first words from the Ezekiel passage had come to pass–Charlie's delight had been taken from his life. And now, the second thing was set in motion, for there would be no usual funeral rituals. From the type of casket to the method of transport to the cemetery to the celebrations, all would be unique to Karen and Charlie.

Charlie detested funeral homes. He wrote, "Funeral homes suck money from the bereaved like an auto-teller sucks our deposits into the bank." Fortunately, one of Karen's last requests was to be buried in a pine box, and Charlie had arranged for a special one to be made with a very simple construction. What happened is so Charlie. He and I went to the funeral home, owned by a casual friend of Charlie's, to see if the pine box would fit in Scott Crews' pickup truck. The funeral director had never had the husband of a deceased wife come to the funeral home to let him know the body would be taken to the burial site not only in a pine box, but in a pickup truck! The director was so confused that he left his soda cup on top of the funeral home Cadillac as he drove off, yelling something at Charlie and heading for Lake Wales, leaving us laughing.

The graveside memorial service was very moving. In Charlie's own words:

> We released purple balloons at her graveside, symbolic of her spiritual journey to her heavenly home, sang *Amazing Grace,* and Brother Henry Smith prayed. And at her request, we lowered the hand-crafted unfinished pine box that contained her body in the ground with ropes, buried that box and went home. That night we celebrated her life and transition in a service of worship at the Presbyterian Church in Lake Wales. We sang songs she requested: *Be Still My Soul, Fairest Lord Jesus* and *A Mighty Fortress is our God....* Her friend and pastor's wife Miriam Rockness spoke, as did her pastor Dave Rockness, Jim Usher and others. I spoke from my heart and then Steve Coder and Mark Shaner lifted our hearts in prayer to the God we serve. And then we partied. The ladies from the Seeker Class wore Karen's favorite color, purple,[38] and served refreshments.

In later years, Charlie wrote of the tremendous impact Karen had had upon him:

> Karen coming into my life radically changed the course of my life. She took me out of my mindless circle. She took me out of Ruston and around the world. She turned my heart to the poor, the needy. She kept my sights on God and on faith in Him. She turned my heart to the needs of the people living in other lands. She showed me how to die and how to view my own death as a transition from this life to another–from a physical, material realm to a spiritual kingdom. She maintained a child-like faith in her God. She condemned no one and simply loved everyone–the rich and the poor, the black and the white, the powerful and the powerless. She believed that love is eternal.

Karen had asked that her "home going" be a party. And it was. It was almost like a dance, as fiesta-like Honduran music played in the background and people rejoiced, laughed and carried on as if Karen were still present with them. Death

---

[38] Not only did they wear purple, but they wore the red hats referred to in Jenny Joseph's poem *The Warning.*

184

for her was not a hole in the ground, but a bridge to something better. What a wonderful tribute to one who blessed all around her, and who was now Twice Blessed as she transitioned to her eternal reward.

Smith Family Portrait
Clockwise: Charlie, Anne-Marie, Felicia,
Karen

PART SEVEN

1993-1997

Accelerating Vision

I think it's fantastic that Tony and his crew with the public utility would give of their time and money to bring electricity to the poor in Honduras. Electricity is a major key in bringing these people a better life.
~Charlie Smith

35
A Ministry Sprouts Wings
Heart to Honduras 1993–1995

Early Staff
Front: Candy Pischel, Merrill & Benjie Esch, Kelly & Monty Harrington
Middle: Felicia Smith, Dave Pischel, Christina Jeppsen, Tony Bayles
Back: Carol Lynne & Jim Usher, Melissa & Gary Mitkowski, Rick & Sue Dike,
Charlie Smith, Miguel Pinell

By September of 1993, Charlie was beginning to return to his old self. The spring and summer of that year had seen Charlie consumed with caring for his wife during her illness and passing, and trying to recover enough emotionally to become fully engaged again in the ministry. Charlie had a small office staff in Florida who took care of the books and administrative tasks, and teams continued to make trips to Honduras to minister.

The good news was that the ministry was so fine-tuned with competent leadership, it hardly missed a beat. In fact, several big projects were completed during that year, in large part because Miguel was very capably serving as the director of all activities in Honduras.

During his years in the States, Miguel acquired a good command of English (though heavily accented) and began to grasp some of the mindset of North American culture. Once he was back in Central America, working as the on-site director of Heart to Honduras, he was an energetic doer with a foot in two cultures. Karen Steves, a nursing instructor at Ball State University in Indiana and member of several May Medical Teams, captured him well:

I waited in immigration at the San Pedro Sula International Airport. A wind was blowing and the air was thick with dust containing who-knows-what kind of disease-causing organisms. The road, the cars, and the people were bathed in a colorless beige. There was a haze across the horizon. Finally Miguel Pinell, the resident head of the project, arrived. "Hi, fren's!" he hollered at us, "Le's go to wor'!"

Miguel was a short, squashed-looking, muscular, gnome-like man of about 35, Nicaraguan by birth but Honduran by marriage. This stocky, unimposing little man with a smile that seemed to slice his face in half, was truly a miracle worker. Once he was on the scene, the situation seemed to improve. "Don' worry. You don' haffa do nuttin'. Jez follow me."

...Later as all 26 members of our team loaded on the back of three pickup trucks, our discomfort on those god-awful roads (and I use the term advisedly) replaced the fear of flying. Our discomfort seemed to delight Miguel and he roared with laughter whenever we hit a hole at high speed, causing baggage and passengers alike to become airborne. "Dey're go'n to hay [hate] me for dat one!" he would chuckle.

Team Transportation – without guard rails!

Karen's description of a team's interaction with Miguel's leadership resonates in the memories of scores of people who bounced in the trucks with a teasing, but focused, on-site director at the wheel. In the early years, Miguel was translator, driver, pastor to the village pastors, guardian of the teams, purchaser of materials, planner of menus, and sometimes a one-man dental team. Without the multi-tasking capabilities of this man, Charlie's vision would have sputtered and wobbled in its beginning stages, and especially so in the trying days of Karen's illness.

But it wasn't only Charlie's dream and Miguel's application that made this ministry flourish. Something marvelous happened when the vision that had originally belonged to Charlie alone began to take on a life of its own. People would travel to Honduras and discover a way that God could use their particular expertise to dovetail into Charlie's model village vision, and soon big and little offshoots were popping up all over. Charlie's vision was so powerful that over the years, more than 50 "spin-offs" would be birthed out of the holistic vision that God gave him.

BLACKSMITH SHOP

One example came through a volunteer named Van Elkins from Louisiana, a skilled blacksmith and maker of knives. He created an ironworks shop in the village of Bartolo with five forges, bellows, and anvils. Blacksmith Chuck Everitt, husband of artist Becky Everitt, from Longmont, Colorado, moved to Honduras in January of 1993 to oversee the blacksmith shop. He became like a father to the five men and taught them how to forge with great skill. The shop used charcoal to heat and shape implements for local sale and for shipping to the United States. Charlie was thrilled with this endeavor, as it gave gainful employment to five men who previously hired themselves out for field work for $1 per day.

MEDICAL

The annual May Medical Team was an incubator that hatched a series of new teams and projects. As Dr. Lilly recruited members for his May Medical Teams through his contacts at Riverside Hospital in Columbus, Ohio, more and more medical personnel began to come on board. Dr. Jennifer White, who first came to Honduras with Dr. Lilly, and Dr. Scott Kardatzke of Wichita, Kansas, would serve on the HTH board and also lead teams from their faith communities.

A very passionate dentist, Dr. Craig Carter from Wichita, Kansas, brought down the first dental team. Later, his contacts

Hernia repair on a young boy, performed by flashlight in the San Isidro office by five doctors & two nurses: Dr. Mark Gittens, Dr. Larry Lilly, Dr. Jerry Girardi, Dr. Lynda Yonker, PA Gary Mitkowski (hidden right). The charge was 2 limperas (10 cents) – which they forgot to collect!

in the dental world resulted in a full dental team from Lincoln, Nebraska. This dental team became a Sister Church team that began working with the local government in community development and added projects as diverse as building homes and teaching nutrition to their original project of providing dental services.

191

The Nelsons with Gorman

Florida physician Dr. Jim Nelson caught the vision. On a follow-up visit to Honduras, he and his wife were key in the adoption, by Miguel and Nilsa Pinell, of a street child named German (pronounced Herman) who later became the person who managed the logistics of all North American visitors to Honduras.[39]

H.E.A.R.T. student Gary Mitkowski became a physician assistant and served on staff for a year in Honduras. Dr. Dave Sperow, the son of Dean Sperow, who was a friend of Charlie's while he attended the University of Kentucky, was a dentist who later became a dentist-in-residence in Canchias.

Anderson University nursing professor Cindy Penhorwood made her first trip in 1992 with the May Medical Team, then in 1996 began bringing student nurses under a program the university called Tri-S (Student Summer Service), exposing scores of young people to the health needs of people in the developing world. Discovering that her heart was in Honduras, Cindy joined the HTH staff as health care coordinator in 2004.

Nursing professor Cindy Penhorwood welcomed Charlie Smith
and Jimmy Usher to the pinning ceremony for one male and four
female graduates of Anderson University's nursing program.

HYDROELECTRICITY

Another great vision Charlie welcomed to the ministry was born when missions presentations were made at Meadow Park Church of God in Columbus,

---

[39] Dr. Nelson became Charlie's personal physician in Florida.

Ohio. A member of the congregation, Tony Ahern, was moved to think about going to Honduras when Dr. Lilly showed his slides of the Medical Trip.

When Miguel came later that year for a missions weekend, Tony approached him and stated his interest in "doing something, but not medical." Miguel had a ready answer when he learned that Tony was an engineer for an electric utility. Correctly believing that it would be many years before Canchias would even be added to the list for eventual public electricity, Miguel said, "We need a hydroelectric system."

In April 1992, Tony and Mark Gray tagged along with the medical team to survey the river in Canchias. They were satisfied that its drop and flow rate would support such a project. With help from his wife Sue, a reference librarian, Tony envisioned a hydro turbine that could generate a few kilowatts of power for the ministry. He calculated that a 10 inch PVC pipe dropping 125 feet over a length of 2,200 feet could create 10 to 12 kilowatts.

Tony was well-motivated to raise funds for the hydro turbine after having watched Dr. Lilly perform hernia surgeries on makeshift tables in church buildings with dirt floors while a team member held a flashlight over the surgery site and insects buzzed all around. He could see how helpful it would be to have a clinic–a clinic with a sterile, well-lit surgical room powered by electricity.

Returning alone in November 1992, Tony worked with Miguel to install the concrete base for the turbine and ponder the issue of how to run that half-mile of PVC pipe. And then there would be the challenge of recruiting a team to do it.

But God was way ahead of Tony. On the flight between Columbus and Houston, Tony's seatmates asked why he was going to Honduras, and his answer was overheard by the men seated behind him. As they changed planes in Houston, these men from Indiana stopped Tony and asked if he needed any help. Darrell Toney and Larry Linneman wrote their contact information and occupations in Tony's notebook, and he hurried off to catch his flight. As he settled in his seat for the flight to San Pedro Sula he read what they had written: "Drill water wells and install PVC pipes." Wow!

In April 1993, while Charlie and his family were dealing with the disease ravaging his wife's body, Tony led a mission platoon of about 40 men, including Tony and Mark, their new co-workers Darrell and Larry, 14 other North Americans and local laborers. Everyone worked extremely hard, and many of the Hondurans walked more than an hour to work for a wage of $1.50 per day plus three good meals. John Maineri stated, "We worked so hard that you could often hear men snoring during the evening meeting! However, we noticed Tony's flashlight on at 4:00 a.m. as he worked on, and worried about, the next day's task."

The men, from the youngest teenager to the oldest senior, worked like mules. They had only one week to complete their project. Tony wrote: "We arrived at the site on Saturday night. Our goal was to lay 400 feet of pipe a day. However, we lost a lot of time moving rocks and boulders out of the way by hand. We also had to build all of the scaffolding along the cliff sides to hang the PVC pipe, using whatever materials we could cut from the surrounding forest. Occasionally, a Honduran with oxen and a cart would help, but the work was tedious and time-consuming. By Tuesday night, we were 800 feet behind. On Thursday, we installed 1,000 feet of pipe."

Late Saturday night, an airlock had everyone stymied, including the educated engineers from the United States. Finally, one of the Hondurans took a screwdriver and punched a hole in the PVC pipe, breaking the airlock. At last, the power of the water turned the turbine and the first light bulb ever in that mountain village lit up the night to the cheers of the weary men. At 5 the next morning, the team worked for one more hour, then started the journey back to the United States, exhausted but happy in knowing the energy they had expended would bless the villagers with the energy it created.

The platoon hanging PVC pipe on the Canchias River's cliffs
Above, right: Tony Ahern pulling the lever to allow water
to flow into the turbine

Charlie was overwhelmed by this hydroelectricity. It enabled surgeries to take place, saving many lives and easing pain for the wounded. It empowered a

194

molina so the women no longer had to use mortar and pestle or a hand grinder to prepare the corn for their family's daily tortillas. It provided a cooler at the village store. It put computers in the school; it provided light for the village church and lit the narrow paths to cabins. Canchias was truly being transformed.

AGRICULTURE: The Esch Family

Merrill and Benjie Esch and their daughters Suzi and Daisy were Mennonites from Ohio who had gone to H.E.A.R.T. to be trained as missionaries. There, they heard about the work in Honduras through Charlie. Arrangements were made for them to work with Heart to Honduras in the village of Montañuela, and in 1993 they moved there and modeled living as a Christian family before the villagers, taught food production and established a rural health clinic. They worked under the umbrella of Heart to Honduras for two years, then started an agricultural ministry of their own.

MORE AMERICANS IN THE FIELD

More and more people committed to Charlie's vision. Rick and Sue Dike, along with their three children, began a tenure of 13 years with Heart to Honduras because of the unconditional love they saw in Charlie—as well as his holistic vision. The Dike family lived in Honduras for four years before returning to the United States, where Rick continued to serve the ministry as a well-loved team leader for groups. Rick shared, "Charlie was a risk-taker with people. I saw this over and over again. And when you made a mistake, he would not second-guess you. He would not look the other way, but also he would never condemn. He never raised his voice. He was the same person as if you never made a mistake. He was the best visionary I have known–the best I have ever known."

At Charlie's request, Monty Harrington, who had begun working in the Florida office and had made a video for the ministry called "The Church Revived," committed with his wife Kelly to live in Canchias for 1994 and do a baseline sociological survey of the people of the community. After hundreds of hours of labor, they completed *Mud and Masonry,* which gave the ministry a greater understanding of the needs of the village (and which was a great resource for the writing of portions of this book). They committed to this project because they believed in Charlie and his mission.

Money exchanging hands for the purchase of the land in Caliche.

195

LAND ACQUISITION

Trying to focus on something besides his grief, Charlie returned to his risk-taking style of leadership. He directed the purchase of almost 700 acres in Canchias which came to be called *La Promesa*, the Promised Land, and over 300 acres of land near the El Cajon Dam. The latter, with its tiny village perched on top of a nearly inaccessible mountain, challenged scores of early volunteers, who braved a dugout canoe, a long hike, and finally a horseback ride up a steep incline to reach the village of Caliche, a little plateau dotted with stick houses capped with grass roofs. Both sites were used for growing corn, coffee, and sugar cane and for raising cattle. Charlie purchased these acres due to their potential to provide food, housing and employment for the poor.[40]

Karen's Hope in "downtown" Canchias

FACILITIES FACILITATE

The number of teams volunteering on various projects in Honduras increased from nine in 1994 to a dozen in 1995. They held rural health clinics, finished the roof on the original medical building within the main compound area in Canchias, and began caring for the handicapped at Karen's Hope. This last was a home established in honor of Karen Smith's desire to see care given to those who were suffering.

Charlie made it his goal to reach out to the *poorest* of the poor–not just the poor. Among the poorest of the poor are the handicapped. In developing countries, these are the ones most without social nets to prevent them from falling through the grid of hopelessness with its endless downward spiral.

Such were these three in Honduras: Crucito, Lydia, and Heydi. Crucito was

Charlie playing with Heydi

---

[40] Eventually the land in Caliche was sold, though the ministry continues to send a Sister Church team to the village.

196

paralyzed after falling from a mango tree when he was nine, preschool age Lillian was blind and malnourished, and preteen Heydi was the size of a preschooler, non-verbal and unable to walk. Charlie gave all three of these children refuge at a hospice named Karen's Hope in honor of his wife.

Another frail child impacted a group of teenagers who visited Chagüitillos in the summer of 1993. Maria Magdalena was born with a cleft lip and palate and was unable to nurse. Her mother wondered if the team had any powdered milk which she could spoon down her newborn's throat. They did, but they had brought it to prepare breakfast for the team the next morning before they left the mountain. Giving the milk to the baby would mean no breakfast for the group, but as one teen said, "How could we eat with that baby starving to death?"

So the next morning at dawn, instead of eating breakfast, the group walked single file down the narrow village paths to a home perched on the side of the mountain. First, a Kentucky teen—whose sister had been born with the same condition— presented the large can of powdered milk to the mother. Then time stood still as an Alabama teen named Ember took the fragile little Maria Magdalena in her arms and prayed that through this little life the whole village would come to know God. Ember's prayer summed up the whole purpose of the Heart to Honduras ministry: that people would come to know God through this holistic outreach. And on this day, a group of teenagers demonstrated that they understood what it means to love "the least of these."

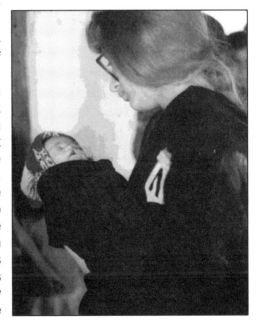

Ember Jeffers holds fragile Maria Magdalena. Her experience that day led Ember to become a nurse.

Merrill and Benjie Esch, Suzi and Daisy

Gary Mitkowski with
Crucito of Karen's Hope

Rick and Sue Dike with
Nathan, Anna and Jon,
posing in front of their home
in Honduras, which later
became the main offices for
Heart to Honduras.

Monty & Kelly Harrington with Lillian,
a 5 year old blind child cared for at
Karen's Hope

FACILITIES SPROUT ON THE HILL: From undeveloped undergrowth to a terraced hillside dotted with housing for North American visitors, students at the Discipleship School, and church members attending conferences, the property in Canchias was slowly transformed into a fulfillment of Charlie's dream.

LEFT: A fence, a winding track, and a water tower were the only signs of development as Charlie (on horse, second from left) surveyed the property and began to dream of what could be.

RIGHT: From the same vantage point a few years later, buildings to educate, house, and care for medical needs dot the landscaped hillside.

LEFT: The first medical clinic in Canchias, finished under the supervision of Benny Dohm, a Florida carpenter, who donated many hours of labor to HTH.

199

What you leave behind is not what is engraved in stone monuments, but what is woven into the lives of others. ~Pericles

36
Impacting Lives, Changing Values
1993–1997

A solemn Crucito is found wasting away with no hope for the future.

When Miguel and Gordon Garrett bring a wheelchair, change is on the horizon.

Crucito's smile flashes often as he thrives under care at Karen's Hope!

I am reducing my work load from 60 to 30 hours in order to spend more time with my family.

I am going to be more honest in my relationships.

I am going back and will love the children of Honduras by loving my own children more.

No longer will I say "What's in it for me?" but rather, "What's in it for Thee?"

I can't remember a week when I have prayed, laughed, wept, learned, loved and experienced life to the extent that I have on this trip. God is working mightily through Heart to Honduras.

We went to Honduras to be a blessing, and we wound up being blessed.

200

These were the words of team members as they prepared to return to the States. As North Americans experienced a week of ministry in the culture of rural Honduras, and were immersed in daily Bible studies and sharing times led by Charlie, they were being transformed just as much as the communities in which they ministered. One church gave their report to their home congregation using kerosene lanterns to light the sanctuary. The church that had a weekly Meal of Remembrance donated the money saved from their fast (about $25 per person per month) to Heart to Honduras. The young girl from Alabama who prayed for the baby in Chagüitillos said, "It was a life changer for me. It solidified in my life the desire to become a nurse, and I graduated in 1998 with a BSN from Anderson University."

As groups shared their impressions with friends and family back home, they often mentioned the gratefulness they observed in the Honduran Christians. One pastor noted one Honduran habits: those who took the offering, led the singing, read the Scripture or had an opportunity to help in some other capacity in the service would afterwards kneel and pray, thanking God for the privilege and opportunity. What a great lesson in gratitude.

The group that gave a VCR and TV to the church in La Joya had been puzzled when there didn't seem to be any excitement or anticipation in the gathered congregation. But when the picture came on the screen and the eyes of adults and children grew round in astonishment, the mystery was solved. The people had never seen a TV in their lives!

Charlie and Miguel pose with a team from Lexington, KY

201

The rural communities had seen schools before, but not one like many neglected corners of Honduras would receive following a series of interrelated events that began in Ohio.

A SCHOOL FOR CANCHIAS

A chain reaction began with the missions conference in Columbus, Ohio, when Jerry Grubbs told Dr. Girardi he could help Honduras by bringing a medical team. Dr. Girardi and Dr. Lilly's tradition of bringing a medical team in May would evolve into at least a dozen medical teams a year visiting Honduras. In the second year of the May Medical Team, engineer Tony Ahern came along to explore building a hydroelectric plant. On a subsequent hydro electrical installation team, an architect with no talent for things electrical reluctantly agreed to accompany his teenage son, serving as a common laborer while additional pipe was laid to increase the kilowatt capacity of the system. Out of that obedience came another far-reaching vision. Bill DeJong relates how he conceived his vision in April of 1996:

> While working on the engineering team, my son Todd and I visited the school in Canchias...There were no lights, very old and antiquated desks, textbooks, each shared by four students, virtually no teaching aids, and no plumbing, just an outhouse...Through this brief exposure to this one-room school came the idea to study school facility needs in rural Honduras and look at the possibility of developing a better learning environment and educational opportunities for the children.

Soon, Bill had recruited his own team to travel to Canchias in April 1997. About a dozen architects came from all over the continent: Canada, Minnesota, Ohio, Texas and other states.

Charlie wrote of his admiration for Bill's team after their second session together:

> This time we talked about philosophy of education, our vision for education for the rural people and the like. How stimulating it was to hear the ideas from these very intelligent and successful educational architects. I cannot remember having such a well-educated group of people together to explore one subject. I expect that the outcome of this time together will be a new paradigm for education that will meet rural needs.

This team designed an amazing learning environment for the children of this village of 300 people. The new facility increased interest in education, and attendance at the school jumped from 40 to 75 students, which encouraged the government to double the faculty to two teachers. The new building was designed to also host community meetings, and it soon drew the attention of the national government.

Original school building in Canchias that inspired Bill DeJong to use his architectural skills to build a new three-building school there.

The team of architects who became the "Ed Team" with leader Bill DeJong (Harvard T-shirt) met with Charlie & Miguel at the Martha House, Fall 1997

On July 15, 1998, the team dedicated the *Escuela (*school*) Rural Bertha L. De Castaneda de Canchias.* But Charlie's prophetic words became a reality as a new educational paradigm emerged, impacting not only Honduras but the world. The *Escuela* became a model for other schools in the country. In May 2003, this team became incorporated as Schools for the Children of the World (SCW). In April 2004, SCW, working in partnership with the Department of Education, the Honduran Army, and national, regional and local educators, used helicopters, jeeps, 4x4 trucks, horses and mules to survey conditions of Honduras' more than 17,000 school sites, and made recommendations to the president of Honduras.

A plan was developed by the Department of Education and SCW for improving the schools, a plan that included everything from painting rooms to new construction, from new books and supplies to teacher training. The tasks were divided between the government and SCW's architectural interns, and the teamwork lasted through that administration. With a new Honduran president came a new minister of education, and their part of the plan was dropped. However, SCW continues to send two or three teams a year to carry out their part of the agreement, and SCW maintains a staffed office in Tegucigalpa. Today, SCW is working in Africa, Asia and Central America, spreading the dream from one isolated mountain village to similar locations around the globe.

Lives were being changed, whether in the little village of Canchias, Honduras, or an equally remote African or Asian village, or in some city large or small in the United States. The influence of Charlie's vision was spreading, and he was humbled and thrilled to be in the middle of it all.

Transformed from a crowded one room/one teacher school attended by 40 students to a complex of three buildings with a large playground for older children and an enclosed playground for preschoolers, the new Canchias school with its sheltered entrance now has two teachers instructing 75 students, and one of the buildings doubles as a community meeting space.

This graphic of the names of people who visited Honduras in the first six years was designed for the back of the T-shirt given to work campers in 1995.

The following people have visited Honduras with Heart to Honduras from the beginning of the first pastors' association through September, 1994:

January: Ed Joyner • Charles Smith **August 1:** Steve Coder • Charles Smith • Jim Usher **August 1:** Buck Brazel • Mary Jean Daniels • Phil Germany • Walt Williams **December 1:** Robin Bauer • Rose Lang • Mark Martin • Evelyn Schumate

January 1: Irwin Bontara-ger • Dan Brown • Broadway Christian • Junior Iden • Leroy Rapp • Larry Wilkerson •J. D. Woods **March 1:** Deryl Johnson • George Rodruguiez **June 1:** Keith Wilkins **June 15:** Doug Wartman **July 1:** Larry Carter • Harold Coomer • John Quattlebaum • Jerry White **August 25:** Marilyn Aleman • Steve Collins • Lilorci Herrera **November 1:** Maryln Aleman • Robin Bauer • Dwayne Joyner • Eddie Joy-ner • Earl Wheatly **November 15:** Steve Birch

January 1: Eleazar Cepeda **February 2:** Dan Brown • Peake • George Rodriguez **May 11:** Marylin Aleman • Lilly • Karen Steves • Lynda Yonker **September 1:** Harrington • Bonnie Hitzeman • Jerry Knisely • Evie Mueller • Dean Pape • Doug Peake • Kim Peake • Kelly Kentucky **November 11:** Betty Allen • Laura Cash • Lester Cash • Benny Dohm • M. D. Elston • Edna Elston • Gary Loar • Myrene Shrewsbury
Larry Wilkinson • Doug Wartman **April 1:** Lorna Kardatzke • Doug Peake • Kim Leah Blagg • Rhoda Bowman • Jerry Girardi • Jerry Grubbs • Larry Lilly • Tara Shawna Barlow • Mike Brewster • Sherry Brown (Rufener) • Larry Carter • Monty Lundstrom • Mike Mawdsley • Chris McKinney • Danny Mueller • Michelle Prescott • Anne-Marie Smith **September 1:** Harold Coomer **October 19:**

January 1: Wanda Augustine • Jean Bell • Janette Flyn • Ann Hiner • Barry Kellog • Rodriguez • Martha Lee Russell • Bill Thrasher • Ron Wilson **February 16:** Terry Burke • Susan Frost • Steve Hall • David Hammer • Kimberly Hughes • Zelma Lam- • Leroy Rice • Robert Smith • Joseph Wright **April 15:** Lester Cash • Mason Crews • Tim Kufeldt • Steve Meggs • Phil Murphy • Paul Phillips • George Rodriguez • Barry Tony Ahern • Rhoda Bowman • Gerald Girardi • Mark Gray • Jerry Grubbs • Kathy Hartsough • Larry Lilly • Joel Lilly • Tara Lilly • Driston Michelson • Lucinda Penhorwood • Mary Snider • Karen Steves • Charles Thurston **June 15:** Keith Wilkins **July 15:** Craig Carter • Carolyn Carter • Dorthea Carter • Dave Helmig • Danny Mueller • Michelle Mueller • Doug Peake • Kim Peake • Elizabeth Ray **August 1:** Doris Berstein • Barbara Hagenmyer • Merrill Kanouse • Chris Linsley • Heath Richards • Carol Lyne Usher • Ron White • Marlin White **August 15:** Jarie Nelson • James Nelson **September 16:** Wayne Baldock • Harold Coomer • Doug Corbin • Leroy Herring • Mel Jacobs • John Lott • Ken Mattingly • Chuck Tatum • William White • Jerry White **November 15:** Daniel Betts • Mike Carrigan • John Harvey • Tim Harvey • Freda Johnson • Karen Longwith • Becky Pickens • Jerry Pickens • Eric Seelback • Dale Seelback • Lynn Speelman • Larry Speelman • Joe Stephenson

February 12: David Andreas • Micheal Anstead • Todd Braschler • Edward Daugherty • Doug Durick • David Hammer • Ronald Hillard • Kimberly Hughes • Christina Lambert • Charles Lambert • Shari May • Tammy Redmond • Rebecca Rwallings • Ed Shonkwiler • Bernie Short • Jane Smith **April 1:** Michael Bennett • Scott Crews • Anne-Marie Smith • Charles Smith • Felicia Smith • Karen Smith • Dean Stone • Ruth Stone • Jim Usher **April 24:** Tony Ahern • Donald Beam • John Cash • James Christy • Charles Coutellier • Becky Everett • Richard Field • Mark Gray • Monty Harrington • Larry Linneman • John Maineri • Gary Mitkowski • Paul Neundorfer • Michael Neundorfer • Carlton Oesch • Gene Scherrer • Barry Shick • Twyla Smith • Ken Smith • Darrell Toney • Dale Vanhoose **May 15:** Michael Barstow • Stacy Biegel • Rhoda Bowman • Chris Bright • Sarah Froman • Gerald Girardi • Mark Gittins • Karen Ledford • Joel Lilly • Tara Lilly • Larry Lilly • Margret (Meg) Maloon • Jeremy Mithis • Kristen Michelson • Lucinda Penhorwood • Michale Samuel • Julie Shorno • Mary Snider • Karen Steves • Charles Thurston • Lynda Tonker **June 28:** Cherie Bolin • Melissa Carroll • Sherry Graham • James Hockaday • Lee Hockaday • Ember Jeffers • Chris Liverett • Tina Lott • Wade Martin • Nathan Mattingly • Jeremiah Mattingly • Tim Mattingly • Howard Megrill • Brandon Rolader • Jonathan Rolader • Carol Lynne Usher **July 3:** Veronica Anderson • Karen Bailey • Michelle Drusell • Scott Gersers • Judy Murphy • Dave Murphy • Mark Shaner **July 8:** Doris Bernstein • Barbara Hagenmyer • Merrill Kanouse • Chris Linsley • Heath Richards • Ron White • Marlin White **July 11:** Tom Barnett • Ricky Butler • Chad Butler • Charlene Cowart • Melinda Cowart • David Cox • Melvin Jacobs • Steve Jacobs • Karl Langley • Joseph Langley • John Lott • Kristina Moore • William Moore • Russ Porter • Frank Stoll **July 24:** Bradd Carter • Carolyn Carter • Craig Carter • Linda Howard • Pamela Lamborn • Thea Mocky • Michelle Mueller • Kim Peake • Doug Peake • Tyrone Sinclair • Carol-Lynn Usher **August 8:** Doris Berstein • Merrill Kanouse • Chris Lindsley • Dwight Looney • Heath Richards • Ron White • Marylin White **September 4:** Wayne Baldock • Harold Coomer • Doug Corbin • Ray Lawrimore • Ron Lowe • Brad Lowe • Chuck Tatum • Jerry White **October 23:** Jim Dickey • Laverne Dickey • Sarah Dickey • Jan Dickey • Dot Dickey • Julie Forsyth • Beverly Hislope • Joe Rice • Nicci Rice • Jason Simms **October 30:** Ann Napier • Russ Napier • Twyla Smith • Ken Smith • Larry Speelman • Lynn Speelman **November 20:** Steve Birch • Jeff Birch • Michael Collier • Terry Collier • Duane Craft • Tracy Hargis • Zelma Lambert • Billy Midkiff • Lora Pennington • Kristy Quarles • Bruce Rawlings • Shelby Rothman • Jeff Rothman • Stephanie Savage • Ed Shonkwiler • Matthew Short • Bernie Short • Sarah Smith • Kristy Thomas • Linda Thomas • Chet Trumble • Jonathan Weber • Joshua Wiber **December 4:** Robin Bauer • Marty Cheeks • Steve Hartsell • Gus Jeenings • Aubrey Matthews • Linda Prescott • Jimmy Joe Pryor • Joe Stephenson • Earl Wheatly • Jim Williams • LeRoy Yates

January 22: Gloria Anderson • Mike Carrigon • Cecil Cooksey • Diana Ellington • Rick Foster • Gorden Garrett • Althea Greene • Wilton Greene • Greg Kendall • Jim McLaughlin • Jerry Pickens • Bob Powlison • Dale Seelbach • Janet Smith **March 11:** Tremayne Batiste • William Bowlis • Howard Briggs • Borita Broyles • Wendell Burr • Kathryn Burr • Teresa Dungey • Heather Holliday • Oda Holliday • Ju-dith Kardatzke • Christina Leonard • Cathy Mercer • Wayne Mercer • Thomas Pelt • Caroline Pelt • Pamela Rhoden • Robert Roy • Barbara Joan Spurling **March 25:** Carolyn Carter • Jayne Crews-Linton • Sandy Dohm • Benny Dohm • Kelly Harrington • Lorna Kardatzke • Ro-bert Kirkner • Max Linton **March 25:** Ben Bergamino • Leah Burdsall • Evelyn Cioccio • Marc Cioccio • Amy D'Albora • Scott Gerlers • Regina Gray • Jennifer Martin • Michele McGann • Judy Murphy • Dave Murphy • Brenda Rogers • Mark Shaner • Vickie Shaner • Kerri Stafford • Beth Testa • Gina Vincent • Ashley Wiseman **April 11:** David Barrett • Gary Bates • Robert Brink • Rick Mooney • Doug Scserba • Jimmy Swogger • Bruce Wilson • Keith Wilson **April 23:** Tony Ahern • Don Beam • Jim Christy • John Cash • Donald Demers • Owen Dewolfe • Martin Dixon • Rick Doran • John Jones • Donald Keith • Margaret Kasten • Sarah Kasten • Ron Leslie • Brittany Linneman • Larry Linneman • John Maineri • Thomas Martin • Barb McVicker • Bob McVicker • Darby McVicker • Ryan McVicker • Jennifer Myers • Carl Oesch • Brian Paris • Darrell Parks • Dale Vanhoose • Robert Walling **May 14:** Carolinda Allen • Mike Barstow • Rhoda Bowman • James Cook • Jeff Gittins • Mark Gittins • Peter Gumma • Barbara Holman • Alexander Ide • Hedy Jansen • Gustav Jeeninga • Angela Lilly • Joel Lilly • Larry Lilly • Tara Lilly • Chuck Thurston • Brian Marshall • Jeremy Mathis • Joshua Mathis • Ryan Rinke • Mike Samuel • Julie Shorno • Cynthia Swart • Jennifer White • Ken Writesel **June 20:** Ralph Anderson • Burnadette Anderson • Troy Anderson • Trent Freed • George Freed • Louise Freed • Ron Lastoria • Don Parshall • John Richey • Wendy Richey • Keith Wilkins • Sharon Bromley **July 23:** Craig Carter • Judy Granheim • Bradd Carter • Jerry Cass • Melanie Fulton • Chris Harbour • Judy Henderson • Linda Howard • Scott Kardatzke • Cindy Kardatzke • Rhonda Krause • Nelson Mar • Russell Mason • Brenda Mason • Doug Peake • Kim Peake • Richard Peppard • Timmie Teppe • Richard Marino • Linda Marino • Michelle Murray • Kim Stevenson

I didn't want to go now.
I wanted to stay and work on the vision that had been given to us.
~Charlie Smith, April 1997

37

I Pleaded for More Time

1996

"Charlie, you are short of breath. You might want to visit a doctor when you return to Florida and check it out." Artist and nurse Judy Rentner and Charlie were walking from the clinic in Canchias to the ministry campus in March 1996 when she made this observation. With no idea of the serious implications of that moment in time, I had walked on ahead, anxious for lunch. Looking back, I saw that they had paused, but thought nothing of it as Charlie was always stopping to talk about some aspect of his ever-expanding vision.

The North American staff had not noticed his shortness of breath, but they had noticed another change. There were two affections Charlie had in Honduras: he loved the poor and he loved the Body of Christ. He valued his visits to the village churches for their worship services, held four or five evenings a week, so he could encourage and fellowship with them. But during that spring, Charlie began to stay behind when a team went to the village churches. Was the backbreaking truck ride getting the best of him? Why was the spiritual leader suddenly preferring his rocking chair at the Martha House over a wooden bench at church?

The previous fall, Charlie had been treated for a persistent cough diagnosed as bronchitis. Now, at the urging of Judy Rentner, he sought further testing and discovered that he had a lung disease for which there was no known cure other than a lung transplant. At first, Charlie felt he was functioning all right, adapting to the lessened intake of oxygen by walking more slowly and resting more often. But in time he began to realize how little time he had left. His words describe this disease:

> I was diagnosed with diffuse idiopathic, interstitial pulmonary fibrosis. This is a rare (3-5 cases per 100,000 people) disease brought on by over 180 known causes such as fumes, pesticides, asbestos, silica sand, wood dust, hay mold, and on and on the list goes. One of these elements is

206

believed to cause the body to protect the lungs by inflaming the inner lining of the lung. That's what it is supposed to do, but when the threat or invader has left, the inflammation leaves and the lungs return to normal. In pulmonary fibrosis, the lungs stay inflamed even though the stimulus that brought it on is gone. The body's response to the prolonged inflammation is to lay down scar tissue over the inflammation, causing the lungs to become hardened or less flexible, to decrease in volume and to prevent oxygen from entering the body through the alveoli, which have been overlaid with scar tissue. The initial signs of the disease are shortness of breath and a hacking, non-productive cough.

Bottom line: this is an ugly disease. There is no cure. The statistics are that after five years following diagnoses, 50 percent of those afflicted with this disease have died.

Charlie followed a regimen of several medicines assigned by his doctors, but they had little positive effect. Meanwhile, he continued to spend as much time as possible on site with his ministry.

Charlie in his newly cedar-lined office. Some thought the cedar to be the cause of his pulmonary disease.

The following announcement was made in the February 1997 *Reminder* (the newsletter of Heart to Honduras):

Please pray for Heart to Honduras Overseer Charlie Smith, who has been diagnosed with interstitial pulmonary fibrosis, or lung-scarring, due to unknown causes. The condition results in shortness of breath, limiting activity, and aside from divine healing is considered irreversible. Charlie is doing well, but needs strength and encouragement as he faces this challenging limitation.

The battle lines were drawn, and they were both spiritual and physical. Charlie recorded the following thoughts:

There were some very difficult days for me during January and February, I would think about the rapid progression of the disease; Dr. Forman said the disease can shut down a pair of lungs in two to three months. I wasn't getting any better. In fact my second full pulmonary function test showed my decline in lung volume and in oxygen diffusion. It seemed as if I possibly was headed to a rapid transition to be with the Lord. I thought a lot about that, and the more I thought about it, the more I didn't want to go now. I wanted to stay and work on the vision that had been given to us. We were just now at a point where the Canchias project could take off. I was using all that I had ever learned in this one situation, and it was working, for a change. I've been like a kid in a candy shop, having the time of my life. Just let me stay a little longer and see some more of the vision become a reality. I knew I was being selfish and that I must relinquish my will to the will of the Father, but I pleaded for a little more time to continue the work. Dave Pischel said that if the Lord took me home now, it would be like playing outside with the neighborhood children, having a wonderful time, when you hear the sound of your father's voice calling you home. You really want to stay and play awhile longer, but you know you cannot. When Father calls you home, you have no choice. You go home.

My greatest anguish and pain still comes from thinking about Felicia and Anne-Marie having to go through the death of their only surviving parent and not to have me or their mother there for them through their lives like "normal" people.

208

Sometimes my pain thinking about their pain seemed unbearable. I weep, moan, cry out to God for help.

God was not deaf to his cries. On March 15, 1997, he officiated at Felicia's wedding to Lyle Graybeal in the park surrounding Bok Towers in Lake Wales, Florida. As he had declared he would do, he conducted the entire ceremony, including his extensive message to them, without the use of oxygen. To all of us who were present to hear his words, it was a blessed but bittersweet day. The sweetness was expressed in Charlie's own words: "The fellowship was divine, the food incredible, the setting marvelous."

But the bitterness came as Charlie looked at his lovely daughter Felicia. "I turned around just for a moment, and I looked into the face of my beautiful daughter, and for an instant saw the face of Karen when I married her nearly 37 years before. It was more than I could bear for the moment, and I began to break down and cry, quickly telling Marie and Lorna that I needed to go home."

In the days just after the wedding, Charlie flew to Honduras, taking with him his daughter Anne-Marie, her boyfriend Scott and Scott's mother Jayne. Soon they were joined by the newlyweds, Felicia and Lyle, and Charlie reveled in sharing the results of the past eight years of ministry building with these dear ones. The girls were able to see that their father was well cared for in Canchias, with Dr. Elsa just steps away from the Martha House (Charlie's residence in Canchias). He treasured the peaceful environment. A certified doctor was available and Paola, a local Honduran caretaker, cooked and attended to his physical needs—a blessing for which he was grateful. The arrangements left the girls at peace about their father's choice to spend as much of his remaining time as possible in Honduras.

Anne-Marie with Charlie's caregiver Paola in the Martha House kitchen

Of his being in Honduras, Charlie said, "I do believe that I am exactly where I need to be right now. Here is my life's work–my meaning and purpose." He could do some work for the mission from his Florida office, of course, but his preference was to be in close proximity to the people he loved and the project he had envisioned as it unfolded.

209

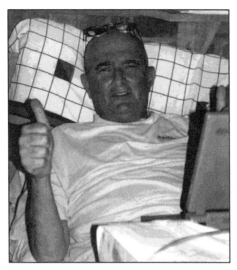

**Charlie and his laptop
in the Martha House, Canchias**

Realizing time was not on his side, Charlie dedicated himself to recording as many of his thoughts as he could type into the laptop his doctor/friend Jim Nelson had given him. Day and night he typed–so much that Paola said, "*Siempre estaba teclando.* [He was always typing.]" He typed a journal of the progression of the disease, the visitors who came to see him, aspects of his vision he wanted tweaked, instructions for his staff, advice to the two beloved daughters he was leaving behind, words of gratitude to people who had blessed his life, and his strongly held philosophies and theologies. One day his fingers flew with joy across the keys as he recorded that day's momentous events:

Friday, April 25, 1997
It's now the end of the day, and what a day it has been. I had two mountain-top emotional experiences I will always remember. Miguel had been saying he was going to take me to see the work on the Assembly Hall and the work that has been accomplished this week, so at about 3:30, Manuel Lemus brought his mule all saddled and ready to go. With the help of a stool, it was easy to get on, and I carried my portable oxygen unit with me. As Miguel led me into the big

View through the screened wall of the Assembly Hall

hall, I was overcome with such great joy that I began to weep. Tears flowed freely as I thanked God for this wonderful new

210

building. One wall is totally open to nature. It almost feels like you are seated in the middle of that natural environment.

[Then] my second peak experience. Today, Friday, April 25, 1997, I, Charles Robert Carver Smith, for the first time in my life had the great privilege of riding an ass. What a thrill!

To understand why this was such an exciting day for Charlie, we need to pause the narrative and let Miguel explain why Charlie loved the humble burro, and why he loved to throw conservative language to the wind and call it an ass. These words are taken from an orientation talk Miguel gave many times to visiting North Americans.

God delights in the humble, but like the Bible says, he opposes the proud. The call for this week, for everyone in this group, is to be a humble servant of the Lord Jesus Christ.

That reminds me of two stories. The first was when Charlie and I first started the ministry. I only had my backpack and Ziploc baggie for my Bible. I asked God to provide me a 4X4. God, having a sense of humor that He does, did provide me a 4X4. A donkey! A burro! A four-legged animal! And I said, "God, why do you want me to have this ass?" It was then that this second story about the humble ass became real to me.

211

When Jesus came to Jerusalem He chose to ride on an ass to enter the city. Maybe you have a problem with that word, but it says in the King James Version of the Bible, "Thy King cometh …sitting upon an ass." Everyone was throwing the palm branches and shouting, "Hosanna, blessed be the name of the Lord!" The poor little ass put his ears up and he said, "Wow! I never knew people liked me so much. I never knew I was so popular!" The little ass did not know that about three blocks down the road, Jesus would get off of him and tell His disciples to tie him back. Then the little ass would realize all the glory and praise was not for him, but for Jesus.

We are all called to be an ass for Jesus. We all must be Ambassadors Serving the Savior. This is why Charlie loved the word ass. Not only was the little ass the symbol of humility but for Charlie it meant we are to be Ambassadors Serving the Savior. That means we must live in humility and service to Him.

Charlie took this symbolism into the logo which he asked Dave Pischel to design for the ministry, and it subsequently became the design for conversation-provoking T-shirts. It stands as an inside joke for group members returning to their conservative churches, but the joke has deep meaning, as Charlie noted in his summary paragraph of his donkey-riding day:

Charlie wearing his AmbASSador T-shirt

The symbol of the ass is the very clear signal to all that Jesus came to the common folk, to the poor, to the struggling masses. We must remember this and keep it before us at all times. Carrying Jesus, that is what we are about. May we carry Him well!

212

On another day during that stay in Canchias in April 1997, Charlie anticipated the arrival of The Ambassadors. This musical group from the local church was coming to give him a private concert to express their sorrow for his illness and appreciation for his love. Each member had been employed by the ministry at one time or another: Pastor Miguel and Manuel played guitars, Santos played the mandolin, Simeon played the bass and Chilo played the drum and gong. Charlie reflected on the experience: "Their music was straight from heaven! Song after song, my soul and spirit (How do you separate the two?) were lifted to new heights."

Another day that week, Manuel, one of the guitarists and the poorest man in the village, came alone to visit Charlie. In his diary, Charlie noted: "I rested for a while, and then Manuel came for a visit. I asked him where his guitar was and sent him to the dining hall to get the ministry guitar. He then sang to me like David sang to Saul. How sweet and tender was his music. It lifted my spirit and strengthened my soul. How blessed I am to be in this place and to have so many simple, humble, poor people as my friends."

Charlie recorded one highlight of April 12: a visit from the young carpenter, Ever. "What a marvelous miracle. Two years ago this young man was in the world; today he is in the Kingdom. After two years of growing in the knowledge of God, he is now beginning to teach the Word. What a blessing! What a joy!"

The following excerpts from other pages of his journal for that April trip give us glimpses into the daily life of a man of vision who is squeezing the last drops of joy out of life on this earth.

Monday, April 28, 1997

I decided to make a pot of coffee this morning and couldn't drink the stuff. Why put that garbage in your mouth when you can have fresh, cold fruit?

I sat on the porch this morning and read [the Word] in Spanish, sometimes aloud and sometimes not. I love to read the Word in Spanish.

The meal [shared with Honduran neighbors Trino and Sabina] was wonderful and we topped it off with a glass of ice water and headed back to the front porch where I had my soft seat. I brought out my camera and after I caught my breath took pictures of my surroundings for that moment.

Charlie, Trino, Jim

213

April 30, 1997

Yesterday Ever brought me a bench for the shower. This helps me greatly as I am able to sit down to wash my legs and feet. By the time I have shaved and showered, I am quite exhausted, lacking oxygen, so I sit for a while to catch up. I encourage everyone who reads this to not take the little things in life for granted.

May 1, 1997

The men and boys are back digging terraces today [on the campus below the Martha House]. The place is beginning to look good. These terraces will be kept clean and hopefully planted once irrigation is in place. A few more months and another vision can be realized: the Small Farm or Family Farm Resource Center. I want to see it.

Manuel came with the horse we bought from Jose, and saddled it for me. It's quite an ordeal to get me around. Someone has to hold my oxygen, get a bench for me to get up on the horse, and then lead the horse down the terraced slopes. It's not too bad, but it is tiring. I sat in the big Assembly Hall and watched Ever and his workers putting the finishing touches on the wood and screen work. Wow! The building is wonderful. The Lord finally allowed me to build a multipurpose building–and a big one at that. I see over and over in my mind, heart and soul the hungry of this area coming to sit down at a banquet prepared for them by the Lord. Banquets with music and special speakers. Videos!!!!! It will be the greatest thing people in this area have ever seen. Entire villages invited to attend with special places for the care of children. Let your Kingdom come, Lord Jesus.

After considering alternatives for the big deck, I got in the red Land Cruiser with Miguel, Chilo, and the lady who Miguel is negotiating with for the 80 acres.[41]

---

[41] This property in Canchias was soon purchased and is referred to as *El Tablón*, The Table–or Plateau.

214

The view from Ambassador Mountain of the ministry campus in Canchias

As we drove onto the property I was in awe. The beautiful mountains from this peak were even more beautiful than I have remembered. Miguel then took me to an overlook, where for the first time I could see the entire ministry development shining like a bright star in the universe. How beautiful, how incredible. The houses, the big assembly hall, the terraced hillside all pointed to something special happening in that place. There are some very beautiful building sites on this 80 acres. It can provide a living for 20 or 30 families. Over a period of time, build houses on defined family plots large enough for a garden, for some small animals and the like. Places for families to live. We can rent them or use them for our faculty, workers and students. All that will be needed is a cable chair system to take people back and forth. Now wouldn't that be a sight to behold. People crossing the valley from way above like ski lifts. It would be a tourist attraction, to say the least, and one of a kind in Honduras.

Coming down from the peak experience on the other side of the Canchias River, we paused at the site for the Canchias Plaza and talked about dozer work that needed to be done. We talked about entrances and exits, where buildings would

215

be built and the like. We can see it completed in our minds, a beautiful, peaceful place to go and be with your friends, enjoy something to drink or some ice cream, and listen to the Canchias Band, The Ambassadors for Christ. I can see also the large screen that will be let down and the video projection center where videos will be shown in living color and surround sound. I think that the focal point should be the *asna* carrying Jesus. Miguel thinks that should go on the mountaintop where one day I want to be buried–Lord, let me be buried on that mountain.

After spending three weeks in Honduras in April, interacting with the team of educational architects, and the Punxsutawney, Pennsylvania team, relaxing on the porch with his many visitors from the village, writing his vision, observing the progress on the Assembly Hall, and dialoguing with God about this disease and his desire to stay around to see his dreams come to fruition, Charlie flew home for a time in Florida. As he made his way through the airport with the help of a porter who managed his luggage, wheelchair, and oxygen machine between planes, he reflected on the following entry he had made in his journal:

Several times I have mentioned to people who have visited me that the machine that produces oxygen for me cost $5,000, to which they replied: "The poor would just die."

Charlie realized that he was blessed to have medical expertise available to him, medicines and machines to give him a few more days of life, and steroids to slow down the disease, though the steroids that slowed the progression of the lung disease caused his bones to be brittle and the resulting vertebrae compressions filled those days with increasingly unbearable pain. There was no longer any room for frivolous jokes, indifference toward the oppressed, trivial lifestyles or feeling sorry for one's self.

Phil Murphy recalled a story that Charlie's friend Keith Cross told to illustrate this point. While Charlie lay in bed with an oxygen mask over his face struggling to breathe, Keith said to him, "Charlie, the world is against me. I can hardly make it through the day. I am going to quit my job." There was a long silence in the room. Charlie proceeded to take the oxygen mask off his face and in uncustomary language said, "Well, damn it, Keith, go ahead and quit your job. I am over here dying and here you are complaining about a job. I won't tolerate this kind of thinking."

In love, Charlie used a little linguistic shock to teach Keith a lesson in perspective. Keith never forgot Charlie's words.

216

PART EIGHT

Philosophies

From the Martha House on the hillside of the ministry property in Canchias, Charlie dedicated the days and nights remaining to him to typing all of the things that were in his heart. This included his vision for the future of the ministry of Heart to Honduras, his opinions and philosophies on everything from education to nature to the church. In his tiny bedroom in the Martha House where he could reach out and touch the walls on either side when lying in the bed, he got his laptop, propped himself up and alternately typed and napped. Squeezed in next to the tanks of oxygen that increasingly sustained his life was a FAX machine attached to a satellite phone. By means of this developing technology, and at the astronomical cost of $3 a minute, his thoughts were regularly transmitted to the Lake Wales office. The following chapters are an attempt to distill these sometimes rambling, often edgy, thoughts.

Charlie delighted in using shocking words to make his listener think, and as is sometimes said prior to a broadcast, "The content of this program may not represent the beliefs of this station." In this case, they may not always represent the firm beliefs of their author, but they are guaranteed to provide fodder for thought.

If you are planning for a month, plant mushrooms.
If you are planning for a year, sow rice.
If you are planning for a decade, plant trees.
If you are planning for a lifetime, educate a person.
~Paraphrase of a Chinese Proverb

38
In the Sandbox
Education

Who would have believed that a man who was intrigued by legends of ghosts would be pivotal in Charlie's personal philosophy of education? Dr. John Ardis Cawthorn, education professor at Louisiana Tech and regional historian for Claiborne Parish, was well-known for his passion for researching the ghost stories of the area. However, in Charlie's mind, he was notable not for his book *Ghost Towns of Old Claiborne* but for the way he led his students to find their own "ghost stories"–their own personal passions. Charlie wrote about the impact of Cawthorn's methods:

Charlie the Educator

His philosophy was to find areas of interest in the student and encourage the student to explore those areas. He would bring to class large stacks of articles on a variety of subjects from the history of civilization to the life of great men and women, pass them out and have us read them, looking for those that interested us. It worked for me. He had a strong dislike of teachers who would begin their classes by saying they were going to "take up and cover" a certain subject, meaning they were going to follow the book, not stimulate thinking. I studied harder and made better grades than ever before, completing the master's degree with A's except one B. I learned under Dr. Cawthorn that grades and points mean nothing, and that stayed with me through the years I taught at Warner Southern College...[Cawthorn] had a strong dislike of the 4.0 grading system.... Grades give students the notion that they are to please the teacher, not learn. When recently looking through [my] book report notes of those days, there were no grades, only encouragement: "Excellent report, Charlie." "You certainly are making a thorough study. It is a pleasure to read your reports." "Splendid variety. You read with pleasure, don't you?" Those little words of encouragement had me walking tall, feeling good about myself and motivated me to study all the harder.

It was in that experience in Cawthorn's classroom, in addition to his Peace Corps stint and his applied anthropology studies at the University of Kentucky, that Charlie began to formulate his philosophy of education. His doctoral studies convinced him of the need for the subject of anthropology to be included in the student's early formative curriculum: "Anthropology should be an integral part of the curriculum, beginning in kindergarten. There are many colleges and universities in the U.S. that do not offer a single course in anthropology! How can we know how to live if we do not know who we are? 'Culture' is the most

Charlie and Felicia in Kentucky

powerful concept ever invented by man to describe and explain human group life."

When Charlie moved his family out to that little country town of Rivals, Kentucky, he put into practice this principle. Their home place, with its seven acres of land, was the greater classroom. He used this setting to let nature teach the girls about life. This future teacher would join his little girls in the dirt as they took their toys to the garden, and together they played, plowed and picked produce. He did not grade them, but he did affirm them by saying, "Felicia, you enjoy picking butter beans don't you?" "Anne-Marie, you are getting good at riding your tricycle."

Charlie believed children need the opportunity to explore God's amazing world that surrounds them–the stars, the moon, the birds above, the earth below, the animals around and the crawling creatures aground. He felt it was difficult for them to do this behind a desk surrounded by four walls of brick:

[Children] need safe areas where they can explore and create. A. S. Neill (Scottish educator and founder of *Summerhill* that encourages personal freedom in the life of children) knew what he was doing when he started *Summerhill* ...School consolidation killed the small community–the backbone of this nation–created mega problems for educators, all under the guise of making the latest technology available in the classroom. The result is that public education is in a terrible mess in this country, a mess that will have to crash before someone has the fortitude to offer alternatives, knowing they will be ridiculed. Teaching has become a chore with few rewards.

In Charlie's opinion, a constricted form of education simply pushes the student away from the love of learning and creates greater and greater disciplinary problems throughout the national educational system of the country. He was disheartened at students who were running amok, searching for a "good time with little interest in learning." He said, "I see two problems with our present educational system: first failing to pass on to our students values that have stood the test of time, and secondly, teaching hard sciences to soft students."

By attacking symptoms and not seeking real solutions, Charlie believed the administrators were no different than a doctor putting Band-Aids on a cancer. They had misplaced priorities. He wrote, "What is being done to remove the cause that leads them to experiment and use drugs in the first place? Nothing! Unless meaning and purpose can be provided [to] these wandering souls, there is no hope."

He wrote, "Education needs to be taken to the countryside, where environments can be built that will challenge them to learn about life. By all means, education must be made fun and enjoyable, or the problems we now have, which are great indeed, will only get worse." He was saddened to see children wasting so much time in environments that failed to stretch their imaginations and broaden their horizons.

Charlie continued: "What a massive problem we are creating for ourselves by not passing on to the youth the values that have withstood the tests of time. But [it is now believed] that school must be 'value-free' for fear that someone of a different culture will disagree with them."

221

Charlie believed as America approached the 21st century, she was entering into a dangerous phase, and he was writing these hard words out of a soft heart, because he was deeply concerned about the future direction of U.S. schools and the nation as a whole. "The most dangerous and greatest problem facing our country today is that children are rejecting the culture of their parents and are creating cultures of their own [that are] highly destructive." He believed the family was broken and the child was left outside feeling unwanted, uncared for and unloved.

As [my wife] would say to me, "Do you have an attitude about that?" It is obvious that I do. I would dearly love to be on a team of citizens to explore alternatives to the educational mess we now find ourselves in. Those in leadership positions would not be able to handle the change I would propose, but I can assure you that there are many young people yearning to be saved from the meaningless morass called "school," and any "solution" would be too "radical."...Teach the fundamentals for living in family and village in a real-life, practical educational program. There students would learn pre-adaptive survival knowledge and skills that will help them throughout life. Not everyone would want to take this option, but I can assure you that the brightest, most compassionate students would jump at the opportunity. And what to do with the students who are so disruptive that they are sent to "opportunity school"? I am assured by my friend D.C. that there is no opportunity there. That school is like a maximum security prison for the bad boys and girls, and there they learn how to "beat" the system.

Teachers matter because students matter. Charlie believed this so much that his educational philosophy was like a sandbox where students could play in the sand of new ideas. He would make available shovels to dig up the secrets of a foreign culture. He would show them where to find buckets of resources with which to construct sand castles of their own design. He would encourage them to venture beyond the security of castle moats to expand their awareness of different people groups. He would provide the sand, but give them freedom to engage each other with creative ideas on building the sand castle of life.

Just as Charlie was an applied anthropologist, he was an applied educationalist. His belief in allowing children to learn in a positive environment was more than just theory for Charlie–it was something he practiced. To teach his girls to drive, he put pillows in the seat of their old VW Bug, showed them the gears, the accelerator and the brake, and let them drive on some private land:

They would head for the ditch, but I would sit back, letting them make their own mistakes to see what they would do about it. ...[T]his approach to learning is the "mistake-recovery" approach. Many parents want their children to act like adults, to do as they would do, and become irritated and even mean when the child does not perform. That's cruel. We all need the opportunity to fail so we can learn to do better the next time.

The H.E.A.R.T. program across the street from his classroom was a prime example. His students between 1980 and 1983 helped develop the curriculum, build the buildings, dig the wells, and plant the crops. They even killed a snake or two in the process of creating an international ministry that has touched thousands of lives. Many of these students went on to build their own ministries and mentor their own students.

And when the day was done, Charlie would invite his students over to his house for cornbread and beans. He had an innate understanding that true education was more than the exchange of ideas in a classroom. It included being relational. This was teaching at its best, and this was a teacher at his best– passionate, hospitable, engaging, and personal.

A teacher/student relationship cannot get more practical than this. It was their grand sandbox, and it changed their lives forever.

Be still and know that I am God.
~Psalm 46:10 KJV

39
A Simple Contemplative
Simplicity

Charlie was a paradox. He was a mix between a social animal and a

Charlie teasing children with his false eyes, ears and nose was a contrast to the man who loved time alone to contemplate.

contemplative monk. With his alter-ego "Martha" he was a social animal, entertaining the crowd like a circus poodle jumping through fiery rings. Charlie would turn his back to a group, slip on large plastic ears, bulging eyes and an oversized nose (made scarier by his bald head) and then turn around to reveal his new persona, scaring and delighting little Honduran children and North Americans alike. Nilsa Pinell remarked on the version of this "costume" that included a female headwrap. "The children of Honduras loved Charlie, and he was always teasing them with 'Martha.'" On the other hand, as a contemplative monk, Charlie could retreat into his cave and meditate for hours on the teachings of Jesus.

A casual knowledge of Charlie would lead you to think he could never sit still. How did Charlie stay fresh with his spiritual insights? What was the source of his anointed visions? Where did his passion originate? Spinning so many plates, how did Charlie keep from burning out? What was the secret of his ceaseless energy?

For anyone who lingered for a period of time around him, it would become clear that his source was his oneness with the Father and his time in the Word.

His life was pretty much on the run, so he had to be intentional in finding a place and space for solitude and contemplation. Instead of a closet as his prayer room, his prayer place in Florida was his swivel chair facing Crooked Lake. In a letter written to Miguel Pinell, Charlie's conclusion was, "Finally, let us all commit to prayer for the ministry of Heart to Honduras and for God to touch the hearts of our many friends who support us. Prayer is the key."

Charlie understood the importance of a daily walk with God. Because he was so relational, the times when Charlie felt most in the presence of God was when he was in the presence of others, especially like-minded Christians. He saw the image of God in all people, from the *jamban* man who removed the contents of their "honey bucket" in Thailand, to rich man who lived in a gated community and generously donated from his investment portfolio. But his primary source of inner strength and inspiration came when he withdrew from the crowd and read the Scriptures.

It would be safe to say that Charlie's life of solitude was grounded in the Word, saturated in the Word and filtered through the Word. There were times when God spoke to Charlie. There were times when Charlie spoke to God. And there were times when both were silent in the presence of the other, just as lovers know and are known.

Solitude for Charlie was also a lifestyle. He could commune with God in a cave or while making a cake. He had much in common with the 17th century Carmelite monk Brother Lawrence, who worshipped God while washing pots and pans.

Because Charlie was in such demand and his schedule was so crowded when ministry teams from North America were present, he became intentional in seeking out solitude. He once wrote:

> Today was a lay-back day. I didn't do much of anything. It was nice having the compound virtually to myself again after two weeks of people. Solitude is very important to me.... I need the time to reflect, to write, to pray, to read the Word and just to rest.

I remember in September of 1995 being with Charlie in the Joshua House, and how the two of us made a contract of silence in order to seek the mind of Christ. My journal recorded that time:

> Charlie and I continue to be overwhelmed by the solitude and quietness in Canchias without a group from the States. It is a time of quiet and peace. On a few occasions, needy Hondurans pass by to purchase eggs or to ask for aspirins, but today the traffic has been slow. I can hear the chickens outside

225

clucking as they lay eight eggs each day. We give them three cups of feed and they return the thanks by providing us with protein...Charlie and I have a "silent contract" with each of us not speaking to the other for three hours so that we will not interrupt each other's thoughts. After the three hours of solitude, meditation, study and reflection, we regroup and bounce ideas off one another. Today he has been reading *The Kingdom of God* by Tolstoy, as well as the Word.

This photo was taken before he became so set on not wearing a tie and is included here because of its rarity. Sorry, Charlie.

Nighttime in Canchias was especially meaningful to Charlie, as he would spend hours on the porch of the Martha House. It overlooked the village of Canchias. Many North Americans recall their most poignant moments were the times sitting with Charlie on the porch, sharing memories of the day and how their lives were being changed through the experience.

Charlie lived close to the people and on their level. His great joy was to experience their closeness in a simple way. His clothes were neither ostentatious nor threatening to them. He wore a simple watch. Usually his attire was a T-shirt, blue jeans, tennis shoes and a cowboy hat. Charlie refused to wear a tie. It made no sense to him that a man would cut off the flow of oxygen by wrapping a noose around his neck just to satisfy some clothing designer's dress code. What a departure from his father who always wore a tie, even while mowing the grass!

Living this way, Charlie was able to think like a poor man and empathize with his needs. He wrote, "Think ground-level in lifestyle. No family living in Honduras has a concrete floor. Do an assessment of housing patterns."[42]

Simplicity enabled Charlie to set boundaries to rein in excess and prioritize his life. His boundaries were grounded in truth and in the Word: being transparent, living a simple lifestyle, making relationships a priority, casting holistic visions, living within the teachings of Jesus and giving unconditionally.

Even without trying, the village of Canchias captured simplicity. It was different from Lake Wales, Florida. Rather than swimming pools sanitized with chlorine, it had a river, clean from tumbling over rocks. Instead of the iconic

---

[42] Obviously, many middle and upper class Hondurans DO have concrete floors, many tiled beautifully. Charlie was referring here to the rural villages.

money-maker Mickey Mouse, it had the humble burro. In Canchias, mountain trails replaced interstates. Stars shone brightly without the competition of neon lights. Jet engine blasts did not overpower the gentle evening breezes. Acoustic guitars settled nerves instead of jangling them. Quiet front porch conversations took precedence over mindless television chatter.

In 1994, Monty and Kelly Harrington were living in the Joshua House in Canchias without access to television or any other electrical amenities. Monty had written Charlie about how God was teaching Him lessons about power and its potential to cloud one's thinking regarding the need to be simple and humble. Charlie responded by sharing how he, too, was learning the power of powerlessness:

Recently I had Felicia disconnect my cable, so I have no TV now, and am enjoying the extra time immensely. Last night I went to bed at 9:30 p.m. and was ready for my day to begin at 4:30 a.m. After studying Span-ish, I took a 50-minute walk and was ready to go to work before 8. I am iden-tifying more with you now that the TV has been removed from my life. Felicia and I watched a video on Mother Teresa the other night, and I, too, was moved by the power of powerlessness...The crucifying of ourselves is the key. We want our way...Felicia and I were pounding ourselves saying, "...and what am I doing?" This is the secret, whether well-fed, with or without water and electricity, to be content to wait on the Lord, for He is the one who is leading and guiding us through this life for His purposes as we surrender our lives to Him. You got it, Monty! Powerless! That's powerful.

Charlie wanted all North Americans to experience the blessing of what he had discovered in these quiet moments. Once, when he couldn't make the trip to Honduras to lead the team from Eastland Church in Lexington, Kentucky, he sent a greeting to them by way of a cassette recording. On this 30-minute tape, he advised walking slowly and quietly through the village, with respect for the people:

> I just encourage you this week to practice the presence of the Holy Spirit in your life. Be still and listen to the sounds of the beautiful valley of Canchias. Get alone. Get alone. Get away from the others. Get away from the noise. Hold down the talking–the loud noises. You are visitors in that country. You don't make loud noises. Keep your mouths shut. Listen! Listen! Open your minds. Open your hearts. There is nothing you can give in Honduras that needs to be done that can't be done by the Hondurans needing the work. God wants to teach you. See what God wants to do in your heart. What does He want you to know about the poor and the hungry? Heart to Honduras is helping them in the name of Jesus. Visit in these homes and touch the little children. Be a Jesus to them. Practice the presence of God. Don't plan it. Never plan it. You will kill it. It is not the work–the physical or material work–that you are going to do in Honduras that will make any great difference in the Kingdom, but it is the work that God is going to do in your heart while you are there. And practice the presence of the Holy Spirit in your life day by day and try to keep in step with the Holy Spirit.... Allow the Spirit of God to move what happens down there–to move you individually and move the group. Allow the spirit to move. Don't get disappointed because you did not get to do what you wanted to do. Just look forward to whatever is going to happen and let God teach you through that situation. Be flexible and listen to God. Open up your heart. Be still and God will bless you. He will bless you. It will be the turning point in your life.

Charlie saw humankind moving further and further away from the lifestyle of their forefathers, who were hardworking and simple. Our ancestors were people who wrote with a quill, milked cows, trapped animals, gathered eggs, drew water from a well and chopped firewood. Man was now living in a plastic world with machines and systems to provide comforts and distractions from the natural world and relationships. This artificiality made Charlie sad, and he bemoaned this change in culture. He was determined to use the ministry in Honduras to prick the consciences of North Americans. He did not want to take them back to the Stone Age, but neither did he want modernity to sweep them up in the New Age.

On one particular May night in 1996, the Hale-Bopp comet was passing overhead as Charlie and several North Americans watched from the Martha House porch. Bluish green in color, it had a tail that incredibly stretched half the length of the night sky. To North Americans who struggle to see even the most common constellations through the light pollution of their cities, observing this comet, so bright it could be seen even in the daytime for three days, was beyond their vocabulary to describe. A wordsmith like King David would have fumbled for adjectives to paint a picture of the majesty of observing this comet that last passed through in 2215 BC! Reflecting on night sounds and sights Charlie wrote:

> Oh, the beauty of God's creation. It is so marvelous. Peace is in this place. It is awesome. Oh, it is so beautiful. In this place, you can get close to God. In this place, you can be alone. You can listen to God. The sounds that He makes as He walks in the garden and you listen to the sounds of God. When you read the Words of life, your faith can be strengthened and you can give glory to God....It is wonderful being here to experience the wonder of the heavens, the transformation of the worm into a butterfly; to see the animal migration of the birds, flashes of light from a lightning bug, the intricate web of spiders and the never-ending activity of the ants. The patterns, structure and function of all these creatures of God are incredible. During the cool clear nights in Honduras, I often gaze into the heavens and marvel at the stars that seem several times brighter than in the States. Could it be that our inability to see the stars clearly clouds our perception of the Creator and has led us into a time of unbelief, if not indifference? In our hustle and bustle of our little lives caught up in maintaining the material world, we have little time to consider God–to look at the heavens.

A textbook Charlie often used in his classroom was E.F. Schumacher's *Small Is Beautiful.* Writing on the theme of simplicity, Schumacher said, "Any intelligent fool can invent further complications, but it takes a genius to retain or recapture simplicity." Charlie was one of these geniuses–one who captured simplicity and encouraged others to do the same.

229

*Girls, if there is anything you need to know about community development,
it is that food brings people together.*
~Charlie Smith

40

Christ and Curry

Food

If a sculptor were asked to take a piece of marble and carve a statue of Charlie Smith, the unveiling of that sculpture would most likely depict Charlie with a Bible in one hand and a spatula in the other. Most every gathering of people in which Charlie was the principal speaker, organizer or planner had food as a social and spiritual bonding agent. Charlie believed food draws people like a shrimp boat draws seagulls. He believed food should be the leading character, not the understudy, in the drama of worship and fellowship, helping to harmonize and realize the "Body" of Christ.

Charlie learned the importance of food from his parents. On a weekly basis, his parents invited students, neighbors, church members, family and Charlie's friends for a Sunday dinner, snacks, or sandwiches. He saw the potential of food in building community, witnessed its power to forge friendships, and observed the warmth it brings to the outsider.

"Our mother always invited people into our home for a meal after church on Sunday," his sister Lorna wrote. "She was a fabulous cook and there was always room for somebody else. There was a lot of fellowship around food."

Karen once remarked, "I just love to come home from work and smell the aroma of Charlie's cooking." And so did hundreds of guests and friends as Charlie and Karen welcomed them to their humble home. Those who were there can never forget those Florida nights when the sun was reflecting off Crooked Lake, the smell of stir fry was wafting onto the patio, and the laughter and conversation blended with notes from *Moonlight Sonata* or *Foggy Mountain Breakdown.*

The real beauty of Charlie's preparation and presentation of food at his home went beyond the taste and aroma to the spiritual lessons and principles he imparted before, during and after the meal. He was always a man of two breads– Jesus, the Bread of Life, and food, the spice of life. "Food is so important in bringing together the

A bald and bearded Charlie [upper left] hosts a typical crowd in their tiny modular home in Lake Wales, Florida.

Body of Christ around the common table," he wrote. "Food calms the hunger in the body and makes the spirit glad." It was this understanding of food that caused Charlie to make "Food for the Hungry" one of the five core values of the ministry of Heart to Honduras.

Dennis Turner, a former student of Charlie's, recalls a time when Charlie cooked a meal that soothed the hunger and made glad the spirit of several men working in the orange groves:

> I remember the time Steve Coder, Eddie Joiner and I went in the old Lake Wales church bus that was used to take people to the airport who were going to Haiti on mission trips. Charlie asked us to go throughout Lake Wales and the orange groves and pick up all the migrants we could find and bring them to the church. He wanted to have a banquet for them. Charlie would always talk about going into the highways and byways and bringing in the poor. He wanted to provide them food. And when they got together there were about 30 or 40 migrant workers gathered in the fellowship hall of the old Lake Wales Church. Charlie came in and made a big announcement and said, "It is great to have you here. This is a banquet for you and I want you to eat this food. I want you to eat until you can't eat anymore, but I want to tell you something about food. There is another kind of food that is better than this." And then he spoke the Word of God to them.

231

Dave Pischel recalled one of Charlie's favorite methods of cooking. "Food reflected his sensitivity to the poor of the Third World. His big thing was a stock pot of beans over rice."

Daughter Anne-Marie was always amazed at how many people her dad could entertain in such a small house, "Cooking was just the center of my house, and you know how small our house was. It was ridiculously small, but those burners were always going, those crock pots were always simmering."

On the other hand, Anne-Marie recalls those times when she and Felicia were awaiting their dates. "It was so hot in there, and we would be sweating when we were trying to be fresh and ready. We were just burning up, and Daddy is out there sautéing onions, garlic and curry. Just minutes out of the shower as we put on our makeup in our rooms, our hair smelled like curry, It was just awful to leave on our dates smelling like curry and garlic. Fact is, that was just the way it was. The stove was always going. The doors were always open. And meals were always a part of our family."

This emphasis on food was founded in the fact that Charlie saw a theological basis for hospitality in the Scriptures and used it to advance the

Daughter Felicia and Charlie enjoy cooking together in their Florida kitchen

Kingdom of God. He took seriously the prophetic words of Isaiah, "The kind of fasting I have chosen is that you feed the poor...." He was convicted by the words of Jesus, "I was hungry, and you fed me." His theology of food was also motivated by the writings of Dietrich Bonhoeffer, one of his favorite theologians. In his journal, he copied one of Bonhoeffer's quotes relating how faith and food work in tandem: "If the hungry man does not attain to faith, then the fault falls on those who refused him bread. To provide the hungry man with bread is to prepare the way for the coming of grace."

Charlie believed that the smell of food, especially coffee, brought unity to the people of God just as much as the actual food or drink did. Living close to the poor in Honduras, sharing a cup of coffee with them in their homes, caused Charlie to understand this reality in a way he never would have had he kept his distance. He came to this understanding while worshipping in a home church in a small Honduran village. Though it was a mystery to him, he became convinced that God uses even the aroma of food to bring his people together:

232

As we sang the last chorus of the service, the stinging smell of the smoke and the aroma of fresh coffee blended the crowded, smoky, home chapel together. The atmosphere transformed from stuffy to united. This smell of coffee made the service complete. I may be giving coffee too much credit, but coffee is a staple of life in these mountain villages; some might even say it is life. And the way it is made on the open-fire stoves in the Honduran homes produces an aroma unlike in my house. I know I cannot explain this aroma, this fragrance of coffee, smoke and Honduran life as it was in that room, but it was unity for me.

One can truly understand how Charlie saw food as a spiritual gift from God by the following videotaped conversation in the kitchen of San Isidro during the early years of the ministry of Heart to Honduras. Charlie was cooking for a group of about 25 people from the Eastland church in Lexington, Kentucky.

Jim: Charlie, could you share with the people what you are cooking?

Charlie: To make a good pot of beans, you need several ingredients: olive oil, chopped garlic, bay leaves, bacon drippings, onions, salt, pepper, vinegar, green peppers and red or black beans. Just as the body of Christ has an identity, so does a pot of beans. Each individual ingredient has its own identity that you put into the pot. You blend them together so they might become one as Jesus prayed, "Father, I pray that they might become one, even as we are one."

Now, you will notice that as we put the individual parts into the pot, they all lose their identity and become a part of the whole. It is like a gestalt, you know, when the whole is greater than the sum of its parts. It is those parts that are blended together in a unique way that make the difference. That is what happens when you cook and when you pray together.

You will notice that when the parts are separate they do not taste very good. Alone they are not worth very much. But when blended together, it becomes something that is tasty and delectable. Now we are putting some more parts into the whole–bell peppers and spices. But to taste bell pepper alone, it would not taste very good. All the parts need to come together to make a tasty whole. As we stir these spices, they

233

add more flavor. Some in the church add more flavor to the body than others.

Note, as I take my knife, I am cutting up the parts into smaller pieces so the flavor can be more radiant, if you will. The lesson here is that to become a part of the body, sometimes you have to be pruned or cut. This is how we become disciples. Sometimes it is hard, but there is no way to escape becoming a disciple except through discipline.

Now, you need to cook the pot of beans real good. Note as I stir the parts, the flavor continues to blend. Now, we will let all these ingredients in the pot cook and blend for a while.

There is something very sacred about thinking about bread and breaking it together and I think it would be very beneficial for the church to think more about breaking bread together, cooking meals and serving food and having fellowship. I think this is important. They did this in the early church and enjoyed fellowship.

In our meal tonight, we've got to take time to be together and not just eat and run.

Charlie leads a group in the San Isidro dining/meeting

A little later the group sat on benches around the tables that filled the room nearly wall to wall and enjoyed both the beans Charlie had prepared and the spiritual food he shared. The team was a living demonstration of the symbolism Charlie had spoken of as he prepared their evening meal. They had come to Honduras, bringing their varied talents and personalities, and had become the body of Christ as they "simmered" together in warm fellowship.

234

Although Charlie's restaurant in Florida, Father's Place, hadn't survived, Charlie's dedication to food as a tool for building community and faith deeply enriched the experiences of Hondurans and North Americans alike as they joined him around a common table. As this happened over and over, Charlie realized that Heart to Honduras had reached beyond his original vision of feeding physically and spiritually hungry Hondurans and was also filling a spiritual emptiness in the North Americans who came on mission.

She say, "Celie, tell the truth, have you ever found God in church? I never did. I just found a bunch of folks hoping for Him to show. Any God I ever felt in church I brought in with me. And I think all the other folks did, too. They come to church to share God, not find God."
~*Alice Walker in* The Color Purple

41
Unity in Community
The Church

Every Sunday, from the cradle to the time he was a popular cheerleader for the Bearcats of Ruston High, Charlie Smith attended church with the regularity of a Swiss watch. Not that this was always his preference, but it was something his father mandated. Three times a week, Charlie would sit under Biblical teaching and preaching, and the truth about the church slowly but surely began to shape his thinking. He reflected on these precious days of his childhood:

> My earliest memories are listening to my grandfather preaching, and sitting through services playing with my father's hands and whatever he would give me out of his pockets. I gave my [Sunday school] teachers headaches, no doubt, but their words and more importantly their lives impacted mine for all eternity. Through those early years, there was being implanted in my heart the Word of God that has stayed with me to this day. I shudder to think where I would be if the church hadn't played such an important part in the life of our family.

Charlie's paternal grandfather, Dr. Charles Wilson Smith, played a huge role in shaping Charlie's belief and understanding of the nature of the church. As a four-year-old boy, the future Dr. Charles severely burned his feet when he kicked his way through the ashes left after he and his mother Lucretia burned yard debris earlier in the day. The burn was so deep he was bedridden for a year with the glow of a lantern burning late into the night as Lucretia dressed his wounds. Because of his burns, Charles decided he would have to use his mind rather than his back to carve out his destiny.

236

Dr. Charles W. Smith graduated from Memphis Medical College in 1906 in their first graduating class. He was very proud of his sheepskin degree (which was actually printed on sheepskin!) but he wanted nothing to do with religion. According to Frellsen, his father was a very vain man who loved diamond tie pins and gold chains and had no place for God in his life. But in 1921, he developed angina and knew he needed treatment. Realizing the frailty of his condition, he packed his bags, purchased a ticket on a Pullman train and traveled to Rochester, Minnesota to the highly recognized Mayo Clinic. At the clinic, the news was not good. The medical team overseeing him spoke directly: "Dr. Smith, our tests indicate that you do not have long to live. You need to return to Louisiana and set your house in order."

Back in his hospital room, rather than asking for his medicines, he gave the nurse some money and asked if she would go out and purchase a Bible for him. This Bible became like a best friend. God revealed to him that he needed to confess his sins, repent and get right with God. After many hours of searching various passages of the Bible, he asked God's forgiveness and was set free from condemnation and guilt of sin. He became a changed man and began to feel a call to preach.

A proud Dr. C.W. Smith before his conversion

His son Frellsen had watched a proud but concerned father board the Pullman bound for Minnesota. When a humbled man returned, Frellsen felt as if he had a new father. News of the proud doctor having "found religion" spread like wildfire throughout the community of Oak Grove.

Since Clara, Dr. Smith's wife, attended the Baptist church, the Baptist pastor went to visit Dr. Smith, hoping that he would become a member. But to the pastor's surprise, Dr. Smith promptly told him that from his personal reading of the Scriptures he could not see the Baptist Church or any organized church in the Bible. God loved all his people, and there was only one church. It was made up of the redeemed who had confessed and placed their faith in the Lord Jesus Christ. He said, "I love all Christians everywhere. I am not going to join any church."

Having heard that Dr. Smith had refused to join the Baptist church, the Methodist pastor set his sights on persuading this prominent member of the community to join his church. However, he received the same response from Dr. Smith: "I do not see the Methodist church in the Scriptures."

Bro. Dan Green, a Church of God minister, heard of Dr. Smith's stand on church joining and took a fellow minister, A.Q. Bridwell, with him to see this new convert. As these two men shared their understanding of the church as being the "Body of Christ" that was an inclusive family of born-again brothers and sisters, Dr. Smith's heart was gladdened with great joy to know that there was a fellowship of people who believed exactly what he believed as he interpreted the Scriptures.[43] There were no Lutherans, nor were there "Church of God-ers," no Methodists, Baptists, Presbyterians—just Christians.

Dr. Smith and his son Frellsen became an "evangelistic team" preaching the Gospel and this concept of the unity of believers throughout Louisiana. And God extended Dr. Smith's life for many more years. "My dad came to God through my granddad," Charlie once said. "I have a little pump organ in my house. It is a little treadle organ. It is a folding organ. My dad would open it up on the courthouse square. He would play and sing, and my granddad would preach. And they started churches that way."

Unity was the one theme Charlie preached over and over to the believers in Honduras, a theme he had learned from his grandfather and father. The Heart to Honduras ministry worked with all denominations, and any pastor who wanted to be a partner was welcomed as a brother in Christ. For Charlie, unity was the point. Though this was the ideal, it did not always bring about the unity that Charlie sought. Often, the original denominational churches that came together under the encouragement of Heart to Honduras struggled with their own beliefs, directives from headquarters and authority issues. But unity was so essential to Charlie that when the church in the village of Chagüitillos asked him about becoming a part of the Anderson Church of God, he counseled against it. Charlie believed it would confuse them as to the true nature of the church, since it was Charlie's observation that Anderson was taking on a bureaucratic organizational structure like the denominational churches. Charlie never wavered in teaching the mandate and prayer of Jesus: "Father, I pray that they might be one even as we are one."

Miguel Pinell recalled the importance Charlie placed on this doctrine that was passed down to him from his father and grandfather:

> His last week in Honduras, there were about 25 pastors
> and he taught about unity of the church and how important it

---

[43] The Church of God of Anderson, Indiana, does not have formal church membership and considers itself a movement rather than a denomination.

was for over 45 minutes. This was his last message to them. He said, "Be unified." His first sermon in 1989 in January to the first pastors meeting was on unity. His last sermon in 1997 was on unity. Be unified. Just like Jesus taught in John 17. Charlie had one message down here. It was unity. He taught it over and over and over again and again.

In addition to his emphasis on unity, Charlie made a distinction between the organizational aspect of the church and the body of believers.

Church with a capital 'C' refers to the institution or legally organized groups of people who typically are part of a larger group of churches commonly referred to as denominations. Church with a lowercase 'c' refers to the many who by faith believe that Jesus is the Christ, the Messiah of God who laid down his life for the sin of the world. No group or organization can properly claim to include all of God's people. The New Testament church includes all true Christians...This New Testament idea of the church transcends denominational lines.

The church also transcends the buildings constructed by man. On a 1994 family visit to Seville, Spain, Charlie strolled through the *Plaza del Triunfo* and entered Europe's third largest cathedral, the *Catedral de Sevilla*. According to oral tradition, the planners had said, "Let us build a church so beautiful and so great that those who see it built will think we were mad."

Charlie was not impressed by either the structure or the boastful words. He was repelled by the way tourists were "worshipping" museum objects while others were trying to worship God. It was a form of religious syncretism as tourists stood in awe of paintings and frescoes while worshippers knelt in prayer. Reflecting on this massive edifice, Charlie wrote, "The righteousness of God is not found in stone, mortar, glass or carpet...what kind of house will you build for me, says the Lord?...I am the light of the world. I am justice and righteousness. You don't build houses for me. You build houses for yourselves. I do not live there. There is nothing sacred about anything material. Justice, mercy, righteousness–that is what I require."

Charlie struggled all his life to balance the institutional Church with what he understood as the true church, in such a way as to avoid alienating the former at the expense of the latter. When Charlie began to chart a new path and partnership with the rural churches and local pastors in Honduras, he saw that the key to this ministry would be the church. He wrote:

It's the church that is the focus of all that we do. It is the church that is the fellowship. It is the church that is the expression of Christ in us, the hope of Glory! It is the church that reaches out to the little children, to the sick, and to the man or woman of God that is bound by sin. It is the church that gives the cold glass of water, or the bowl of hot bread and rice, the warm embrace of acceptance into the family of God. Lift high the cross of Christ Jesus, the head of his Body, the church of God, the family of God, the Kingdom of God on earth.

Five times Charlie used the phrase "It is the church…" It was the church that was the focus, the expression of Christ in us that reached out to the little children and gave a bowl of oatmeal to the hungry. It was the church. Other secular agencies do these things in the name of their government, their flag or their country. But the church does all in the name of her Lord. And Charlie believed if all churches would unite, there would be no need for welfare checks, social security or other government subsidies for believers.

Rarely did he speak in a village church in the country of Honduras without referring to the church. His theme was always the unity of the believers. His favorite book in the New Testament was the Gospel of Luke because of the teachings of Jesus on themes of justice and reconciliation. His favorite book in the Old Testament was the book of Isaiah because of the prophetic calls to feed the poor, care for orphans, house the homeless and clothe the naked. His favorite chapter was John 17, in which Jesus calls the disciples to unity.

All things believers do, in Charlie's opinion, should be done through the church–God's people. The church ought to be the distribution center, the clearing house, the Goodwill store, the medical clinic where miracles of healing take place, the elementary school and the university where wisdom is taught. It should be the epicenter for the meeting of all needs, just as in Acts, when the Apostles appointed seven wise men full of the Holy Spirit and faith to administer the distribution of food for the Hebrew and Grecian widows. His thinking was derived from the Apostle Paul's words, "Now all glory to God, who is able, through his mighty power at work within us, to accomplish infinitely more than we might ask or think. Glory to him in the church…."

My mother would sing all the time at home, and she would put a calm in the house. She knew all the words.
~Charlie Smith

42
Hymns, Harmonicas, and Harmony
Worship

The Church of God, Anderson, in which Charlie was raised, is an evangelical group with a strong musical tradition. With just over 2,000 congregations and 250,000 members in the United States, the Church of God is a small group, but its notable musicians of modern times include Sandi Patty, Bill and Gloria Gaither, Doug Oldham, and Steven Curtis Chapman. Even from the pioneering days of this church movement, when Charlie's grandfather first became a Christian, the hymnology was a strong and distinguishing characteristic of its camp meetings and revivals.

Charlie's cousin, Judy Hicks, remembers how much Charlie and the whole Smith family loved music:

My first recollection of the Smith family was in Simpson, Louisiana at my Grandmother Carver's house. I remember that they were a singing family. I remember Charlie stood up and sang, "Old woman, old woman will you do my washing?" and the girls came back and sang, "Speak a little louder, sir, I'm very hard of hearing." That went on for several verses. And then I can remember the girls singing, "Charlie is my darling, my darling, Charlie is my darling."

They were a godly family, with Uncle Frellsen setting the example. And they had devotions every night. Frellsen led the devotions and Marie would play the piano. And when Charlie came to visit us in New Orleans, he would sing at the Lakewood Baptist Church where I attended, and I would play the piano for him. He had a beautiful tenor voice.

I remember one day he hitchhiked to New Orleans. He had his Navy uniform on. Now in those days, Mom and Dad always found things [for us] to do around the house. We had these parquet floors. Mom wanted them waxed. With Charlie there, this was absolutely terrific. We got a Broadman hymnal, as we were Baptist, a rug for our knees, a piece of cloth and a can of wax. And we would wax those floors while we sang those Baptist hymns.

His cousin Sharon McGuire wrote, "I remember two songs that Charles sang in church especially well: "Ye Must Be Born Again" and "Ship Ahoy!" I loved them both...I thought Charles communicated the Gospel very effectively in his singing. He sang like he really believed the words he sang."

While a professor at Warner Southern College, Charlie formed his own singing group with some friends and some students. This group of seven called themselves The Gospel Pioneers. They sang in the churches throughout Florida, and Charlie was the prime mover, getting them excited, organized, and committed for the discipline it took to practice and travel.

Often, Charlie would extend his classroom outside the institutional doors of the college and practically live among the students by teaching them at church, feeding them at his house and singing with them on the weekends. Shari Pugh Mayfield, Florida neighbor and childhood friend of Felicia during those days, remembered Charlie's love for the harmonica:

> I have to admit that Felicia's dad, Charlie, frightened me a bit, but it all changed when he got out his harmonica. He could play that harmonica in such an effortless way and lift everyone literally with his music. He would dance around and stomp like he had the music in him and it couldn't escape fast enough. He sang as well. I remember his deep voice singing, "I load sixteen tons and what do I get? Another day older and-a deeper in debt...St. Peter don't you call me 'cause I can't go...I owe my soul to the company store." Not sure of the words but those are the ones I remember him singing. Those were such good memories.

This love for the harmonica had begun during Charlie's graduate studies at the University of Kentucky. He was lonely, depressed and wondering where life was taking him. He was unsure if the many years of graduate study would be wasted. He was physically exhausted, mentally tired and spiritually drained. Then one day, his loving mother sent him $5 in the mail, and what Charlie did with this money changed his life. In later years it proved to Charlie the power of worship when it flows out of a desperate heart earnestly seeking to reach God. He described this huge spiritual "paradigm shift" in his life while doing both academic and field work on his degree:

> Mother sent me a five-dollar bill so I could go out and get me something to eat. I mean, I had sent my family away to my mother's so I could study. Instead of getting something to eat, I bought myself a harmonica. And I was driving back and forth from Lexington to Taylorsville at 60 miles an hour in my little VW with my elbows resting on the steering wheel, playing my harmonica. Songs began to come out. What songs? Songs of the church. That's the truth, and I believe this is how God got me back to trust Him. Otherwise, I think I could have lost my mind and killed myself. The pressure was so great. I don't think I would have. But this music that was put in me was my salvation.

Because Charlie loved to play Gospel hymns on his harmonica and enjoyed bluegrass music, he was sometimes prejudged as provincial or lacking in urban sophistication, which was far from the truth. He was eclectic in his music and his diversity ranged all the way from Appalachian hoedown music to baroque-era opera. One of the fondest memories from their return trip from their Peace Corps service occurred when he and Karen were spellbound by Leontyne Price in the lead role in Verdi's opera *Aida* performed in Rome's *Teatro dell' Opera*.

As an adult, Charlie loved the hymns of the church, and he believed that congregational singing of hymns was being given a back seat to praise choruses. He felt many worship leaders were seeking to advance their careers using the concert circuit to make money rather than being called to make music that glorified God. He recognized the theological depth of hymnology and lamented that, in his opinion, "Praise choruses have become more important for generating feelings rather than the hymns that teach truth." Charlie sought to revive congregational singing. He believed a singing church was one of the keys to a growing church, and if people would be willing to put their heart into their music and worship, they would be amazed at the power singing produces.

He felt much of the worship on Christian television and in charismatic churches was pretense, hypocritical, because so many pastors and leaders failed to back up their words with their lives. He wrote this caution:

> Performance is the death of spiritual worship....A word to my charismatic brothers and sisters, who when caught up in the spirit, are working mighty hard to convince God to do something for them: quit trying so hard in prayer. How does an apple

ripen? It just sits in the sun. Do not allow non-scriptural emotionalism to destroy worship and praise. Slaying in the spirit is not scriptural. Tongues are for personal edification, not for corporate worship. It is confusing and divides the Body. Unity, unity, unity is our theme.

Charlie was suspicious of the charismatic movement and saw both good and bad in its style of worship. It was good in that a dead church was given renewed spirit, because Charlie believed religion without emotion was dead and he could observe that countless believers had found spiritual meaning in charismatic churches. The downside was that their message focused more on what Jesus could do for the individual rather than how the individual believer lived as a follower of Jesus.

Charlie loved bluegrass hymns, especially instrumentals. He loved barbershop quartets and congregational singing. He loved *a cappella* singing and the unamplified sounds of heartfelt songs in the small village churches of Honduras. He loved to sing out of the old hymnals. He loved the simple strumming of a homemade guitar. For Charlie, congregational singing unified the believers in the sense that individual voices were blended into the whole and the believers were unified through the theology of the lyrics. He felt it was difficult if not impossible to tell the difference between contemporary sacred and secular music.

He doubted that Christian rock or pop music had any lasting value for the church. Possibly this attitude was due to his sensitivity to the eternal things of life, as his death was on the horizon. On the other hand, it might be that Charlie truly loved the simple congregational music that could be sung by simple people with simple instruments or no instruments at all. Thinking of the calming effects of hymns, he wrote:

Turn down or turn off the amplification–the sound system– and let the congregation of God's people sing together in unity the songs of the church. It is far better that the churches sing the hymns that have been passed down through the generations, as well as the new hymns that are being written in this day. And to sing those songs without loud instrumentation for ego-centric leaders who want to be seen as cute and in control rather that facilitating the congregation in her singing of the hymns where no one individual stands out above the others. If the church would return to congregational singing in the Spirit, she would be revived and unbelievers would be attracted to the music.

244

The kind of spiritual ecstasy in worship that Charlie favored – soft, slow and simple–was illustrated in a letter dated September 29, 1989 to his sister Marie following a Wednesday evening service at the South Lake Wales Church:

Last night, I had seven brothers and sisters read Scripture, which was interspersed with singing. My instructions to the readers: read with feeling, slowly. My instructions to the music leaders: soft on the piano...very soft to no instrument. Do not wave your arms. Focus on the words, the music and the singing in the spirit. It was wonderful!

The Ambassadors making music on the Martha House porch
Photo by Charlie, his pillow-padded chair in foreground

Late one night, Charlie stopped by Simeon's small house, at that time the meeting place of the Prince of Peace church in Canchias, Honduras. Simeon was the village patriarch and a member of the worship team Charlie had dubbed The Ambassadors. When Charlie heard The Ambassadors play on their homemade instruments, he was transported back to the days of his singing group The Gospel Pioneers.

I learned that this group is a wonderful treasure for the ministry of Heart to Honduras. When I played some of the old songs of the church on my mouth harp, they jumped right in and made me sound good. It was a wonderful time together. It reminded me of the bluegrass gospel band we had at Warner Southern....This group has got something very special–a

245

genuine, down to earth, honest presentation of music from the soul.

That was something Charlie valued highly. So it was a sad day for Charlie when the government began to bring in the naked pines that provided support for the tentacles of electrical lines that branched off like spider webs into the rural mountain villages. These lines attached themselves to houses, huts, hamlets and houses of worship. Tattered JBL and Peavey speakers imported from the United States were connected to steel guitars, and the sounds of the simple string guitar faded into the background. This loud, raw, screeching sound was as decadent as the devil himself for Charlie. He dreaded the day when those electrical lines would connect to Canchias.[44]

When North American teams came to Honduras, he insisted they have morning and evening devotions with a time of singing, reading of the Word, sharing and prayer. Along with the orientation manual, Charlie printed a 25-page worship manual he referred to as "The Sayings of Jesus." It included hymns, prophetic writings and numerous psalms. This worship manual was passed out for corporate worship. In the early years, the devotional times took place around the large table in the dining area in San Isidro. After the Canchias campus was developed, groups would gather on the porch of the Martha House, Charlie's residence whenever he was in Honduras. On their evaluation forms, team members frequently mentioned that these overflow times of sharing by candlelight, often with a spirit of brokenness and tears, were their most memorable experiences in Honduras.

Charlie's diary from the spring of 1997 mentioned this devotional time with a team from Punxsutawney, Pennsylvania:

The singing was good as we sang and praised the Lord. It always helps when groups can sing. Singing is so good for the soul and the spirit. Songs unify the body and put everyone on the same topic. There is wonderful teaching in the songs of the church.

Charlie was open to the Spirit's leading from other forms of worship, but struggled with extreme attempts that surfaced out of human emotion and effort. His theology of worship was like a four-legged stool—teaching of the Word, soft instrumental music, singing of hymns and stillness before the Lord.

---

[44]The church was provided electricity through the ministry's hydroelectric system in 1993, but as of 2013, there was still no public electricity in Canchias.

In the beginning was the Word
and the Word was with God
and the Word was God.
~John 1:1 KJV

43
Life's Frame
The Word of God

When Charlie's life on earth was drawing to a close, he wrote with a determined pace at his cabin retreat in the village of Canchias. He reached deep into his spirit and mind to bring all the loose academic, experiential, social, religious and anthropological threads of his life together into one theological motif. It would be a triangular canvas with three theological concepts in what he referred to as *The Mother of All Frameworks*. This framework would provide answers to the fundamental questions about life. It would be simple and easy to understand. It would be broad. It would be complete. It would address every need spiritually and physically, and hold the basic concepts that would provide meaning, passion, truth, joy and purpose for life.

In a telephone conversation with his sister-in-law Kathy Smith, Charlie said: "We need to have a framework on that which addresses the broader issues of life. When I share with others, I paint with broad strokes, filling the canvas with the story of creation and God's means to reconcile all things back to Himself and how he pulled it off." He also informed Kathy that for anything to make sense, it had to fit within a framework that answers all the essential questions about life from the beginning to the end.

For many years, Charlie had dreamed of putting these thoughts in a book. Now was the time. He felt he only had a short time to compress all his knowledge into a concise, succinct document in hopes that others might read or publish it in the future. He began to recall profound thoughts, embedded ideas, insightful theories, unforgettable memories and simple truths.

Charlie believed that all of life could find purpose and meaning in three eternal truths: 1) in the beginning was the Word, 2) the Word became flesh, and 3) the Word of God is eternal.

IN THE BEGINNING WAS THE WORD

About the first frame, *In the beginning was The Word (Jesus),* Charlie wrote, "The written, spoken and lived Word is humankind's most powerful possession. Without the Word we would live not differently than the great apes, the orangutans or the chimpanzee." He believed people should value words and The Word. His understanding of the nature of God was derived from his anthropological training. Anthropology teaches that symbols are necessary in the process of creating words, which in turn allow people to formulate concepts and communicate their meaning to others in understandable ways. He saw intelligent design in God's craftsmanship of man by the use of symbols as contrasted with the use of signs and sounds in the animal kingdom. Words constructed out of symbols are powerful because they introduce humankind to The Word (Jesus).

He wrote, "The creator empowered humankind with the mind and the ability to symbolize, which enables me to write these words…in such a way that you will understand the message and perhaps use it to your own advantage for higher purposes." He suggested that words lead to The Word, which is the higher purpose. Words are good, but The Word is greater, for it leads to the eternal.

THE WORD BECAME FLESH

The second frame was *The Word became flesh.* Charlie believed this was made possible through the message and life of Jesus, the relationships and missionary journeys of the early disciples and by defending the poor. This could only happen when "…the Word became flesh and blood and moved into the neighborhood." (John 1:14 MSG) He believed it had to happen in the neighborhood at ground level so that the Gospel could be preached, the church birthed, relationships embraced and the poor defended. This is why *The Word* had to leave His heavenly kingdom and enter the neighborhood as a man. Charlie practiced this truth by identifying himself with the poorest of the poor as he chose to live among them. Later he took this truth a step further by dying among them.

THE WORD STANDS FOREVER

The third frame was *The Word stands forever.* Charlie believed that the Word is eternal. There is no time or space with God. There is no beginning or end with God. The Word spoke and things came into existence. Charlie wrote, "It matters not how this was done, for this we can never understand, nor does it matter how long it took, since time is a human-created concept. There is no time with The Word. The Scriptures state that a day is as a thousand years, yet even this view is limited. There is no beginning and there will be no end."

The Word spoke, and the sun, moon and stars appeared. Creation ideas such as the Big Bang theory of how the universe came into existence did not concern Charlie. It may have happened that way, but however it happened, Charlie believed all things created that lived, moved and had their being came from the eternal, spoken Word of God. It was simple for him. He never went looking for the "God particle" [45] that so many scientists say is the missing link to understanding the universe. He continued, "For reasons known only to The Word, out of the infinite universe, The Word created a world, a planet, and gave it an environment compatible with life, and gave that world living things: plants, insects, animals on land and sea, birds in the air, mammals, primates, and human beings, male and female."

Charlie believed that the creative power of The Word that brought all things into existence was comparable to the physical healing of the body through its natural process. Creating through the spoken Word was as natural to God as the healing of a wound was for the human body. Charlie wrote:

> We cannot comprehend a God so powerful that The Word can be spoken and things come into being, they are created. I do know that the creation is incredibly intricate and complex. This last week I scraped my arm and with my fragile skin, about a one-inch piece of skin was lifted off my arm. [Doctor] Elsa began to come every day to change the bandages, first cleaning the wound and then applying antibiotic ointment and a bandage. I watched the sore every day as she changed the bandage, and observed marvelous things taking place. Finally, after about seven or eight days, a large piece of protective crust shaped like a honeycomb biscuit fell off and I had new skin–beautiful, pink, new skin. What a miracle of healing.

The secret of Charlie's final framework can be found in his great love for the living Word, the spoken Word and the written Word. He marinated himself in the Scriptures. The Bible was to him as Mao Zedong's *Little Red Book* was to the Communist Party. But it was the red-letter Words of Jesus[46] that arrested Charlie's attention and captured his heart.

---

[45] The Higgs boson, a sub-atomic particle nicknamed "The God Particle," was the focus of a successful 40-year quest by an international team of scientists using the 17-mile-long Large Hadron Collider in Geneva, Switzerland.

[46] Some versions of the Bible print the words of Jesus in red letters.

Charlie's daughter Anne-Marie gives a unique perspective on Charlie's love for the Scriptures:

Oh, for [my dad's side of the] family, Christ was the center of all things–always. It was there that Dad came to love the Bible. We would study the Luke story, and I guess you know that Luke was Dad's favorite book of the Bible. Well, at least it was his favorite of the four gospels. Dad was always in the Bible. I used his Bible for my message at his funeral. His Bible was a workbook. He never understood thin pages trimmed in gold. You are supposed to use that Bible–the thicker the pages, the better. Thickness prevented ink from bleeding through so that you could mark it up. He was offended by thin pages with gold trim. For him this was just senseless. Why would a Bible be trimmed in gold? That showed riches. Dad was so practical. He was always in it and he quoted Scriptures. He memorized Scriptures all the time. He knew the Bible backwards and forwards. Felicia has his Bible and the spine is broken. The pages are coming out. It is all underlined and marked up. He used it and knew it.

Charlie's older daughter, Felicia SmithGraybeal, now an Episcopal priest, commented on her dad's love for the Word:

It was huge. I think his two passions–for the Scriptures and for the marginalized–impressed me the most. He knew how to communicate with the people. This inspired my preaching. He was down to earth. He did not engage in fault finding. He had a good education. Often I saw him reading his Bible. I would attend his Bible studies. Even though he was my father, it was not boring. He made it come alive.

Charlie searches in his tattered Bible

Charlie even used his love for the book of Luke to improve his skill at speaking Spanish. "I sat on the porch this

250

morning and read the first four chapters of Luke aloud in Spanish," he told me in the spring of 1997. "I want to be able to read it with great clarity and with meaning."

Staff member Monty Harrington recalls the many times he would enter Charlie's study and see him pondering over the Word of God: "Charlie had a great love for the Scriptures. He would make you stop so he could share his reading with you. He would almost have tears in His eyes going over certain Scriptures. He would say to people, 'Here is the Word of the God of Abraham, Isaac and Jacob,' and that always stuck with me."

Charlie was so passionate about Scriptures that often he would lose his awareness of other important things around him. One time he was driving and was stopped by a policeman. His daughter Anne-Marie recalls the incident:

> Daddy was quoting Scriptures and I am sure his hands were up in the air and he was getting into the Scriptures with everything he had. He got pulled over and got a speeding ticket. He tried to use the quoting Scripture thing as an excuse and it did not work.

Charlie had a real problem with preachers manipulating the Word of God for their own self interest. Modern-day preachers were making God's Word complex and confusing, he said. It needed to be down to earth like the teachings of Jesus who spoke in the vernacular of the people, using words like bread, water, love and light, or if in Honduras, *pan, agua, amor* and *luz*. He wrote, "Preachers or pastors rarely teach the Word, pure and simple. Rather, they preach words that tickle the ears of the hearers, what the hearers want to hear, such as the false teaching that Christians will be healthy and wealthy. Love not the world, seek His Kingdom. You do not need 10 steps to prosperity. You need only to seek His Kingdom."

As the ministry of Heart to Honduras began to grow and more and more facilities were necessary, Charlie envisioned an effective

Cornelius House with nameplate on porch

251

means to keep the Word before the people. He began to name these facilities with Biblical names such as Joshua, Tabitha, Martha, Maria, and Cornelius. Charlie shared his "Theology of Names" as follows, "We have come to the conclusion that giving Biblical/spiritual names to houses is probably a good practice–it keeps us in the Word. Each house should have a small plaque telling about the person after whom the house was named." Charlie named his own retreat house the "Martha House" to communicate the importance of fellowship around food. Naming one house "Mary" communicated the need for prayer. Naming another house "Joshua" conveyed a pioneering spirit and naming a house "Cornelius" communicated equality.

Putting into practice the commands and teachings of Jesus was one of the cardinal tenets of Charlie's faith. He was encouraged one day when he saw a couple from Pennsylvania walking down the road to Karen's Hope to visit the handicapped children being cared for there. This couple, for Charlie, was a living letter, as the Apostle Paul referred to in the New Testament, walking as The Word to put into practice the teachings of Jesus. His diary records his observation of this couple: "Perhaps they are taking Lillian and Heydi to the river for a dip in the cool water. It is obvious that they are going to put into practice one of the commands of Jesus, to attend to the needs of the least of these. That is what the Discipleship Center is supposed to be all about. Learning the commands of Jesus and putting them into practice in daily life."

There were rare occasions when Charlie had time to be alone. Charlie *was* Heart to Honduras. He was needed. Thus he was always surrounded by Miguel, the staff, the workers and the poor. But on those rare occasions when the village of Canchias stood still, Charlie would slip away to spend time in the Word. "It is now about 7:30 p.m. I sat out on the porch most of the day, reading the Word from the Ambassador Hand Book. The selected passages touched my heart many times, several to the point of my being broken, knowing that our God cares for us, loves us, and is there to help us through any and every situation...."

Scott Crews, a close friend of the family, recorded in his journal after dinner with Charlie: "Charlie and I finished reading the book of Luke and started the book of Acts. He told me these two books are the best ones to start with when studying the Word. They lay the whole story out. Luke tells about the life of Christ from his birth to His resurrection. Acts explains the beginning of the organized church."

On his desk in Florida, Charlie kept many different versions of the Bible at his fingertips. He always took God's Word with him to Honduras. Most of his visions were Word-based. With less than 10 days to live, he brought his staff to his bedside and shared two priorities with us: "There are two things I want you to continue after I am gone. I want you to teach all the commands of Jesus and feed the poor." The Words of Jesus served as Charlie's manifesto to engage the hearts and minds of the people to be about the Father's business.

Charlie became so intimate with Jesus that he began referring to Jesus as "The Word." One can note in Charlie's journals that the reality of Jesus as best friend, confidant and lover, was expressed in how he increasingly addressed his Lord as "The Word" as he approached his exit from his deteriorating body. Reflecting on his impending physical death, Charlie mused, "...and if The Word calls me home...." He understood this as correct theology based on what the Apostle John wrote in the fourth Gospel: "In the beginning was the Word and the Word was with God and the Word was God. The same was in the beginning with God."

Contemplating his future and reflecting back on his life, Charlie wrote, "I am thankful to The Word who was in the beginning for giving me life and purpose for living." Thinking about the first events to be held in the new Discipleship Center, he wrote, "I want the best video possible of all of the events surrounding the opening ceremony/dedication of the Discipleship Center, the first banquets with the poor, and my Home Going Celebration, should it not be in The Word's plan to heal me of this infirmity."

Charlie's concepts for the *Mother of all Frameworks* did not occur overnight. They developed starting the moment he met his mission-minded wife Karen. They were stretched when he joined the Peace Corps. They were questioned when he was a PhD candidate at the University of Kentucky. They were surrendered when Karen died. They were refined when he contracted a serious illness. And they were completed the last year of his life, when he realized God was calling him home. He wrote:

> I came across this note in my files: My life has been characterized by intensity, by a solid sense of purpose, meaning and motivation. I have been driven by a search for Truth and the living of the Truth. As I searched, I found my understanding deepened over time. I am so different than I was 20 years ago, but that same voice has been behind me saying, "This is the way, walk in it." And I have taken that path with few diversions.

Charlie lived out this truth by walking this path with integrity. That path was framed with three planks to give it purpose and meaning. They were labeled:

In the beginning was The Word
The Word became flesh
The Word is eternal

253

Dad was a friend of the underdog.
He was always the champion of the underdog.
It was something Jesus would do.
~Anne-Marie Smith Dezelan

44
Friend of the Underdog
Compassion

Charlie ate with the poor, took coffee with the handicapped, slept next to the oppressed, cried over the rejected, and loved the unlovely. True, he was a member of a state champion high school basketball team. He did woo and win the "most gorgeous woman I ever laid eyes on." His goal was definitely to make Father's Place the best restaurant in town. He set out to take the best black-and-white photographs he possibly could. But being "top dog" was not something that characterized his life.

For the most part, Charlie was a humble person who made a decision early in his life that he would identify himself with the plight of the poor. Charlie took literally Christ's admonition: "When you host a banquet in your home, invite the poor, the crippled, the lame, the blind, and you will be blessed…"

One thinks of Charlie as associating with the underdog, even at times BEING the underdog–those considered to be on the fringes of society, marginalized by institutions, used until their usefulness has run its course, lacking authority, and even homeless.

Charlie's compassion eventually led him to the loser, the boxed in, the hurting, the insolvent, the injured, and the broken. It was not that he did not care for the wealthy; he cared for all people. He would be the first to admit that if it had not been for a few family and friends with deep pockets, some of his visions would never have gotten off the launching pad. But he was never awed by the opulent lifestyle of the rich and famous. His compassion led him—not upward, but downward–to the underdog.

Charlie's compassion was birthed as he observed his father visiting folks on the other side of the tracks on Saturdays to invite the poor to church. Riding with his dad in the front seat of his Ford sensitized Charlie's heart. He began to connect with the excluded, seeing in them not only the *imago Dei* but the worth of that image of God in all of humankind. He once described the impact of his

254

mother's love for the hurting, "At 86, she still visits the sick and the lonely...Mother taught us how to care for children and how to love all peoples, regardless of our differences. She did not see color of skin or nationality as having any relevance to the character of a person."

His close friend Wiley Hilburn said of his warm love: "We all felt so comfortable around him. If you were sitting in the back seat with Charlie ... it just made you feel good.... He was just a good shoulder to cry on."

The most visible example in high school of Charlie's acceptance of all persons was his friendship with Robert Barham, who was crippled by polio. In the Peace Corps, he befriended the man who emptied the honey bucket. He fought for the underdog in a wider way as director of the Community Action Center in Ruston, defending blacks against elements of the KKK and a system of racial injustice. He was the defender of the underdog against the Army Corps of Engineers when they proposed relocating poor farmers from the valley of the Salt River.

Sitting in his office on the Warner Southern campus, Dr. Malcolm Rigel, former professor of counseling and psychology (1968-1975) and pastor of the South Lake Wales Church, fondly recalled:

> On the Warner Southern campus Charlie was just a good old country boy.... Culturally, he was out of it except for an identity with people who were out of it.... In psychology the underdog always wins. He has to do it in a subtle way but he always wins. When we take the underdog role we strip the overdog of his instruments of warfare. You take the Jesus road. That is the road that Charlie took. The underdog takes away the top dogs' attack weapons and they can't touch him. Jesus was the underdog to religion, politics and culture.
>
> The fact that Charlie refused to accept the finest medical facilities in the States [during his final illness] and leave his two daughters and family and separate himself totally from his roots, he took the underdog position, the underdog role and willingly gave up. ...The world is full of overdogs. Enron failed. Saddam Hussein failed. You do not have to fight them. They will fall on their own. Just read the Psalms, the prophets and the Old Testament. They will tell you that the overdogs are going to crumble.

This "good old country boy" image Charlie projected at Warner Southern College enabled him to connect to hundreds of students and underdogs who

255

walked the campus and city of Lake Wales. He was a man on a mission. His mission was to be himself and connect with real people.

Anne-Marie recalled several incidences when she observed her father ministering compassion to those that others ignored:

> There was this man we called Sneaks. He was a man who was real thin. He wore Converse high-tops on his feet and that is why we called him Sneaks. We would see him at the grocery store. He was always buying cat food. We believed that was what he ate, because he was always buying it. He would ride his bike around town and on the highway. I remember one day when Dad and I were driving down Highway 60. Dad saw him and right then and there he made a U-turn and went back and gave him twenty bucks.
>
> And there was also the little Mexican man who sat out front of the post office with a sandwich board with Scriptures. Dad would always stop and talk with him. Dad would talk with anybody, especially anybody that people ignored.

Then there was Richard–the guy with some sort of mental disability who would walk around the grocery store and say, "Hello! Nice day, isn't it? Think it might rain?" Charlie would patiently listen to Richard say the same things over and over. Charlie would call his name and treat him as a person. Richard would look at him and Charlie would hug him. Others would avoid him, just like the priest and the Levite ignored the Jewish traveler who was beaten and robbed in the parable of the Good Samaritan. Charlie would shake Richard's hand, demonstrating that he valued and respected him.

Charlie believed the church also bypassed the "Sneaks" and the "Richards." He felt the church was full of super-righteous priests and Levites, but short on Good Samaritans. He wanted to bridge the gap. Anita Bradley, who began a long term as church secretary at South Lake Wales Church of God in 1983, remembered that he was "a very caring person," opening the old church building as a place for homeless migrants to spend the night when the Florida nights turned cold, modeling how the church should serve the underdogs. However, the congregation was not always fully behind him. Anne-Marie shared:

> There is another instance that I will never forget, when the hierarchy of the church talked it but they did not live it. This was when Dad was on the staff at the South Lake Wales Church of God. A Mexican family...ran out of gas on Highway 27.... A church service was going on and they needed help.

Dad [was] on the platform. He took a love offering for them. And that to me is what Christ would do. And it is what the church should do. They had a specific need. It was not like a repeat family that goes from church to church trying to scam you. And Dad just got ridiculed by the church leadership for taking that offering. They said, "How could you do that?" This happened to Dad all the time. He would do something for someone, and those in authority would object because he wasn't following their protocol. That was where he was being seen as such a rebel when that to me is just what you do. This is what Jesus would do.

As Mark Shaner, then the youth pastor, remembers the incident, one of those who thought it was a scam went so far as to follow the family for 30 miles, surprised to find that they did not stop at any other churches. The family later sent a sweet thank-you note.

Charlie would also refuse to buy certain vegetables and fruits at Publix grocery store, because on the return trip back to his house on Highway 27 was a black man with a fruit stand. Charlie would stop and purchase watermelons, tomatoes and cantaloupes from him, regardless of the price. In Charlie's eyes, this man was his brother, a prince in the Kingdom created in the image of God.

In Lake Wales, Charlie showed compassion and true love to Mike, Jim and Max, the three homosexual men who lived next door. In a time when most Christians were shunning all contact with gay people and the world was still sorting out the dangers of being around someone with AIDS, Charlie, Karen and Anne-Marie visited Max when he was dying. Because Charlie had befriended these men, he earned the right to ask Max if he was ready to meet God, and to pray with him when he said he wasn't ready, but he wanted to be. And when Max died, his mother and Mike and Jim invited Charlie to speak at the funeral, where he shared words of life with those in attendance, an audience perhaps full of underdogs.

When he guided the founding of Karen's Hope to care for the severely

Crucito and Heydi, residents at Karen's Hope, a facility in Canchias for handicapped children

handicapped, and thus underdogs, of Honduras, he was following this calling to reach out to those whom others rejected. Heydi, Lillian and Crucito were benefactors of his compassionate nature.

This love for the underdog was noticed by his daughter Felicia in her own life. On February 1, 1995, she wrote Charlie a note:

> Have I told you lately that I truly love you? You are precious to me. You model behavior I desire and long to emulate. You support the underdog, give people opportunities, forgive wrongdoings and encourage people's directions. You not only do this for those you love but also for those you don't even know. You accepted me back after I did not honor your counsel and continue to make me feel just as loved as always and just as loved as Anne-Marie. In my own life, I cannot fathom forgiving someone who I feel has wronged me so blatantly. Thank you for accepting me as I have sinned and continue to do so. You are my earthly father and model. My heavenly Father and I love you very much. Your # 1, Felicia.

Compassion was a mark of Charlie's life until the end. The deep compassion he felt for others was recorded by Scott Crews in his journal during his September 1997 visit to Charlie in Canchias:

> I heard the FAX machine turn on, meaning there was a message coming in from the States. A few moments went by before I heard a sound like I had never heard before. It was a moan coming from Charlie. At first I thought he had read a joke in the letter. When I opened his curtain, I saw he was crying. I had seen him cry many times in the years that I had known him, but never like this. I thought, *What could he have read that would make him react like this?* He then told me the terrible news that [his friend's son] had died due to a bad reaction to his treatment for cancer...Charlie loved everyone...He had a meaningful connection with everyone he met, from the most simple to the most complex and difficult.

Charlie's love for the weak and the oppressed came naturally for him, because his parents consistently modeled compassion before him. From the time he was a little boy until he left home for the Navy, the Smith household on a regular basis opened their home to lonely Tech students, the poor of Ruston, and

258

needy families of their church community. For many a Sunday dinner, these needy people became a part of the extended Smith family.

Charlie witnessed these strange faces, sat next to them and listened to their life stories over and over again. He surmised that they were part of the universal family of God and on equal status as his parents and siblings regardless of their cultural, racial and socio-economic differences. It impacted him greatly. And later, when he met Karen, her exemplary life redirected him to the things of God, especially to the teachings of Jesus. These teachings became the centerpiece of his personal value system, leading Charlie "downward" to the poor, not "upward" to the clever and powerful. An overdog lifestyle was his for the choosing, but he opted for the role that his great Teacher lived out on earth. This courageous, counter-culture decision by Charlie not only impacted Charlie's life for the good, but thousands of others' lives as well.

In many circles, Santa is more believed than Jesus.
~Charlie Smith

45

Room for One More

Christmas

The way Christmas is celebrated bothered Charlie. Even the way the church celebrates Christmas disturbed him. He was saddened that December 25 was designated as the birthday of Jesus, but when it came time to dispense the gifts, rarely was the Name of the Christ Child called out. Recalling an early awakening to this idea, he wrote about an algebra teacher who captured the imagination of his students by sending them throughout the parking lot of the school and the neighborhood putting bumper stickers on cars with the words, "Put Christ Back into Christmas."

But as an adult, Christ became so central to Charlie that he went beyond that slogan and similar catchphrases and advocated keeping Christ in every day of the whole year. Concerned that the true meaning of Christmas was being commercialized out of the manger, he often expressed his dismay over how the spirit of *getting* had eclipsed the spirit of *giving,* even in the church. As he matured in his Christian faith, he became so passionate about it, that most everything he did was through the true spirit of Christmas, which was giving. He once made the statement that he did not believe in tithing 10 percent to the church. When he pondered the cross, Charlie did not see Jesus giving just 10 percent. His giving philosophy was, "We need to give 100 percent."

He was bothered by holiday commercials that began their enticements long before Americans had finished digesting their Thanksgiving turkey. It depressed him to see people loading shopping bags and carts with superfluous gifts when a billion people live on a dollar a day. He couldn't bear seeing gifts purchased out of obligation rather than out of love. He was saddened that once Christmas was over, the giving stopped. For Charlie, the spirit of Christmas was eternal—you celebrate it July 25 and October 25 just as you do December 25. This is one reason the Smith family left their brightly colored Christmas lights, which they called party lights, lit all year 'round on the patio. The Spirit of Christmas was an unceasing adventure of giving.

Regarding the date of Christmas, Charlie had reservations. He knew that not even Biblical scholars had been able to figure out the exact date when Jesus was born. He recognized that some credited Pope Julius I with choosing December 25 as the date to celebrate Christ's birth to appease pagan religions, and Charlie felt that the current celebrations of the holiday were pagan in that the emphasis had gone from Christ to cash registers.

We Christians give assent to this pagan holiday, and even teach our children to participate in the rituals. Why don't we believers put a stop to it? Why don't we Christians withdraw from this pagan celebration and let the world know we don't want any part of it? It is our holiday, and the world has taken something good and made it into something evil. Jesus would drive the money changers out of the Christmas tradition. Shouldn't we do the same and start a new tradition around the birth of Christ?

During his trip to Spain over the 1994 Christmas holidays with his daughters, he saw something he liked. Though he was upset by the touristy atmosphere of the cathedral in Seville, he felt the Spaniards had chosen a better practice for exchanging gifts. They exchange gifts on January 6–Epiphany–the day that commemorates the Wise Men's bearing of gifts to the Christ Child. He observed all the children coming not to the lap of Santa, but to the lap of one of the Wise Men. This seemed more genuine to him than what is done in the States.

As a boy, Charlie anticipated special gifts like any normal child at Christmas time. He received those gifts with delight. But he had a unique spirit of giving that went beyond the holiday that would be characteristic of him throughout life. His twin sister Marie cited the gracious attitude Charlie displayed when he gave her not only forgiveness, but something beyond that:

When I was 16, I asked Charles if I could use his car. It was a 1921 with a stick shift. He had paid $125 for it. I was not a good driver. I pulled out in front of this truck, and it hit us broadside. Our family doctor came along just after it happened and picked [Lorna and me] up, put us in his car and took us to the hospital. He said we were just fine. Anyway, our hair and blood were on the ceiling of the car. I had this turquoise ring Daddy or Mother had bought me while we were in Colorado that summer. It was so smashed up, they had to cut it off my finger. Charles bought me another one. Not only did I wreck his car, but he bought me another ring. And I have had that ring since I was 16.

His gifts were not always material. Some of the best gifts Charlie gave were just thoughtful and practical ways of giving to others: playing a song on his harmonica, cutting onions and slicing carrots for a special meal, or making a guest feel at home on his little porch in Honduras or in his office in Florida. Staff member Dave Pischel recalls the number of times he went into Charlie's large downstairs bedroom, which doubled as his office, and interrupted him. According to Dave, Charlie always stopped his desk work to give him–or any visitor–his undivided attention. "I never remember going into his office when he did not put his work aside, roll back his chair, look at me and be receptive to me. I always felt welcomed. Never did he say, 'Well, Dave, I have a lot of work today and I need to get back to it.' He was very relational." This gift of time was a frequent gift to the many who desired to be in his presence.

This generosity of self was instilled in Charlie by his parents, and one particular example which was recorded by his sister Lorna in an essay titled "Room for One More" illustrates the Smiths' point of view on sharing. With a house crammed to overflowing with children, in-laws, and grandchildren, Frellsen and Myrtle came home from a brief grocery run with more than a bottle of milk. They had spotted Shon Li Fong, an international engineering student, huddled lonely and sad in the rain, and had invited him into the warmth of the family's Christmas dinner. Even a house full of family was no excuse for not reaching out in this season, or any other. There was always room for one more at their table.

In 1997, Charlie's daughter Felicia expressed her grief over his impending death–including how it would change the holidays to come. She was remembering wonderful holidays in Ruston, like the night Shon Li Fong had joined the family for dinner. Charlie later sent her his thoughts on traditions:

The answer is really quite simple: begin building your own traditions based on memories that will stay with you and yours forever. Look at it as having a wonderful opportunity to be creative, drawing friends and family to you in memory-building activities. As we all know, it will never be the same again. The past is over, the memories are stored in our memory banks to draw from throughout our lives, and you make memories to go into that bank throughout the rest of your life. Life is continually unfolding into the future, and you cannot go back in time except through memories. You know that I would dearly love to be with you for the next 20 or so years, building memories with you, and that may happen. But if it does not, then you will go on into your own future with the memories of me and your precious mother.

Learning well from parents who demonstrated the true spirit of giving that Christmas epitomizes, Charlie carried on their tradition of finding ways to put Christ in every day, giving generously to those around him, and exhorting everyone to eschew the giving of "expected" gifts for the glorious blessing of giving year-round to those who expect it the least.

When you come, bring the cloak that I left with Carpus at Troas,
and my scrolls, especially the parchments.
~Paul in II Timothy 4:13 NIV

46
Friends on the Shelf
Books

The books on a person's bookshelves give a glimpse of their interests and personality. Evangelist Oswald Chambers expressed great emotion about his books: "My box has at last arrived. My books! I cannot tell you what they are to me—silent, wealthy, loyal lovers. To look at them, to handle them, and to re-read them! I do thank God for my books with every fibre of my being. Friends that are ever true and ever your own." Though Charlie may not have expressed this level of enthusiasm about his books, he did love them, purchasing and reading thousands over the years. And Charlie's books indicated a serious demeanor, even a somber temperament, that contrasted with his fun-loving personality.

Two books Charlie referred to often were *Small Is Beautiful: Economics as if People Mattered*, by British economist E.F. Schumacher, and *The Life of the Beloved*, by Henri Nouwen. Schumacher derided the notion that "big is better" and "growth is good." The author was prophetic as he denounced the unlimited use of fossil fuels, those non-renewable natural resources. Charlie was deeply influenced by this book and applied its principles in his H.E.A.R.T. and Heart to Honduras visions. In *The Life of the Beloved*, the seeking individual is taken, blessed, broken and given by Christ to bring about healing.

Charlie also enjoyed works by Tolstoy. He knew how it felt to be snubbed by formal church institutions and he found a kindred spirit in Tolstoy's rejection of the ritual trappings and traditions of the Russian Orthodox Church. Tolstoy's renunciation of his publishing rights to such acclaimed writings as *War and Peace, Anna Karenina* and *The Resurrection,* and his desire to give all royalties to the peasants, played a powerful role in formulating Charlie's value system.

I was sitting next to Charlie as he lay in bed in the Martha House. Observing his meager possessions, I noticed his blue jeans, Honduran T-shirt, shower shoes, Bible, pens, and toiletries. Then my eyes scanned Charlie's bookshelf. The books he had brought to Honduras on this last trip were like old friends to him. Surprisingly, there were no books in the field of anthropology. The eight books there were written with eternity in mind. *God's Order, Halley's Bible Handbook, Unto the Last, The Inner Voice of Love, Christ and History, The Christ of the Indian Way, The Cloud of the Unknowing*, and his personal Bible. These friends on Charlie's shelf tell us much about him in the final days of his life.

God's Order was given to Charlie by his father. Perhaps this was chosen because Charlie wanted Frellsen's presence near him in his last days.

Halley's Bible Handbook by Henry Halley and George Buttrick's *Christ and History* would fill Charlie's need for historical facts in his final writings about the church. Charlie loved church history and cherished the many copies of *Church History* magazine that his dad gave him.

Unto the Last by John Ruskin influenced Gandhi's social and economic theories. From Ruskin's ideas, Gandhi began paying the same salary to all men regardless of function, race or nationality. Charlie had a bent toward this economic concept, and believed the poorest of the poor should be treated as well as the richest of the rich.

David Crippen, fellow WSC professor and director of Thailand ministries for Project Global Village, had introduced Charlie to Henri Nouwen, a priest in the Catholic Church who taught at Harvard and Yale. Nouwen spent his final days as a pastor at *L'Arche* (Daybreak) in Canada near Toronto, working with children with developmental disabilities. In *The Inner Voice of Love*, Nouwen explores the nature of holding, lifting and drinking the cup of life. Holding the cup is savoring its sorrows and joys. Lifting the cup is reflecting on one's life, even as one offers it to others. Drinking the cup means intimacy and celebration, salvation and finally death–emptying the cup. This book brought Charlie comfort as he was drinking from the cup of suffering.

Christ of the Indian Road by E. Stanley Jones emphasizes deep spirituality and that wherever we are, in India, in the United States, or in Honduras, we are to share Christ in a personal way. But the book's main motif was that in sharing Christ with both the Brahmins and Dalits [Untouchables], Jesus Christ could be accepted without embracing Western civilization and its culture. Charlie also desired to contextualize the Christian faith in the Honduran culture without forcing the "American Dream" upon them.

The Cloud of the Unknowing is by an anonymous English monk who seeks to teach a student that the way to God is not through knowledge or reason but through love. This book was written around 1375 as a primer for freshmen monastics, encouraging them to "hide their thoughts beneath the *Cloud of Forgetting*" and pierce God's heart with love beneath the *Cloud of the Unknowing*.

Out of thousands of books Charlie read over the years, he chose these to be with him in his final days. They mentored him. They assured him. They encouraged him. They were his friends on the shelf.

265

The trees are God's great alphabet:
with them He writes in shining green
across the world his thoughts serene.
~Lenora Speyer

47
Two Trees
Nature as Nurture

Charlie's bedroom window (left) in the Martha House

One has to visit Canchias and stand on the porch of the Martha House to understand why Charlie found so much peace for his soul in that place. During the rainy season, a person can sit on that porch and count 11 shades of green on the mountainside beyond the Canchias River. At night, the sounds of katydids, tree frogs, birds and crickets harmonize in symphonic agreement. This is what attracted Charlie time and time again to seek refuge from a culture motivated by greed, speed and feed.

During the late night, many of his creative thoughts would come to him. And now, in the final season of his life, Charlie was putting the finishing touches on the canvas of his vision as he typed away in his mountain cabin with the nocturnal sounds as his companions.

Darkness was his friend, as Simon and Garfunkel called it in *The Sounds of Silence*:

Hello darkness, my old friend
I've come to talk with you again

266

Because a vision softly creeping
left its seeds while I was sleeping
And the vision that was planted in my brain
still remains, within the sound of silence

One afternoon, as he lay ill upon his bed, Charlie's attention was drawn to a tree outside his window. He saw God's creative love in this tree. He saw beauty and purpose. But something was wrong. Charlie was disturbed because he noticed the tree was growing in the midst of weeds. He felt that God had provided this tree for him, and those weeds were a hindrance to his enjoyment of its beauty. Charlie asked the workers to cut the weeds so he could freely enjoy the beauty of the tree.

Charlie was more of a naturalist than a materialist. He had a simple appreciation, much like his wife Karen who loved roses, for the natural beauty of all of God's creation. Money meant little to Charlie, but he loved to sit beneath a full moon. Treasury notes meant little to Charlie, but trees were valuable to him. Power meant little to Charlie, but a patio laced with palm trees and plants brought him great pleasure.

This tree outside Charlie's window reminded him of the time when he and I drove to Taylorsville, Kentucky to reclaim a large bell he had left with a mountain homesteader. He had acquired this bell while living in his house in Rivals, Kentucky. After founding Heart to Honduras, he decided he wanted to use this bell in the village of Canchias. He wanted to hang it outside the Assembly Hall to call all the workers to communal meals from their fields or for village-wide fiestas.

After loading the bell in the car, at the request of Anne-Marie, we visited Elsie–her beloved babysitter who always kept a supply of orange marshmallow circus peanuts. Charlie knocked on the door of a badly battered little house with a rotting porch, broken windows and a tattered roof. No one answered. In town, he learned that she was in the local nursing home, and we went to seek her there.

As we walked down the hall, we came to a room with the door slightly open. There was Elsie, 90 years old, lying on her back facing a window. Charlie rested himself on the side of her bed and spoke softly to her. She did not recognize his voice, face or name, but she said something that day which made a real impact on Charlie. As Elsie gazed out the nursing home window, she murmured, "If it was not for those trees, I would not have anything."

Elsie had affirmed what Charlie already believed. Life without trees...and birds, flowers, people, family and friends, was meaningless. Nothing. Elsie taught Charlie a lesson that day. Little did he know that someday, as the curtain of his life drew to a close, he too would have his own little tree to sustain him.

PART NINE

1997

Farewells

Mother, you always said, "All things work together for good to those who love the Lord...including the times when we walk through the valley of the shadow of death." Walk through, Mother, walk through with your head held high, into the open arms of our Lord, and I'll meet you on the shore of our heavenly home. ~Charlie Smith

48
Travels with Charlie
May 1997

John Steinbeck's *Travels with Charley* recounts a trip he made with his dog to revisit the 38 states and people he had first met doing research for his novels about our country. One Saturday afternoon in May 1997, I received a call from Charlie Smith that resulted in my own "Travels with Charlie."

In light of his deteriorating health, Charlie had already been sensing a need to visit his mother. A phone call in May 1997 made the visit seem even more needed.

So much has happened so fast.... Marie called to say that mother had been admitted to the hospital and would be undergoing surgery Monday [May 12]. I knew it was time to go, and began thinking about how I was going to get there. Now that I am oxygen dependent, all of my planning revolves around how I am going to have that oxygen with me.

His physical situation certainly left him incapacitated for driving himself from Florida to Louisiana. He phoned me at my Alabama home and said, "Jimmy, I know I don't have much time left. I would like to go and visit my mother one last time. Anne-Marie has another commitment, so I thought I'd ask you."

Like everyone connected to the ministry, I was so grieved over the prospect of losing our Overseer that I was quite willing to spend extended time with him, helping him visit his mother and accompanying him wherever else the Lord led. My wife concurred, and I called the airlines (no computer purchases in those days) to buy a ticket to Florida for the next day.

I found Charlie in a good mental state as he anticipated our drive to Ruston. The next day, I drove the first 500 miles, and we passed the time with Charlie

271

reading chapter nine from John's Gospel, listening to worship music and a cassette recording of the testimony of former mafia enforcer Tom Papania. In Pensacola, Florida we got a hotel room and went to supper at Bob Evans. After ordering his meal, Charlie stood up to go to the restroom. Declining my offer of help, he slowly walked away, struggling to open the door. When he returned, he was weeping profusely. His journal entry recorded the reason for his tears, with a touch of humor:

> I had this incredibly moving, emotional experience. I was in the restroom in a stall equipped especially for handicapped people. I was sitting on the Jon (I spell it this way in honor of my brother-in-law Jon K.) with my arms resting on perfectly placed bars for helping one sit down and get up, when I realized how much effort and money went into providing these facilities for me, never knowing that I would be the recipient of their diligent, and I am sure frustrating battle, to get America to consider her physically impaired people. I was so grateful when it came time to stand that I had those bars to help me get up. A sincere, belated thank you to all who gave so much of themselves to stand up for the rights of less-than-perfect physical beings.

The next 500-mile leg ended at our destination, Ruston, Louisiana. Late the next night, he journaled about his time with his mother:

> Mother is in a hospital bed, approaching her 89th birthday, weighing only 94 pounds where once she weighed 140 lbs., close to making her transition to her eternal home. I pray that she will not have to suffer. In times past when I have asked Mother if she is ready to go home, she would say, "Even now, come Lord Jesus." I will meet you in the morning over there, Mother.
>
> It was a strange feeling being wheeled into a rehabilitation center for some people who were no worse off than me. And it was somewhat strange to be wheeled into my mother's room in a wheelchair with supplemental oxygen being fed to me through a tube. I wondered who was the weaker, until I saw Mother for the first time. She is about as frail as a person can be.... Several times I pictured her in my mind in a casket, not looking much different than she did today.

272

Mother made no big deal about my oxygen. In fact, she never mentioned it. I wheeled myself into a position where I could be as close to her as possible, put my hand through the bars on the guard rail, and held her cold, worn hand. We held hands through most of the visit, and talked directly to each other, eye to eye.

Mother was always a natural storyteller. I can't believe a child has ever forgotten the story titled *Worms for Sale* that she told from time to time at church. It was a story of a bird who would buy worms in exchange for one of his/her feathers– taking short-cuts, not realizing that one day there would not be enough feathers for the bird to fly. It was a sad story, but had a strong punch line.

It was an intense emotional time...saying goodbye to her.... I said that I didn't know which one of us would make our transition first, but if I did I would be there to meet her with Daddy and Karen, among all the others. She understood, and after I left she told one of the workers at the rehab center that I was her son and that she probably would not see me again on this side of life. She probably thinks she will outlive me several years, and she just might do it, but from her present condition, it will not take much at all to take her on over.[47]

We wept together as Lorna wheeled me down the hall to the elevator. My tears were not only sad tears because of the impending separation...they were tears of thanksgiving for having a mother who loved me so much that she prayed for me continually. Thank God for praying mothers.

That evening we were at Marie's house, and with the help of Anita and Lorna, she served an incredible meal. It was a lovely summer night with the moon out and a cool breeze. The family had a great time being together again – all five of the children and in-laws Joe Womack and Dave Riggs, along with Anastasia and Ksenia, two Russian girls who were living in the Smiths' old home place as exchange students. Since we spent our nights in that house, we had many good conversations with these girls, who had many questions about Christianity. Foreign missions and home missions in one place.

For the rest of the week, Charlie rested and spent time with his family. His back continued to plague him with excruciating pain. Marie took him to the

---

[47] Myrtle died a year later – on June 18, 1998, six weeks short of her 90th birthday.

hospital to have it X-rayed, and the diagnosis was compressed fractures of his vertebrae due to the intake of steroids. He was prescribed medications to strengthen the bones, but it was too late. Later, Charlie wrote a letter to the doctor who had prescribed the steroids, begging him to never prescribe them without warning the patient of the need for bone-strengthening medications. He felt he could have avoided a lot of suffering if this had been done for him, and he didn't want anyone else to suffer as he had.

The Frellsen Smith family in 1988 celebrating Myrtle's 80th birthday
Alvin, Lorna, Marie, Charlie, Anita

The pain was not allowed to hinder time with the family. It would be the last time they would share together as brothers and sisters. They all sensed this in their spirit, because Charlie was hanging on by a thread. But the family had no idea that Anita, who sat among them that week in fine health, would also be gone within two years. That decade was a sad one for the Smith family. Frellsen, Karen, Charlie, Myrtle and Anita would all "graduate" during this season of time.[48]

As the week with family came to an end, Charlie had to make a decision. Would he return to Lake Wales, or would these "Travels with Charlie" take us on to some other place? Jon and Lorna invited us to stay in their retreat house on Beaver Lake in Arkansas. The idea of that restful setting appealed to him, so on Wednesday, May 21, we headed for Eureka Springs.

As we turned onto Highway 167, it was raining. Charlie began to weep, as he thought about his family and Karen. Reality began to set in that he would never see his mother again. Later, he wrote her a letter:

Dearest Mother,

How wonderful it was being able to visit with you while I was in Ruston. I was pleased to see you doing so well after such a major surgery, and enjoyed our conversations. More than that, I just enjoyed being with you, listening to you share about the significant events of the past in our lives, and I especially enjoyed the songs you sang.... You are absolutely

---

[48] Frellsen Smith passed away on July 25, 1992 at the age of 84. Anita Smith Womack died April 18, 2000, of complications from a pulmonary embolism. She was 63 years old.

274

the greatest mother that a son could have. Your love for me through the years has been a solid foundation for my life, and I know that your foundation is Christ Jesus, the Solid Rock on whom we can depend; in whom we put our faith. I thank God for a godly mother.

I admire you for your spirit that stays strong even though your body is weak.... I admire you for enduring pain, for suffering with the Savior, during your time of trial. Just recently I, too, have had to endure pain, so I know a little about what you have been through...I know it was hard saying goodbye to Daddy...and I, too, grieved because Karen was taken from us at such a young age.

As you know, I have contracted a lung disease that has no cure and will likely, if the Lord does not intervene and heal me, cut my life on earth shorter than any of us had planned. The doctors say that unless I am healed or have a lung transplant, I don't have very long to live. Doctors say that if the disease becomes aggressive, I could die in a matter of months. If that is required of me, then I am ready to make my transition whenever my Father calls me home. It has been a wonderful life. Regarding my own transition, my prayer is for our daughters, Felicia and Anne-Marie–that they will be sufficiently strong and spiritually mature to live life to the fullest without my presence. And should the Lord favor me with healing, pray that I will be able to continue in the center of His will for however long He allows me to live.

I love you, Mother.... I am eagerly looking forward to our reunion on the other side in glory with the saints of the ages and with our Lord, and there we will have all eternity to sing praises to our Savior who died for us so that we might have this life eternal.

Your son who loves you with all his heart,
Charles

That afternoon, after roller-coastering our way through the Ozark Mountains, we finally made it to the Kardatzkes' retreat house. With Charlie unable to do any lifting, I hauled the luggage, 10 plastic bags of food and the portable oxygen concentrator down to the lower level of the house. Charlie took the downstairs bedroom near the kitchen to avoid the stairs, and I took the upstairs bedroom with a beautiful view of the mountains.

The house sits on a 13-acre peninsula surrounded by black walnut, sassafras, white oak and persimmon trees. Herbs, shrubs and various wild flowers bloom throughout the landscape. This was such a blessing for Charlie, who was in so much physical and emotional pain that he needed time away from people, conversation and other demands so his body and mind could rest.

Friday afternoon we talked about how close we were to country music haven Branson, Missouri, and decided to drive over. He pulled himself together in spite of his pain and dressed to go. I juiced him some pineapple to boost his energy and to moisten his dry mouth–another side effect of steroids. Attending a show called "Country Hoe-Down" was relaxing for Charlie. He was comfortable in his seat, but it was sad to hear him breathing heavily, and he asked me to move his oxygen up to level 5.

Sunday night, Charlie wanted to visit Branson again to hear the Braschler Music Show under the leadership of Cliff Braschler. Cliff's son Todd, former member of this family singing group, had visited Honduras many times with Heart to Honduras and was a favorite of Charlie's. Todd had called his father in advance and gotten us free tickets to the show. The piano player for the Braschlers came down to see us after the show. Having grown up in Louisiana in the Church of God, Anderson, the pianist had once stayed at the Smiths' house during an overnight youth rally held in Ruston. He told Charlie: "I remember Frellsen fixing me and my friend a wonderful breakfast. And during the breakfast, your dad reached for his Bible and began reading it to us. When it was over and we left the room, my friend looked at me and said, 'Is that man the prophet Jeremiah?'" Hearing of his dad's Christian impact on these two boys was worth the trip for Charlie.

Tuesday night, May 27, was the most trying night for Charlie. It was the night we designated *Beauty and the Beast.* For two hours, there was a storm over Beaver Lake. The lightning reflected off the mountain tops for miles. Huge bolts flashed their elongated fingers over, and seemingly into, the lake non-stop. It was as if one were attending a Fourth of July fireworks display, but this one resonated with the voltage of God. Charlie and I were both in awe of this beauty.

But in the bedroom where Charlie lay was the spirit of the beast. He could not move without excruciating pain in his back and legs. And then, about 30 minutes into the electrical storm, the phone rang. It was Anne-Marie. She called to share with her dad that she had just broken up with Scott. In the six years of their relationship, Charlie had loved Scott and come to feel like a father to him. Not long after Charlie hung up with Anne-Marie, Felicia called. They began to weep together over the phone as he told her Anne-Marie's news. Felicia said, "It is like a death in the family." I wrote in my journal:

Charlie wept throughout the night. He is most fragile. He said the thing that grieves him the most is when his girls say, "Daddy, we need you. Daddy, we need you." I told Charlie I wanted to pray. I turned out the light in the room. I knelt by the chair near his bed and prayed as the flashes of lightning lit up the night sky.

Charlie and I slept late due to the intense emotional evening and because of the six-hour drive we were planning to Wichita to visit with Jon and Lorna. We timed our arrival for late in the evening, when Lorna and Jon were free, and after a while their adult children joined us, reaching out in love to their uncle Charlie.

The next day, Dr. Craig Carter, who headed up our first dental teams to Honduras, came by. Then Monty and Kelly Harrington, former staff members, brought their newborn daughter over and fellowshipped with Charlie. In fact, the whole time at the Kardatzke house was filled with a stream of visitors, including the mission pastor of Central Community Church, a group from that church which was planning a trip to Honduras, and Dennis Turner, a supporter of the ministry. Noting these wonderful ministry connections, Charlie said he felt this was the reason our trip had brought us to Wichita.

As a doctor and as a brother-in-law, Jon was deeply concerned about Charlie's deteriorating physical condition. He wanted Charlie to take advantage of every possible medical procedure that might preserve his life. Jon scheduled an appointment for May 29 with a Dr. Reed, who was the recipient of a lung transplant and had survived for five years. The meeting was cordial, straightforward and personal. Dr. Reed shared with Charlie 10 somber things to keep in mind regarding a lung transplant, including the fact that a transplant is not a cure, the surgery takes eight hours, and that you must be close enough to the hospital to arrive there with only three hours' notice of the availability of a lung. Dr. Reed noted that there were major expenses involved: $10,000 per year just for medicine and hospital visits as follow-up to the transplant (which he could afford, but many people could not).

That night, Jon extracted a promise from Charlie to go for a three-day evaluation to see if he qualified for a lung transplant. There was also talk of the financial needs of the ministry, and Jon and Lorna made a very special gift from their collection of gold coins. These dear people were the lynchpins for the ministry of Heart to Honduras in its formative years, and their steady financial and emotional support gave Charlie encouragement to stay the course.

Our three week journey ended on June 3. Dave Pischel met us at my Alabama home so he could drive Charlie back to Florida. With the family visits behind him, Charlie now turned his attention toward other priorities in his life: juggling ministry responsibilities with his deteriorating physical condition, being with his two daughters, and contemplating a return trip to Honduras. A third priority was beginning to surface in Charlie's mind. It was emotionally troubling and a bit scary. It had to do with a specially called meeting.

Board Members at October 1997 Meeting

Jerry Grubbs, Charlie Smith, Jim Usher,
Gordon Garrett, Jayne Crews-Linton, Miguel Pinell,
Lorna Kardatzke, Jim Nelson, Dean Flora

There is so much to do and so little time–pray for patience in my affliction.
~FAX from Charlie to Dave and Candy Pischel, Sept. 5, 1997

49
The Last Board Meeting
August 1997

Questions tripped over each other in the minds of the Heart to Honduras board members as they gathered in the living room of the double-wide trailer across from Charlie's house. Was Charlie really dying? If so, how much longer did he have to live? HTH had so many doctors–why couldn't they do something? Why doesn't God intervene and heal Charlie? Can the ministry continue without him? What will happen to his daughters? Why would God take away both parents in the prime of life? Can Charlie still function as Overseer in his present physical condition? Who will take his place?

And in the mind of Charlie loomed a fear that the board would replace him as Overseer before he was finished laying out his plans for the ministry. Would they allow him to continue to lead in whatever time he had left?

The regular board members–Jerry Grubbs, Lorna Kardatzke, Miguel Pinell, Charlie Smith and Jim Usher–were being joined that day by newly elected members Jayne Crews-Linton, Dean Flora, Gordon Garrett and Jim Nelson.

The massive cloud whose shadow moved slowly over the freshly cut yard mirrored their feelings of a heavy cloud hanging over the ministry. When the sun peeped out on this August day, the men and women who had big decisions to make hoped it was a sign that God would shine on them the light of His wisdom.

Pastries and fruit were on the table. Pots of Nicaraguan-style chicken and rice were steaming in the kitchen, where Miguel's mother Pastora was preparing the noon meal. The aroma of coffee wafted into the living room as board members took their seats around the long wooden table. Charlie was seated in his wheelchair near the head of the table. Everyone was there for the 9:00 gavel except Jayne, who was caught in traffic. Board reports and minutes in three-ring notebooks were passed out.

Jerry Grubbs welcomed everyone, and a couple of items of business were covered before he turned the meeting over to Charlie. True to his nature, Charlie passed out a responsive reading from the Bible.

Then, for the next hour, Charlie shared his vision for the future. He knew it would be his last board meeting unless God intervened. His extensive report reached all the way back to his days in Malaysia with the Peace Corps, his social science studies at the University of Kentucky, the successes and failures at H.E.A.R.T., his five years with Project Global Village and every tidbit of information since December 1988–the beginning of Heart to Honduras. This was his final chance to cast the Grand Vision into the future leadership of Heart to Honduras.

Charlie had each board member take turns reading a section of his report. The vision was complex in its detail, broad in its outreach and compelling in its challenge. It began with a model village, placing emphasis upon holistic healing for the entire family and community. Charlie wrote, "For years I envisioned and yearned for the opportunity to build a model village totally self-sustained for the impoverished masses."

His plan was to do this in Canchias, Honduras. Canchias would be his model village for the world. Charlie never thought small. He recommended prototype developmental elements. Clean water for Charlie was the number one priority for the health of any village. In Charlie's vision, home improvements–potable water, *pilas*, toilets, showers, concrete floors, interior furnishings for homes, no-interest loans, and stucco and paint for the exterior walls with pleasing colors to brighten up the village–these components were crucial to his vision. Once these components were completed, his desire was to teach the people how to raise family gardens and livestock–chickens, goats, sheep, pigs and turkeys. "I can envision us putting together a complete manual on how this can be done...It makes sense to me, but then I am a simple person...Einstein's theory of relativity is an example: E=MC² started a new paradigm in physics and

Charlie with the storekeeper of the newly opened, well-stocked
pulpuria (general store) in Canchias

281

**Charlie watching the bulldozer create a flat space on a
steep hillside for the Discipleship Center in Canchias**

astronomy. 'Simple' answers to complex problems is the goal…"

Charlie then challenged the board with other key elements to village development. His desire was to keep the general store filled with commodities to meet the people's basic needs: salt, sugar, flour, corn, beans and coffee. He had also installed a diesel-powered *molina* (corn grinder) for the villagers, saving women countless hours of labor with mortar and pestle, or with a hand grinder to reduce the grains of corn to the flour needed to make the many tortillas required daily. He had worked with the local *patronata* (governing council) and built a community hall where they had begun holding their meetings.

His report then turned our attention to the infrastructure of the compound. He had made a bold decision during the rainy season of December and brought in a bulldozer at the cost of $20,000. This machine had smoothed roads and leveled ground for an assembly hall with seating capacity for 400 Hondurans. Architect Jerry Pickens of Denver, Colorado had designed the large hall, as he had ably designed several other campus buildings in Canchias.

In the center of town, the bulldozer had carved out an area for a community plaza where Charlie pictured a future amphitheater, medical, dental and eye clinics, an arts and crafts center, a blacksmith shop, a woodwork shop, a bank, a leather shop, a barber shop and a vocational trade center. In his mind's eye, he could see students from the Discipleship Center being trained with vocational skills so they could be employed and products might be sold right there in the village.

After listing all these components, Charlie reflected on how all this would be accomplished, for it was indeed an extensive list. First and foremost, it would be done through the local church with the assistance and partnership of North American believers. "Empowering the indigenous church is the approach to missions that makes sense. Missionaries are needed at times to help in this process, but not to pastor congregations. What we are doing in Honduras can be a model for the church universal, especially the unifying of various denominations for one central purpose: the building up of the body of Christ. We will do all that is within our power to emphasize this truth in all that we do in Honduras."

The centerpiece of his dream was the Discipleship Center. Charlie was a strong believer in secular and Christian education. Making disciples, teaching all the things that Jesus taught, and feeding the poor–these were the purposes for the Discipleship Center. It would be a Bible school to train apostles, prophets, evangelists, teachers and pastors to be able to teach all that Jesus taught. Charlie left Project Global Village after five years because he felt it lacked this component. His thought was that too often, development organizations go through local and regional governments rather than God. His vision would go through the church, which for Charlie was the greatest change agent on the face of the earth, especially in the personal transformation of humankind. Charlie's plan was to go through a church with leaders trained to have a holistic outreach– including evangelism along with education, the Bible as well as bread, preaching as well as *pilas*, instruction in the Word as well as digging wells, teaching Christ as well as growing corn.

Charlie longed to be part of the future administration of the Discipleship Center. Yet, like Moses who failed to enter the Promised Land, Charlie would not live to see the hundreds of students who would eventually graduate from the School of Discipleship. He encouraged the board to let Canchias and the Discipleship Center be the educational center of the ministry. His desire was that the students would utilize the outlying buildings to learn about food production: preservation, processing and preparation. His curriculum plans included teaching construction skills with components like working with concrete, making blocks, using the *Cinva-Ram* block-making machine. He saw students being taught child care, sewing, manufacturing and repair of clothes, and leather work that would include making and repair of saddles, belts, and footwear.

Canchias Clinic – built in 1999 as the first step in the Canchias Plaza project

He expressed his longing to empower the poor by giving them options that went beyond awakening in the morning and going far from home to slash and burn their rented fields. He wanted to liberate them from back-breaking labor beneath the burning sun, where their only skills were hoeing, planting and harvesting. He envisioned a curriculum being taught at the Assembly Hall that included pottery, candlemaking, weaving, basketry, toy making, broom making, interior and exterior design and landscaping, iron and metal work, small engine repair, money management, music, animal husbandry, and energy alternatives such as solar, wind, water and wood.

This report to the board was a 50-page document with 10 indexes. He gave his final words of appreciation to each staff and board member. It seemed that his eyes were moist for the entire session. He broke down twice and wept.

Charlie coughed intermittently throughout the meeting. As the board neared page 38, Charlie's cough became so bad it seemed as if he were choking. The coughing persisted. Board members sat silently, waiting for him to finish. As each board member empathized with Charlie, his sister Lorna said with a firm and concerned voice, "Can we take a break?"

After everyone enjoyed a bit of fellowship over some snacks, the meeting reconvened, and Charlie brought up the work that Dave and Candy Pischel were doing for the ministry. Dave and Charlie had met years ago in Thailand. At the first board meeting, Charlie had expressed a desire to have Dave come on board as a graphic artist, even though he lived in Oregon. Eventually, Dave and Candy made the decision to come to Florida, and Candy was now working as the ministry's bookkeeper. On this day, Charlie tearfully made an appeal to the board:

Dave and Candy are totally committed. They are only making 500 dollars each per month, but are giving full-time to the work. Candy needed a crown on one of her teeth but could not afford it, so I made it possible. They serve us so diligently. I have never seen anyone serve us like that. It is incredible. Dave is in the Word all the time. Every morning, he is in the Word. They serve me.

Dave and Candy Pischel in the Florida HTH office

They are true disciples of Jesus Christ and we are so blessed to have them. They are always there for me. I get so emotional when people care for me and they care for me. They were up all night putting this [Board Report] together. They called me at 7 this morning. I said, "What time did you go to bed last night? I went to bed at 1:30 a.m." They just said, "We got it done." They stayed up almost all last night for you and me...they are beyond reproach.

After this impassioned appeal, the board voted to raise the salary of these fine servants, who ended up becoming Charlie's caretakers in Honduras during the final days of his life.

Following this vote several board members began sharing their appreciation for Charlie. Dean Flora could hardly speak through his tears as he spoke of what Charlie had meant to his life, closing with, "I thank God daily for Charlie." Likewise, Jim Nelson, who was Charlie's personal physician, wept openly as he described how Charlie had been a great encouragement to him during recent personal trials. It seemed as if the board had gathered not to make decisions but to hear the heart of Charlie and to share their hearts with him.

For this board meeting, there was more weeping than work. There was more brokenness than budgeting. Taking a group photograph was forgotten in this solemn moment.

Recognizing that the leader was very ill, though still in possession of a mind that was keen and alert, the board had to think about his position as Overseer. How much longer did he have to live? And in that time, whatever length it was, did he have the strength to continue to lead? Was there anyone to whom the baton of leadership could be passed?

When the board decided they would approve Charlie continuing as the Overseer of the ministry, he wept with relief. Though he was aware that the time was approaching when he would no longer be able to function, he was not yet prepared to give up his life's purpose. He had come to the meeting worried they might replace him. What a blessing to know that he could continue visioning with the days the Lord allowed him to live.

As the board meeting began to wind down, Jerry welcomed the new members, which would normally have been done at the beginning of the meeting. Jerry shared that Heart to Honduras was an informal ministry, much like a family. It was a young and small organization with a great deal of trust and freedom. He explained that he and Lorna Kardatzke served as the executive committee while Charlie, Miguel and Jim worked the field. The board did not involve itself with day-to-day operational activities on the field, but set policies and provided resources.

It was time to adjourn and give the Overseer a rest.

I was walking alongside as Lorna pushed a weeping Charlie in his wheelchair toward his home across the street, and asked, "Charlie, why are you weeping?" He sobbed, "Because I love life so much!"

He had conducted his last board meeting. His body was fragile, his emotions frayed. But his mind was good; his will was strong–strong enough to make one more decision. As many of his decisions in the past had been, this one would also be risky. He was relieved that he could continue as Overseer for the time being, but his heart was more broken than his lungs as he recognized the fulfilling joy of the past eight years was being cut short. At 59, he was not ready to quit this life that he loved so much.

Suffering is God's megaphone to man to get his attention.
~C.S. Lewis

50
From Dependency to Dependency

Not included in the things Charlie shared with the board at that final meeting in August 1997 was his plan to return to Honduras to live his last days. In fact, he practically sneaked out of the country, confiding only in his daughters, the Pischels and Miguel. The girls understood that his heart was truly in Honduras, and they released him to follow this tug.

He knew that many people would judge him crazy for giving up the fine medical care available in the United States, particularly since he had doctors in the family, but he had been called crazy before. He had done as he had promised his brother in law, Jon, and had an evaluation for a lung transplant. He was not a candidate because of the osteoporosis brought on by high doses of steroids. With the exception of being separated from his daughters, there was no reason to stay in the states.

Over the past few years, his heart was increasingly in Honduras, and so, no matter what other people thought, he would be in charge as much as possible of his final months of life. He left without telling his possible detractors where he was going.

On August 29, he was greatly relieved to have succeeded in his escape plan and to have found himself in San Pedro Sula's airport being picked up by Miguel, who had made the appropriate arrangements for oxygen. However, neither Charlie nor Miguel had fully realized how excruciating the trip to Canchias would be for a man with a deteriorating spine. Every pothole, every rut, every hairpin curve, no matter how carefully maneuvered by Miguel, brought horrific pain. It was a trip Charlie didn't think he would survive. Hours later he laboriously climbed the path to the Martha House and settled into his room. He was relieved to be there, but the physical cost had been great.

Charlie brought along a laptop, a printer and a FAX machine that worked off a satellite phone, and he was determined to continue refining his vision for Honduras as long as his fingers could tap the keys. Ensconced in his little cabin in Canchias, he recorded his vision and his philosophies on various topics, journaled his physical deterioration, and wrote out instructions to be followed should the Lord not choose to heal him.

In the midst of focusing his energies on recording his visionary thoughts, Charlie was not forgetting the fact that his young adult daughters would soon be orphaned. Drawing on the closeness of the family, he used the technology he had brought with him to send his four siblings a letter just days after his arrival.

Anne-Marie, Charlie, Felicia in 1994

Who would have ever thought or believed that our daughters would be left without living parents, parents to be there for them during all of life's joys and pains? This has by far been the greatest grief I have experienced through this travail. I have cried more tears over this one thing than anything else.... We have enjoyed more quality time than most fathers and their children spend in a lifetime, but that still does not remove the pain of separation.... As they have said so often to me, "Daddy, if we didn't love you so much, it would not be so hard to say goodbye."

Charlie loved his girls as much as any father could. They were soon coming to spend a week with him, and he was looking forward to this final visit so he could impart more of his core values to them. He had already done this by the life he lived before them, but he also wanted to leave some words on paper that they could reread after he was gone. An agreement had been made that the girls would not stay and watch him die. Charlie had watched them endure their mother's final sufferings and he didn't want them to have to do that again. They would visit while he was still in a relatively good state, and then they would return for the funeral when the time came. On September 6, 1997, Charlie typed out a response to a recent letter from Anne-Marie:

Now to the reality of my situation about which you asked. My lungs are small and hard, and breathing is increasingly difficult. The steroids calm the inflammation in my lungs somewhat, but have the terrible side effect of sapping energy out of my body, especially my legs. It is with great difficulty even to stand up.... When I fall into unconsciousness, I want all the oxygen tubes removed and the machines turned off so I can go home peacefully. This is as difficult for me as I am sure it is for you. But I am trying my best to face reality as directly head on as I can. I do not want to die struggling for air. What an awful way to go. I hope you understand where I am coming from in this regard.

...I still believe in miracles and know that the all-powerful God who made me can heal me, but as Jesus prayed when facing his own death, "Lord, let this cup pass from me, but not my will, yours be done." With no fear, I submit my life into the loving arms of our heavenly Father. And be assured, like the Apostle Paul, that nothing, absolutely nothing can separate me from the love of God that is in Christ Jesus our Lord. I love you, Anne-Marie, with all my heart. Your Dad

Ten days later Charlie wanted to encourage Felicia and sent a FAX with these thoughts to her:

Dearest Felicia:
Suffering and death is the hard side of life, but such has been since the beginning of humankind. Our pain is great and no one can take it away from us.... We have hope, Felicia, hope! And we have faith that the Word is, and that it is true and all powerful, and loving, enabling us to make it through even the darkest of nights when the loneliness surrounds us.

The Word that was in the beginning is love, now and forever. Love, Felicia, love that envelops us in warm and tender arms like I used to hold you close as a small child and tell you that it's all going to be OK. "It's OK, Felicia! It's OK!" I can hardly wait to hold you in my arms again and tell you those same words, the same words your mother told us when she was making final preparations for her transition home to her Father. "It's OK, it's OK, it's OK!" I can still hear the ring of assurance in her voice.

What you are now experiencing will make you stronger with roots driven deep.... As a tree on a mountain top that is blown almost beyond recognition, the roots hold it solid to the ground that cannot be uprooted. Believe that and build your life on that Truth. Begin searching the Scriptures for His commands, all that he commanded us to put into practice, and then live these Truths through your life and you will find joy the world has no way of knowing.

Candy and Dave Pischel had joined Charlie in Canchias to care for his physical needs and be present as staff members to help him as he recorded his final instructions for those who would follow him in the ministry.

Paola was there as his faithful caretaker, cook, and housekeeper. He appreciated so much her care for him, though one day in late September she inadvertently hurt his feelings. She asked him when he wanted his bath, and innocently remarked that it was like taking care of a baby. These words hit Charlie hard, though he didn't let her know. When he shared the incident later, he said he felt like he was turning back into a child, and wanted to fight against that. He even thought of a title for a paper he wanted to write: *From Dependency to Dependency,* dealing with the progression from a child to an elder in need of assistance in his dying days.

The Pischels, Paola, and Dr. Elsa, who tended to his medical needs, made up his personal hospice team. With these caregivers and the people from the village surrounding him with their music, their visits and their prayers, Charlie was as happy as one could be in those circumstances. He was happy that he had been able to make the trip to Canchias, happy that, should the Lord not heal him, he was going to die among these people he had grown to love, and happy for the hope of what was happening just below his cabin as the Assembly Hall was nearing completion.

The Discipleship Center was the quintessential piece of Charlie's vision. Without indigenous leadership trained and discipled, the vision God had given to him would be swept away as debris in the wake of a tsunami. From his cabin, he could hear the carpenters sawing and nailing. From the porch, he could see trucks bringing in supplies. He longed to go down there to feel the wood, see the progress and smell the food. He typed the following plea:

> I can feel the kitchen below at the Discipleship Center. O God! Let me live long enough to see the Assembly Hall completed. Then I can say as Simeon, "Sovereign Lord, as you have promised, you now can dismiss your servant in peace. For my eyes have seen your salvation, which you have prepared in the sight of all your people, a light of revelation to the Gentiles and glory for your people Israel."

290

It is not the years in your life but the life in your years that counts!
~Adlai Stevenson

51

Come on Down

In early October 1997, I received word that Charlie was in Honduras and had taken a turn for the worse. Knowing that many would want to visit him and that his family was limiting his visitors, I hesitated to go, but how could I let Charlie slip away without sharing with him one last time? Charlie and Karen had opened their hearts to me from our first meeting in Kentucky, and I had always felt fully accepted as family. I gave him a personal call on the satellite phone, and he said, "Jim, come on down."

It was strange flying to Honduras that first Monday in October without Charlie in the seat beside me. It was stranger still to ride into the village without him in the truck, wearing his signature hat and being welcomed by the poor believers. It would be a very different thing to do ministry without our founder.

As I walked up the hill toward the Martha House, I was cheered to hear happy voices in the distance. I could hear Felicia and Anne-Marie singing to their dad, "O, Daddy, I love you! O, Daddy I love you! Yes, I do! O, Daddy we love you! O, Daddy we love you! Yes, we do!" The girls had come to spend a week with their father. They had grown even closer since the death of their mother four years earlier.

When Charlie saw me approaching, despite his struggle to breathe, he gushed with excitement, "Jimmy, would you believe that God gave us a song? The music is already there. It was a long time in coming. Then, in 15 minutes, it came to me. The music is from the opening instrumental of the *Forrest Gump* movie soundtrack. Do you remember the little feather falling? Hang on, and I will sing you a verse or two." Soon we were all gathered around him, singing his new song, "Ambassadors for Jesus."

In the heat of the afternoon, the other visitors retired to their cabins for a siesta, and Charlie said to me, "Jimmy, this week I want to read a lot of Scripture, especially on heaven." And so we did. Sitting on the Martha House porch, with a panoramic view of the mountains and river, we read about how Jesus left planet Earth to prepare mansions for His children. Since Charlie's body was wearing down, he wanted to hear the Apostle Paul describe how this earthly body was

291

like a tent destroyed, and that in the future, all believers would have an eternal house in heaven not made with hands.

Then, he wanted to share Scriptures on some other themes. He quoted Matthew 28:18 from memory as the verse to support the theme of discipleship. "Therefore, go and make disciples of all nations, baptizing them in the name of the Father and of the Son and of the Holy Spirit..." Undergirding the theme of reconciliation, Charlie quoted 2 Cor. 5:20, "We are therefore Christ's ambassadors...." And because the little burro represented humility for Charlie, he quoted the prophet Zachariah, "Rejoice greatly, O daughter of Zion...see, your king comes to you, righteous and having salvation, gently and riding on an ass, the foal of an ass."

It had been decided that while I was there, I would sleep on the couch in the Martha House, to give Dave and Candy a much-needed break from caring for Charlie throughout the night. So after everyone else retired to their cabins, he and I had some more time to ourselves. Charlie began to share gratitude and ideas on many topics. Taking note of his laptop propped on a pillow in his lap, Charlie spoke, "Jim, we have gone all out with this high-tech stuff. What a blessing to have the satellite phone and the FAX machine. Thank Mack Bramlett for his donation."

His mind wandered to the School of Discipleship, and he began to imagine it completed, with all its décor, furniture and lights. "I really love the beautiful tablecloths Lorna brought down for the dining hall tables, and the decorative clay bell lights Tony Bayles selected to provide ambiance for our gatherings. I love candles, because they teach us the soft side of life."

Then he turned his attention to the harvest. As he thought about the students and pastors who would, someday soon, attend the School of Discipleship, he quoted Jesus: "Greater things than these shall you do because I go to my Father in heaven." Charlie believed the greater things that Jesus spoke

Ambassadors for Jesus
(Tune: Forrest Gump theme song]
We are Ambassadors for Jesus
Savior to all the world
Sent forth to all of His disciples
Sharing the news of His love
God does not hold your sins against you
Accepts you just as you are
Welcomes you home with open arms of love

Sent to all peoples of all nations
Living the truth of love
Calling creation to Creator
Be reconciled to God
God made him who had no sin
To be sin for us
So we might be the righteousness of God

292

about were the ingathering, or fruit of the harvest, that would be brought about by those called to enroll at the Discipleship Center.

His sister Marie had loaned him a book by psychiatrist Scott Peck. Charlie began to integrate his and Peck's thoughts on suffering. Charlie quoted Peck's words, "[Suffering] is a stripping-away process, and there is no peace until we accept this stripping away." Charlie loved life so much it was difficult to submit to God's shredding machine. He admitted that Karen managed her suffering better and accepted her impending death with more grace and poise than he.

As night sounds filtered through the windows and the humming of the oxygen machines sputtered and crackled, the clock signaled it was past midnight. Both of us were sleepy. Charlie broke the silence and said, "We must mourn with those who mourn and weep with those who weep. My tears are many. I anticipate a home of glory. I anticipate a mansion, a place in heaven. But it is still hard to go. Life is good!"

I miss Felicia and Anne-Marie. Please ask them to write me. I want to hear from them whenever they get a chance to write. I have thought of them every day as I remember the time we spent together here in the Martha House.
~Charlie Smith

52

Juntos

Wednesday, October 8, 1997 turned out to be a gorgeous day. As the sun peeked over the mountain, the village came to life. Farmers in their black boots, machetes dangling at their sides, walked briskly to their fields. Skill saws and hammers kept time as the ministry carpenters Naldo and Ever supervised the men busy completing the Discipleship Center. In the cabin on the hill, Anne-Marie was cooking her tasty scrambled eggs, and the entire box of southern grits that I had brought down at Charlie's request.

After his daughters helped him with his bath on this October morning, Charlie was carried onto the porch, where he loved to take in the view and watch the village people go about their daily tasks. The porch was his living room, where he entertained visitors from as close as the village and as far as North America. Today, it was where he and his daughters would spend precious hours together.

As soon as he was situated, Felicia and Anne-Marie began to trim Charlie's eyebrows, as each one took photos of the other manning the scissors. They took pleasure in kidding about finding a few hairs to trim on his bald head.

Though they were attempting to be light-hearted as they teased their father, all that day a somber feeling permeated the air on the hillside. Felicia and Anne-Marie's departure was set for the next morning.

In the evening, Dave, Candy and I went down to sit on the deck near the Canchias River, allowing the girls to be alone with their dad. We reflected, wrote in our journals and pondered life, death, relationships, love, suffering, loss and hope. The stars were bright that night. The wind blew gently across the deck, and the river faithfully flowed over endless rocks as we waited in silence. Nature was beautiful and we knew God was good, but it was sad for us to think about the pending loss for these girls, whose father's life was hanging by a thin plastic cannula feeding oxygen to his increasingly hardened lungs.

Thursday morning was bright, with clear blue skies above. From the porch, we could hear the Toyota truck grinding its way through the village on its way to pick up Felicia and Anne-Marie and take them to the airport. The girls were alone with Charlie, wrapped in his arms, sharing last words.

When the girls came out of their father's bedroom, their hair was disheveled. Their tears overflowed. Wheeled onto the porch, Charlie gave them each an Ambassador hat, and they requested one last photo with their dad. As they prepared to walk away, he sought to encourage them by saying, in as strong a voice as he could manage, "Keep your heads high!"

I watched the girls walk down the stepping-stone path to the waiting vehicle. Dave and Candy would provide comfort by going to the airport with them. They had Lyle (Felicia's husband) and Jason (Anne-Marie's boyfriend) to lean on. I was reminded of Karen's words to the family when she first learned of her terminal illness. "Hey, guys! We have never been here before. Let the party begin!" But no one was blowing horns, eating cake or lighting candles on the Martha House porch this day. Karen was gone. Charlie was going. And for the girls, the candle wick was flickering out at the base of the frosting.

Anticipating this moment of separation from their dad, Anne-Marie had sensed the need for solidarity and strength and had come up with the Spanish word "*juntos.*" It means "together." As the six of them headed to the airport, "*Juntos*" gave them hope. *Juntos! Juntos! Juntos!* Candy thought back on this truck ride:

> We used "*juntos*" because that's how we would get through it—together. We rode a lot in silence, crying and touching and letting our tears say it all. Our tears for them, their tears for what they had to do…. Etched in my mind were the emotions.
>
> As we parted at the airport, I remember Felicia standing there with tears streaming down her face. That's one thing about the whole experience that really impressed me…how Charlie and both of them were just unabashedly free in the expression of their grief. And though I am not a big emotional person, I sure was all about emotions that day!

Though it was a time of deep grieving, Felicia remembered: "In the immense pain of leaving, we experienced a peace, knowing that Dad was where he wanted to be and that he was being cared for by people who loved him dearly."

I have brought you glory on earth by finishing the work you gave me to do.
~John 17:4 NIV

53

Glory

The sound of the truck faded as it rounded the mountain and the Toyota engine could no longer be heard in the distance. Charlie said to me, "It is hard to say goodbye. I wrote letters to my sisters and brother to take care of the girls." His shirt was wet from the mixture of his tears and the girls'. I left the room to give him space to grieve, yet I did not go too far, because he said, "I will need someone nearby."

As he was sleeping, a short Honduran farmer named Trino came to the Martha House and slipped in to stand by his friend Charlie's bed. He had just returned from his corn field and sweat was on his face. He wore dusty black rubber boots, brown pants with a patch on the seat, and had removed his New York Yankees baseball cap and set it on the couch. Trino began to pray. A cool breeze was blowing through the windows of Charlie's room. "*Gracias Señor...Espiritu Santos...*" was all I could comprehend. It was a fervent prayer, as most prayers by Honduran believers are. Charlie did not hear this prayer, but heaven did.

Later in the evening, I had another chance to be alone with Charlie. He shared from the depth of his soul what the essence of life itself meant to him. "It is hard to go and leave this world. I have no desire to return to the States. These are my people. I love it here. In the night, I learn things. In the stillness, I learn things. Sometimes I raise my hands." Charlie was not raised in a denominational tradition where worshippers raised both hands in praise and worship. However, the more his physical body began to be squeezed by the vise grip of death, the closer he moved to the inner sanctum of God. And the nearer he came to this divine presence, the more he focused on the eternal. He was never one to let denominational dogma or ecclesiastical ritual dictate his conscience. This tiny 8-by-10 room was now his little chapel, and at night while the sounds of nature droned outside his window, he thought of Karen, his two girls, his family, and all that God had accomplished in his life. As he reflected on these memories, he would raise his hands and weep.

The next morning, I learned something about gratitude when Charlie asked me to help him shave. Often, it is difficult to notice the true limitations of a person or to appreciate the blessings of being able to manage the tiny details of daily living, until you have to assist someone in some small detail. He could still shave himself, but Charlie was so weak that he was unable to press the button on his Edge shaving cream can to release the foam.

Moments after he finished shaving, the satellite phone rang. It was Gordon Garrett, HTH board member—and though no one but God knew it at that point, the one who would eventually take the helm of the ministry. Gordon was calling from Denver to check on his friend. Charlie was unable to pick up the heavy satellite phone, as he was worn out from shaving. I held the phone up to Charlie's ear and he managed to say, "I love you, Gordon."

Felicia sent word from the States that she had just read out of the Bible Charlie had just given to her. She and Lyle were going to spend the weekend at her aunt's cabin in Breckenridge to process how they wanted God to use their lives. Upon receiving this message, Charlie began to weep and asked me to pray for Felicia and Lyle. Candy, Dave and I knelt down, and I led a prayer for this beloved daughter and her husband as they sought God's will for their lives. In the struggle and emotion of the moment, with my friend's life slowly slipping away, I felt my words were inadequate for the task. But God took over and used Charlie's caretaker Paola to rescue this stumbling pastor in my feeble attempt to pray for my friend. In the background, Paola began singing beautiful Spanish choruses to the accompaniment of the wind chimes. The harmony of the chimes and Paola's singing brought a sweet rest to Charlie's spirit, just as David's harp soothed the spirit of King Saul. Those prayers were answered, as Felicia became an Episcopal priest with a congregation in Colorado, and her husband Lyle worked many years for Renovaré, a Christian ministry.

My wrist watch indicated 11:16 p.m. on Friday night. Charlie called me into his room and said, "I need more oxygen." I moved the arrow from 10 to 14. Charlie wanted to talk. We talked for almost an hour. Realizing it was long after midnight, I told Charlie I needed to let him get some rest. As I was leaving, he said, "Jim, thanks for listening." I wish I had stayed and talked for another hour. Those were precious minutes we spent together, and my time with him was coming to an end.

The next morning, we were both groggy from our late night and the frequent interruptions to our sleep when he needed help with a drink or oxygen or a visit to the bathroom, but his mind was still clear enough to gently lecture me. He knew that often, my sermons were out of the Old Testament, while Charlie always preached and taught out of the New Testament. He told me I needed to start preaching Jesus.

The more I thought about this, the more it made sense. Charlie's entire life and his core values were centered in Jesus. Jesus was the Great Anthropologist for Charlie. Charlie would always vision with a holistic perspective, seeking to minister to the whole man. Preaching Jesus and applying the anthropological principles learned at the University of Kentucky were Charlie's quintessential means of bringing hope and healing to a desperate humanity.

Sunday, October 12, was the final day of my trip. I remembered how Charlie had walked into my life at a time when the Lord was just awakening in me a call to missions. It had been 28 years since a "chance" meeting in a morning church service in Lexington, Kentucky had redirected my life more than any other human encounter. Time was short for us to say whatever we were going to say to each other. He again asked me to read some portions of Scripture to him to begin the day, noting that "My Bible is getting heavy in my hands."

I was to leave at 9 a.m. About an hour prior to my planned departure, Charlie called Miguel, Dave, Candy and myself into his room. We made up most of the staff of Heart to Honduras in those days; only Rick Dike was missing. Charlie had some final words for those of us who would carry on together after he left us. With his ever-decreasing breath support, speaking was difficult, but this was important, and he wanted to impart these words directly to us. Gasping between short phrases, he spoke and then prayed:

> Anytime...God is at work...Satan is at work.... I want to be sure...that we...stay together.... Stay a family.... We have...a simple purpose...for this ministry.... There are two things...I want us...to always do:...help the poor...and make disciples.... That's all.... If we do that...we have fulfilled...our purpose.

Man...what a joy!...What a joy!... What a joy!... It has... been great! Lord...thank you...for all...the good things...of life. You have...blessed us...beyond...our wildest...dreams and visions.... We give you thanks...honor and glory.... We pray...for souls to be won...and nations to be discipled...for you.... We pray...you will...bless each life.... You have called...each of us...into this life.... We all...have been called...to live pure...clean...and holy lives.... And we will...do our part....Amen.

With longing in his voice, Charlie remarked, "I wish God would give me 10 more years-one more year. The Lord has played brinkmanship with me. He is going to say, 'Charlie, get up and go back to work.'"

As my last moments with Charlie came, I went to his bedside. "We have shared some great memories, and I do not know how to say goodbye." He asked me to read Paul's farewell to the Ephesians in Acts 20 and the last part of Romans 8. We looked at each other with tears.

He took my hands, and the final word he said to me was, "Glory!"

A few hours later, when I sat down on the plane, my mind and heart were unsettled. I could not get Charlie's word out of my mind-the parting word, the last word-"Glory!" Surely the last words a person shares as he nears death are the most important. I pondered over and over his word to me. Why the word "Glory?"

I thought about it on the way to the airport. I thought about it on the plane. I thought about it as I prepared my next sermon. I thought about it when I awoke and when I went to bed. Why did Charlie take my hand and say, "Glory?"

Two weeks later, I was reading the seventeenth chapter of John's Gospel. And I came across the words of Jesus: "Father, the time has come. Glorify your son as your son has glorified you.... I have brought you glory by completing the work you gave me to do. And now, Father, glorify thou me in your presence with the glory I had with you before the world began."

Eureka! Now I knew. Charlie in his wisdom and love was communicating to me that he had done all he could do for his Lord. His time and season had now come to an end. He could now confidently say that he had completed the work God had given him to do. And now, more than anything else, he was asking God to glorify him with His presence.

With this revelation pressed into my spirit, all I could do was thank God for such a man who knew he was faithfully completing the work God had given him to do. "Glory!"

I have no greater joy than to hear that my children are walking in the truth.
~3 John 1:4 NIV

54

The Greatest Joy

A Farewell Message to the Pastors

Late one afternoon, a week after I left, a small group of farmer-pastors came to the Martha House, lifted Charlie into a makeshift litter and transported him carefully down the steep trail. At last, the day had arrived, a day Charlie had feared he would not live to see. The kitchen and the deck on the Assembly Hall had been completed, and he was being carried down the mountain path to see the finished product. Adding to the joy (and the bittersweetness) of this October Tuesday was the opportunity to share his heart with a group of 32 pastors who led congregations in the Meambar, Comayagua region and beyond.

From the time Charlie arrived in Honduras at the end of August, joy had flooded his heart, as he realized he would soon see the ful-fillment of his vision for a building that would serve as a center for disciple-ship. It would be a place where people would gather around the two breads of tortillas and the Bible, the one to nurture the body, the

The deck for the School of Discipleship began with wood planking, but was later changed to stone pavers

other to nurture the soul. It would be in this building that believers could be discipled and sent forth to share the Good News of the Kingdom. And now the moment had arrived. He could hardly contain his excitement.

After the farmers lowered Charlie's litter gently to the ground, he was given a grand tour of the facility, being wheeled first to the completed deck with its unobstructed view of the tumbling Canchias River. Then he was taken to the end of the building to see the 40-foot Ambassador flagpole. Charlie was already delighted, but when they brought him into the newly finished *Cocina de Charlie* (Charlie's Kitchen) with its commercial gas stove, gleaming stainless steel work table and buffet serving line, he was absolutely beside himself. His body was frail, and he slumped just a bit in his chair with his head cocked to the right. And from that position as he was gently and slowly wheeled into the kitchen, it was his eyes that communicated all that Charlie was experiencing. They were eyes of wonder, as if he were staring at the Grand Canyon for the first time. His "Simeon" prayer had been answered. He had lived long enough to see the kitchen completed.

Dressed in shorts, his favorite "I Am an Ass for Jesus" T-shirt, white socks and house slippers, he was wheeled into the large fellowship hall. He rested his hands on the white towel that lay across his lap. The plastic tubes that fit snugly in his nose would provide enough oxygen to his increasingly hardening lungs to sustain his life for only seven more days. There was scarcely enough oxygen to give him the energy and breath support needed for making a speech. But Charlie was determined to share his heart with these men and women who were doing Kingdom work.

Taking advantage of Miguel's translation time to rest his lungs between his words to the 32 assembled pastors, he spoke in a whisper and used shorter phrases than are customary even when using a translator, but he still managed to speak for 45 minutes. There was weeping among the many Hondurans as they clung to every word he uttered. These extemporaneous words, spoken in an atmosphere that felt like the Upper Room, would be Charlie's final ones to them. The words he had pondered throughout the week as he anticipated this moment echoed the final themes spoken by his Lord to the disciples:

> It is a great joy and pleasure to be with you tonight. I have looked forward to this meeting for a long time. When I left Honduras [last spring], it was in my mind and my spirit to come back to Honduras. I wept because I did not think I would make it back, but Miguel said, "You will make it back." This was a prophecy by *Hermano* Miguel.
>
> It is hard to believe that eight years ago, we had the first pastors' meeting in Palmital. We invited a few pastors to put aside their little differences for the Kingdom of God and work together. And this is largely what we have done–to unite–for there is only one church. There is only one Lord, one Spirit,

and one Father over all, in all and through all. Just one Lord, and He loves us. He gave us His Son who died on the cross for our sins. God no longer holds our sins against us. Isn't this good news? Just think where you would be if God had not forgiven you of your sins! Families beat each other. Husbands beat their wives. Wives beat their husbands. People get drunk. They go crazy. But God in His great mercy has forgiven and accepted us. He puts His arms around us and wants us to be reconciled.

I asked God last night, "Why this disease?" I don't understand it, but I do not have to understand. I just have to be obedient. David said, "Yea, though I walk through the valley of death, I will fear no evil," I do not know what the outcome of this will be. He may raise me from the dead. He has the power to do it. He made us and He knows everything about us. We are fearfully and wonderfully made. I think it would be a great thing if He raised me from the dead, because I think a lot of people would put their faith in God and trust in God. Some would say this is a selfish prayer. But I would rather stay around for a while and advance the Kingdom of God.

I would like to do this for three reasons. Keep these reasons in mind. Do not ever let them leave you. The first thing I want to share from the Word is: *go make disciples*. Jesus said, "All authority is given unto me in heaven and earth. Go and make disciples of all nations, teaching them to do all the things that I have commanded you." Jesus said to put into practice all the things I have commanded you. Now, it would be a useless command if we taught this but did not put them into practice.

The second thing: in order to do this, *you must be sent by the Father* into all the world, not just Honduras but the entire world, and that is God's call upon our lives. You know the story of the wise man who built his house upon the rock. The rains and storms came, but the house stood, because it was built on a rock. The other man heard the Word, but did not put it into practice. You have to put it into practice.

The third and last thing is to know that the Father said, "I will be with you always, even to the end of the world." And He is with us tonight.

What a special place the Lord has given to us. Who would have dreamed of this 10 years ago? Oh, the Lord has done a great work among us. But we know this is not the church. The building is not the church. The building is a place where the church comes to meet and eat and fellowship, and that is what we do. It is a place where we learn and go forth.

It has been wonderful being with you tonight. I did not think I was going to make it down. But with God's power and your help I made it. Does anyone have any questions?

A Honduran pastor asked, "How did you become a Christian?"

I was so blessed to be born in a loving Christian family. What a great blessing that is to be nurtured in the Kingdom by parents who show their love. As a young boy, I accepted Christ into my life as the center of my life. Many times I failed God, like you. I was up and down. That is the way I was. But when I was, I guess, about 19 years old, I met Karen, and through Karen the Lord planted a seed in my heart, and it has been my joy to follow Him all the days of my life through all these years. I have not been perfect.

Another Honduran pastor said, "*Hermano* Charlie, our greatest joy is to be sitting with you here in this room."

Charlie's rejoinder corrected him gently:

The greatest joy, the greatest joy, the greatest joy by far that any of us can think or imagine is the joy of the unity of the brothers and sisters and with all the *mundo* [world]. The Scriptures tell us that by unity, the world will know that Jesus is Lord, and this is the cry of the church every day, "Jesus is Lord! Jesus is Lord!"

With these words, Charlie folded his hands together, leaned back on his pillow, and closed his eyes. After a few seconds he opened his mouth to ease his breathing and said, "Heaven!"

PART TEN

October 20, 1997

Home

I was going to say, don't weep for me, but from time to time
I weep for myself as I think about my own death.
~Charlie Smith

55

Chimes

After speaking to the pastors on Monday, Charlie was taken back to the Martha House where six more days would pass before the heaven he longed for became a reality. But he was at peace. His peace came from knowing his dream had been completed. His peace came from knowing that he had delivered a great challenge to the humble leadership of the Honduras church. The baton had been passed.

He called Dave into his room on Wednesday and asked him to pray that he would have the courage to face his final days on earth. Dave prayed, and then he read Psalm 27, which begins:

The LORD is my light and my salvation, whom shall I fear?
The LORD is the stronghold of my life, of whom shall I be afraid?

Over the next couple of days, Charlie received FAXes from his daughters that Candy read aloud to him. She also read FAXes from his young nieces Rachel and Hannah. She then attached their little drawings with messages to the wall to brighten up Charlie's room. Charlie wanted to continue typing on his computer, recording his thoughts for posterity and sharing encouragement through correspondence with those he loved, but now he was too weak even for that. Candy noticed two words at the top left of Charlie's computer screen: "Dear Lyle." These words to his son-in-law were the last Charlie would ever type.

Friday, October 17 brought the last visitor from the United States to Charlie's bedside. His brother Alvin, the father of Rachel and Hannah, came and served as chronicler of Charlie's final hours for the entire family. He sent regular updates to their sisters, children, nieces and nephews, and their still-living mother.

Charlie's face lit up when he saw the gifts his brother withdrew from his luggage: paintings from Rachel and Hannah, toilet paper and his favorite brand (Community) of tea and coffee. Though by this point he could barely speak two or three words without taking a rest, his response to his brother's bringing a six-month's supply of each item was, "Isn't God wonderful!"

Dr. Elsa, her husband Baltazar, and Miguel

One of the first things Alvin recorded in his journal was the dedication of the Assembly Hall for the Discipleship Center. Miguel and all of the workers had felt the urgency of finishing the building and holding the dedication as a final gift to Charlie. Now it was ready, and the people gathered that Friday night for the celebration. At one point, Charlie had said he was ready to be carried down for the service, but in reality, he was far too weak. He had to be content with listening from his bedroom to the sounds of the joyful singing and the series of preachers who spoke to the 300 assembled below. Later that night, some of the people gathered on the porch to sing for their friend. They knew how much he loved simple music accompanied by simple stringed instruments. The night sounds of the rainforest and the soothing music of God's people were Charlie's lullaby.

On Sunday, Doctor Elsa said Charlie's breathing condition was one tenth what it had been on his arrival eight weeks prior. Near the end of Charlie's bed, three tall green cylinders filled with compressed oxygen stood like Green Berets at attention, sustaining Charlie's life. Six months earlier, Charlie had been able to function with a portable machine pumping out two liters of oxygen per minute. On this Lord's Day, he needed 16 liters per minute to keep him alive. Recalling Charlie's desperate need for oxygen in the Martha House, Dave wrote:

> The last two or three days, he had two cannulas running to his nose. Miguel would send a truck into San Pedro Sula every two or three days to pick up new tanks. He would pull up in front of the Assembly Hall and a couple of the Hondurans– including short little Markitos–would take those heavy tanks up to the Martha House on their shoulders. May God bless and reward them greatly! We were having trouble with the power [from the hydroelectric system] shutting down at times, and when it did, Charlie's floor-standing unit would no longer work,

308

so we would have to hustle to hook him up to one or both of the tanks.

That Sunday evening, Charlie noticed Miguel's wife Nilsa among those visiting him, and he asked her to pray for him as Miguel translated. After the prayer, Charlie said, "I am going through a great struggle, and I need the help of all of you who are so close to me." Gathered around Charlie's bed, in addition to Miguel and Nilsa, were Alvin, Dave and Candy, Ever Andino and his wife Gloria, Paola, Doctor Elsa and her husband Baltazar–an unbeliever who was witnessing some pretty powerful "how to live and die as a Christian" lessons. Together, the North American group began to sing some of Charlie's favorite hymns, *Victory in Jesus, Trust and Obey, In the Light of God* and *Amazing Grace.*

The satellite phone rang. Felicia and Anne-Marie had called, wanting an update on their father. When they were told about the singing of the hymns, they requested that the group sing *This Is My Father's World.* As the group was singing the last verse, the wind chimes on the front porch begin to ring. Over the years, Karen loved the sound of wind chimes and had several hanging at their home in Lake Wales. As a reminder of his wife, Charlie had them hung on the Martha House porch so he could feel her presence when they rang. Candy referred to the ringing as "visitations from Karen." In the peace that followed the singing of the song, the chimes rang vigorously again. Alvin wrote, "Charles was pleased to hear from Karen."

During their phone call, the girls also requested that Candy give Charlie a kiss for them. Charlie requested that one of the kisses come through Candy and the other through Alvin. So Candy and Alvin both kissed Charlie on the forehead, and the expression on his face indicated he was quite pleased with the results.

After the simple time of worship, several of the group gathered around Charlie and held him close. As Charlie received this closeness, he muttered quietly, "I'm ready!" He indicated that he did not know when the Lord would take him, but he was ready. Around 11:45 p.m. he asked for Dave and Candy to spend the night with him. Honduran staff worker Markitos stayed on the Martha House porch throughout the night, ready to be a messenger to Miguel and to Alvin, who was sleeping in the Maria House about 20 yards down the hill.

Between midnight and 4 a.m. on Monday, October 20, Charlie was restless. But when Alvin returned at 6:30 a.m., he was sleeping peacefully. At 7:30, Candy asked Charlie a question, and he indicated that he both heard her and understood. When Dr. Elsa examined Charlie, she noticed that his fingers had a blue tint to them, indicating his body had begun shutting down. She estimated he had between four and eight hours to live, and would soon slip into a coma. Alvin wrote in his journal:

Candy knew that Charles had said if he became comatose, he wanted all the oxygen sources to be removed. Candy knew and understood Charles' wishes, but she wanted to speak with Felicia and Anne-Marie to inform them of his wishes... As Candy prepared the FAX, Anne-Marie called and Candy relayed the information. Anne-Marie wanted to consult Felicia. They called back and said that Charles had not discussed this with them, and if he became comatose, they wanted to ride it out for a little while. All agreed that it was the right decision to leave the oxygen on... It was now 8:45 a.m. I was seated on one side holding Charles' hand and Miguel was seated on the other side. Miguel tried to sing a song, but was unable to finish it. The rest of us were unable to join in... Charles' breathing began to slow...There was no gasping for breath... It was now 8:50 a.m., and Charles breathed his last breath... Miguel asked for the stethoscope, which I handed to him. He checked his heartbeat. It was still there, but was starting to beat more slowly. At 8:55 a.m., Charles' heart beat for the last time, and he was home.

We cried, but for Charles there was peace. At 9 a.m., Karen's chimes rang for the first time that day...

At 10:15 a.m. I noticed a red truck racing up the road. Miguel said, "That's Dionicio with fresh oxygen tanks." Dionicio ran up to the Martha House, talked with Miguel and then walked slowly into the house and wept at Charles' bedside.

Word spread quickly among the people of Canchias that their beloved friend had made his transition. An atmosphere of solemnity hovered over the village as tears fell from the eyes of men and women like tender raindrops on banana leaves.

Give all that is within you to others–
to those who need what you have to give.
Be the best you can be in the army of the Lord.
~Charlie Smith

56
The Last of the Best

When Charlie passed away in the village of Canchias, people whispered a phrase of deep respect. The phrase, uttered only of the most esteemed individuals, was, "Charlie was the last of the best." With the news of his passing, they began streaming up the rough road to pay their respects to this beloved member of their community. Here are some of their stories.

Leonarda and Nicolas

Leonarda lived just outside the ministry's *Gates of Justice.* Her special memory of Charlie's love for her brought tears to her eyes. In 1994, her son José had been dying in Santa Elena, about a two-hour drive from Canchias in those days. He had stomach cancer, and it was spreading fast. She sent her son Eduardo to ask Charlie if he would use a ministry truck to go and pick up her son and bring him home to die. Without hesitation, Charlie said "Yes." He personally drove the family to Santa Elena, where the family members placed José in the back of the truck. Until José died two weeks later, Leonarda's neighbors, as well as anyone sitting on the Martha House porch with Charlie, could hear the cries of José in pain. Charlie requested Elsa, the ministry doctor, to administer what little Demerol the American doctors had left in the ministry clinic to ease his distress.

311

Now, three years later, Leonarda's two surviving sons, Eduardo and Wilmer, had been asked to lead the donkey in the funeral procession for Charlie. And her husband Nicolas was one of 36 men digging round the clock to prepare Charlie's grave on top of Ambassador Mountain.

Paola

Another person who loved Charlie unconditionally was his caretaker, Paola. She lived for five years in Canchias as the ministry cook at the Esther House. But when Charlie came to live out his last days in Canchias, she became his "nurse." She is caretaker now of a house instead of a man, but she keeps something special of Charlie's to help her remember the impact he had on her life. On the porch of the San Isidro house of a well-to-do Honduran who lives abroad, she keeps Charlie's old wicker chair, full of memories of her months in Canchias. She remembers how generous Charlie was, and how she counted it a privilege to carry him to his bed, turn up his oxygen, take him outside to hear the birds sing, and watch him type away, transcribing his dream.

She said, "I would carry him to the bathroom and rest his head on my shoulder and clean him before taking him back to bed." For her, this humble task was a privilege that could not repay the generosity of a man whom she remembered as never coming to the village with his hands empty.

Estella and Victor

Meals needed to be prepared for visiting teams from North America, and Estella recalls the love that Charlie extended to train her to be the ministry's cook. She and her husband Victor lived in the village of Los Globos. Victor was hired to work for the ministry and

312

would be gone from Estella for three days at a time, performing his duties as driver. He pleaded with Charlie to hire Estella too, so that she could be with him in San Isidro. Charlie understood Victor's heart, as he missed his wife Karen on his many jaunts to Honduras. He sent word to Miguel to bring Estella to San Isidro and hire her as a cook. She knew nothing about cooking for groups, but Charlie said he would teach her. Charlie believed in the potential of others, especially the poor. Soon, Estella could prepare a pot of beans Charlie's way and knew how to figure out shopping and cooking for large numbers of people. Because Charlie was sensitive to Victor's request, Victor said of Charlie, "He is the last of the best."

After many years of working for the ministry, Victor and Estella opened their own restaurant just up the street from the ministry offices in San Isidro. Today, her baked chicken and fries, along with her rice and beans, are favorites of customers in their community. Moved to tears in his living room attached to the restaurant, Victor shared, "Charlie was like a father to me. If it were not for him, I would still be working in the fields. Our daughter loved him and his wife Karen so much that they named their daughter 'Karen,' and today she is an electrical engineer. Charlie loved the poor of Honduras so much because God put His heart in him, and that is how he loved, with the heart of God."

Trino and Sabina

Trino and Charlie were harmonica partners, often enjoying playing this simple instrument in the quiet Canchias evenings. Trino's property abutted the ministry property, and the two men often visited each other, sharing a cup of coffee and their love for music. Charlie helped Trino and his jolly wife Sabina obtain a better house with a good roof and a concrete floor. Years later, Trino and Sabina still cherished a framed photo of Charlie, a memento of the days when he was just a short walk away.

Markito

One rainy evening in 1994, as Charlie cooked "chicken spaghetti" in the Joshua House, there came a knock at the door. It was Markito. Charlie's guest was small in stature but powerfully built. His face was square and his jaw tight. His unshaven face appeared to be covered with the deep black bristles of a shoe brush. There were large gaps between his brown teeth. His face was hard until he smiled, and then the furrowed wrinkles on his forehead looked like the grid inside a toaster. On this night, he stood in the  doorway holding Junior, his preschool son, on his shoulder. Charlie invited them in and gestured toward the couch. They sat closely on the sofa. Junior's legs dangled over the couch and Markito's feet barely touched the floor. They were wet from the drizzle outside and hardly visible in this unlit room as the setting sun drew a sheet of darkness over the village.

Markito not only lacked the formal education that would have taught him to read or write, but may have lacked the ability to learn those skills. He was once asked, "How many children do you have?" He held up his left hand and began to count, "*Uno, dos, tres, cuatro, cinco.*" But Markito was loved by Charlie, and

**Markito with his family
Junior is in the very back, behind Jim**

Markito loved Charlie. He represented the treasure in Honduras that Charlie committed himself to on his knees the night in 1991 when Heart to Honduras was formally founded.

Charlie had special affection for this man, because he had always been a loner until he met Sarah. The child with him that night was actually her child, born out of wedlock to another father. When this happened, Sarah

314

became the village outcast. Her chances of remarriage were slim, even though she was beautiful. Being rather shy, not particularly good-looking, and for sure poor, Markito also had slim chances of marriage. Somehow, these two had found each other and married. Perhaps it was because Markito had such a loving, accepting nature that Sarah decided to marry him. Though they eventually had four children of their own, of all who observed Markito, none would have suspected that this child he so lovingly carried everywhere was not his own as well.

Knowing how much Markito loved to serve others and realizing that he and Sarah and Junior were probably hungry, Charlie thought of a little errand that would help Charlie and also enable him to "pay" Markito without patronizing him. He paused in cooking his spaghetti and said, "Markito, would you take this money and go to the *bodega* and purchase us some candles?" Immediately, Markito put Junior on his shoulder and left.

When he returned with the candles, he and his son were damp again from the drizzling rain, but his big smile showed how happy he was to have helped his friend. Later, as Markito and Junior prepared to leave for home, Charlie reached on top of the refrigerator and took half a loaf of bread, a can of tuna and some eggs and gave them to Markito. These two friends, who shared a mostly wordless friendship, had blessed each other with an errand in the night and a bit of food—small tokens of their strong bond.

Charlie's loving kindness was poured out to Markito, Trino, Nicolas, Leonarda, Paola, Victor, Estella, and many others in this remote place. It is because of this love he became the "last of the best" in the hearts of all the villagers of Canchias.

Love feels no burden, thinks nothing of trouble
and attempts what is above its strength.
~Thomas à Kempis

57
A Pine Box

In keeping with his belief in simplicity, Charlie wanted to be buried in a pine box, just as his wife had been.

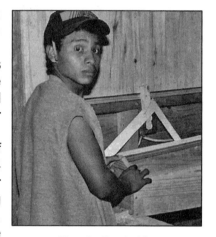

When it had become obvious Sunday evening, a few hours before Charlie's death, that the pine box would soon be needed, ministry carpenter Ever Andino began his labor of love.

Burials in the rural mountains of Honduras typically take place within 24 hours of the person's passing. The poor have no means of preserving a decaying body in the intense tropical heat. However, in light of the need to allow time for Felicia and Anne-Marie to arrive, the desire of the pastors scattered across

Ever Andino in his carpentry shop

Honduras to be present for the funeral, and Charlie's instructions regarding a pine box and burial on top of Ambassador Mountain, it would be 48 hours before his final interment.

Ever and his wife Gloria had been frequent visitors at Charlie's bedside, and Ever was honored to have been chosen to construct his friend's coffin. He owed so much to this man. Before Ever met Charlie, he was a teenager with a bleak future, living without hope in a culture ready to snare him with the repressive tentacles of disease, ignorance and poverty. Now Ever was healthy, had been trained as a carpenter through Charlie's encouragement, and had steady work, as his expertise was needed in the expanding projects of Heart to Honduras.

Ever was also becoming recognized in his community of San Isidro as a skilled carpenter. He could make furniture and cabinets, and he had recently framed the 20-foot-high screened wall of the Assembly Hall in Canchias. He loved his work and did it all carefully, but there was a different love being poured

316

into the construction of this pine box. Charlie had introduced him to the Kingdom of God by example, and Ever's value system had totally changed. He had recently given up spending his Sundays playing soccer and had committed his life to following the Jesus that had brought Charlie Smith to his community.

Ever worked through the October night not only to complete the box, but to make sure it followed the requests of his friend and met the requirements of the plan God had given to him. In Ever's vision, the box would be rectangular in shape, with a slight extension about a third of the distance from the top, giving it the appearance of a cross. There would be no gold or silver or bronze on this box. The Heart to Honduras logo of a donkey would be painted on the sides to communicate how the ass, being the poor man's animal, symbolized the spirit of humility. The Spanish word *embajador* [ambassador] would be painted on top.

After many hours of loving labor, a truck drove up to the woodworking shop in San Isidro. Six men lifted the beautiful box onto the back of the truck, with Ever giving careful directions. The truck then headed for Canchias. When it arrived, the men carried the box up the steep path to the porch of the Martha House.

While the men were preparing the egg-crate lining of the casket, a woman who worked for the ministry slipped into the room. She was weeping and praying, and the men waited respectfully until she finished before they carefully lifted Charlie's body, took him out to the front porch and gently laid him on the soft cushion in Ever's box. Charlie had instructed that he be buried wearing his shorts, so that some poor man could have his jeans. A beautiful Guatemalan blanket was strategically placed over the body so his special T-shirt with the Ambassador logo could be clearly seen.

Lifting the box with its precious contents, the men began a careful journey back down the winding path. The first of the mourners could be seen making their way up the road to begin the wake, and the braying of a little female ass, which had been a special gift to Charlie from Miguel, could be heard, as if sadly acknowledging his departure.

At the bottom of the hill, the box was taken inside the huge, just-completed School of Discipleship building that had been Charlie's central vision. The box was placed on top of three sawhorses. Charlie's Bible, tattered from much use, was laid across his legs, opened to John 17 in recognition of Charlie's love for the unity that Christ prayed for in that chapter. As Charlie had requested, there was a photo of his wife Karen beside of the casket. Charlie's "Indiana Jones" hat, given to him by his daughter Anne-Marie, was placed below the open Bible, and symbolizing his great love for the music of the church, his harmonica was placed on top of his hat.

As the plain box with its precious treasure rested on the three sawhorses, Ever gathered his tools and quietly left the hall, humbled that God had honored him with the task of making this simple pine box.

317

58

A Stubborn Boulder, A Proper Burial

With his usual expertise, Miguel was managing all the logistics a death entails. He had made arrangements for someone to pick up the arriving North Americans on Tuesday. He had sent Baltazar to the 20 churches associated with Heart to Honduras, notifying them of Charlie's passing and the time of the services. In those pre-cell-phone days, all contact with churches was made by personal visit, and Baltazar's trip over the rutted roads was his own labor of love. Leaving in the afternoon, he did not return to Canchias until the wee hours of the morning. Too late, Miguel realized that in his haste to get the word out, he had put the wrong day for the services on his note to the pastors, and many of them would arrive on Wednesday evening, instead of Tuesday evening. The best he could do would be to have a second service on Wednesday afternoon, just before the processional to the gravesite.

Arrangements for one task remained—one enormous task, as it turned out. But no one realized that at first. Miguel had spread the word for volunteers to come to the mountain to give Charlie one last gift, and men flooded in from the surrounding villages to dig his grave on top of Ambassador Mountain. Beginning at 7 p.m. Monday, 36 men cut down three trees, leveled out the top of the mountain, and began to dig the grave. Three feet into the task, they hit solid rock. The spot Charlie had chosen for his final resting place was the top of a small mountain, which consisted of an enormous, impenetrable boulder! Determined to honor his request, the men began taking turns hitting the rock with a sledge hammer and a pickaxe, breaking the rock apart bit by bit.

But they could not break through the rock. Fifteen hours into the task, they realized that their progress was far too slow to be able to bury Charlie by the next day. On Tuesday afternoon, Alvin observed some of the discouraged men trudging past the mourners in the Assembly Hall and recorded in his journal: "There was a hopelessness and sadness in the men's eyes about their apparent failure."

When Miguel came to assess the situation, he explained to Alvin what it appeared they would need to do: level the grave at the depth it was—about three feet—put in the casket, cover it with cement, then bring all of the rocks that had been tossed out of the hole back up the mountain and build a six-foot-high cairn with them. Miguel said that putting concrete over a grave was a common way to bury the rich, and Alvin worried about what Charlie would say about that.

Alvin had blessed his brother by his visit, the giving of the Community Tea, hugging him, kissing him on the forehead, weeping with him and holding his hand. But perhaps the greatest gift Alvin gave to Charlie was his warning to Miguel. "Miguel, if you bury Charlie on top of the ground, he will haunt you for the rest of your life."

Alvin made this composite panoramic photo of some of the men who worked so tirelessly to dig Charlie's grave on Ambassador Mountain.

Into the second night, 16 men remained working on the task. At 3:30 a.m. Wednesday morning, Miguel climbed the mountain in the dark to check on their progress, only to discover that the main chisel had just broken. Miguel sent a man to San Isidro to repair it and brought the workers down to the Assembly Hall for a meal. By 4:30 a.m., the men had a freshly sharpened chisel in hand and renewed energy from the food as they set off to chip away at the boulder again. They told Miguel, "This is our last expression of love for Brother Charlie. We would never do this kind of work for money. This is our love for him."

Mid-morning on Wednesday, Miguel trudged up the mountain again to check on the gravesite, dreading what he might find. But soon he came running back with exciting news. Some men who worked in the silver mines near Tegucigalpa had been located. These miners were able to analyze the rocks and come up with a solution that involved heating the rock by burning tires on it, then pouring cold water on the heated boulder, breaking it apart so that the debris could be removed. They were making rapid progress, flinging the remaining rocks over the mountain. The grave would be six feet deep by burial time that afternoon. It was good news to discover that Charlie would not have to haunt us for burying him like a rich man.

319

I want a buck wagon or a jolt wagon like the one Martin Luther King used.
Not like President Kennedy who had a fancy bier on wheels. I want a
procession led by an ass followed by a casket borne by men, with a procession
of the poor singing simple music without instruments.
I want it simple.
~Charlie Smith

59

If You Loved Them, They Will Come

The two-day wake had begun. Inside the Discipleship Center, the mourning of the people of the village masked the distant sound of pickaxes chipping away at the top of Ambassador Mountain. Many tears were shed as people stood in front of the plain pine box, though Charlie's desire had been that the memorial services were to be times of worship and praise. As he was coming to terms with his fatal illness, he had written:

> I was going to say, don't weep for me, but from time to time I weep for myself as I think about my own death. I feel sorry for myself that I have to die now when the work of the Kingdom is going so well, and I don't want to be the cause of mourning, of tears, but this is the way of all flesh, and how blessed I am to know that there are people, children of God, who love me and who will carry parts of God's love from my life in their hearts for the rest of their lives.

Confusion had been generated by Miguel's erroneous message that had announced a Wednesday, rather than Tuesday, evening funeral service. This was to have been followed by a morning burial service on Wednesday, but Miguel knew that many pastors from the more distant churches would be profoundly disappointed if they arrived after all the celebration was over. Eventually, a decision was made to continue with plans for a service on Tuesday evening, and then postpone the interment service from early morning to mid-afternoon on Wednesday, hoping that the guests who were coming for what they thought was to be an evening service would arrive early and be able to participate. And so it was that Charlie's life was honored with a wake that began on Monday afternoon, simple music that continued into the night from the

Ambassador band that he loved, a service on Tuesday night, and a Honduran burial on Wednesday morning. In addition, two North American celebrations of Charlie's life would be held: one at First Presbyterian Church, Lake Wales, Florida on Sunday night, November 2, 1997, and a second, smaller one in Wichita on November 30, for those in that area who had been to Honduras under Charlie's ministry.

THE WAKE

Those who came to Honduras to pay homage were a testimony to how Charlie Smith's life had brought God's love in very practical ways. Old men with wrinkled foreheads, little children clutching a mother's hand, pastors respectfully dressed in white long-sleeved shirts in spite of the heat, farmers in rubber boots and straw hats, the crippled, the paralytic, women wearing dresses permeated with the smell of their cooking fires, the barefooted and those with flip flops, some wearing North American T-shirts with slogans they didn't understand, the poorly educated and illiterate, the pregnant teens, the toothless with time-worn and hard faces, ladies with  river-washed black hair, those carrying flashlights, the hungry, the weary who slept on dirt floors, and mothers with suckling infants. Poor people. Good people. God's people created in His image. They came because of this one man who loved them and gave himself for them.

Alvin's journal spoke of the children who gathered in curiosity around him as he either typed his journal on the ministry laptop or scribbled it by hand in his

321

notebook. He noticed the children who sat quietly through the long services or fell asleep on the tile floor, the dozens of men who assembled on the deck and peeked in through the screens, and a special teen who sat next to him and moved him to tears:

> A boy who looks to be about 15 years old has come in to the service. He has a handicap that has affected his legs. His legs are only bones and skin stretched over them. He is able to propel himself by holding his hands on the floor with his knees bent straight up. He moves by his hands to the back of the hall where he focuses his eyes on Nilsa as she sings. As I watch this boy, tears start flooding my eyes again as they have done often and at unplanned times all day: when a villager came in to Charles' room and began crying and praying; when Karen's chimes rang; when Charles' ass brayed; when I stood alone on the porch of the Martha House and looked at the village; when I think of the love Charles had for these people; when I see the boy walk in on his hands and take his place in the assembly, when I listen to the singing tonight and think of Charles' glorious spot on the top of Ambassador Mountain.

Long after midnight, when Alvin had retired to his cabin, he continued to hear these first-night visitors "flooding the valley with wonderful music." He fell asleep on the night of his brother's passing, listening to the loud sounds of the crickets, the braying of Charlie's donkey, and the gentle sounds of the five-piece acoustic band. He had to agree with something his brother often said: "Isn't God wonderful?"

On Tuesday, the mourners continued to arrive. In the afternoon, Alvin wrote:

> Two children, probably ages 3 and 7, walk slowly up the hill holding hands. Grandmother, mother and three other children follow behind. All are going to one place–to see their friend Charlie. A truckload of people from San Isidro arrived about 30 minutes ago... There has been a steady stream of people coming here all day. No one is having people sign in at the door. No professional funeral directors greet you when you arrive. No one is rushing in for quick condolences between busy schedules. There is just a lot of love here.

Dave Pischel had set up a keyboard, and as the mourners gathered, he played from Charlie's list of favorite hymns: *Onward Christian Soldiers, When the Roll Is Called Up Yonder, The Love of God, Revive Us Again...* The new kitchen was the scene of much activity. Jimmy Pinell, brother to Miguel, with the help of a pastor from San Pedro Sula, was

Charlie and a campesino

installing a filter on the new ice machine. Paola and Doctor Elsa were directing a kitchen crew of women patting out hundreds of tortillas, cooking chicken and rice on the newly installed eight-burner gas stove, and brewing a 20-gallon pot of coffee so that Charlie's desire to make this a festive occasion could be honored, with all who came hungry able to be fed, and so that the men who were working around the clock digging the grave could receive sustenance.

As Alvin observed the kitchen activity, the San Pedro Sula pastor struck up a conversation, asking if Alvin would be coming to take Charlie's place in the ministry. A counselor with his own ministry back in Louisiana, Alvin was briefly silenced by this question, then replied, "No one could take Charlie's place." The pastor looked sad at this response, and Alvin realized that down deep the question really was, "Who will come?" Alvin would miss his brother dearly on a personal level, but these men and women were grieving the loss of a man who had brought hope to an impoverished people. They were wondering if the whole project would collapse in his absence. They had lost a friend, true, but were they going to lose even more than that? Were they going to lose the hope for a better life that he had kindled in their hearts?

Later in the afternoon, Felicia and Lyle, Anne-Marie and Jason, and Dr. Jim Nelson and his wife Janie arrived from the United States. Through tears falling from red-rimmed eyes, Anne-Marie gazed at the body of her father and said, "He's not here. It's just a shell." She and Felicia walked around the Assembly Hall, hugging all the people who were special to them because they were special to their father. During their visits to their dad, they had made many friends, and they thanked each one for loving Charlie and taking care of him.

By 7 p.m. on Tuesday, around 300 poor Hondurans, ranging from little children to the old and feeble, were in the Assembly Hall. The people who came

323

to pay their respects knew this man had choices. They knew that he had a thousand options they could not even imagine. Yet, he chose to die among them. He could have had his body shipped back to the United States and "done it right," but he chose to be buried here. He could have chosen a sleek, black hearse with a powerful engine to transport his body, but he chose a humble ass to lead the funeral procession. He could have chosen a stainless-steel Batesville casket, but he chose a pine box. His body could have lain in state in a cathedral with stained glass windows and a pipe organ, but he chose instead the Assembly Hall in Canchias, with its view of the mountains and the homemade instruments of The Ambassadors.

Miguel invited the people to come forward and share their thoughts about Charlie, and for an hour, they did so. Jimmy Pinell gave Alvin a summarized translation: "Charlie always kept his eyes on the simple things." "Charlie did not call the ministry 'Heart to Honduras' just as a name for the ministry. He meant it. His heart was here. He showed it by coming to die here with us." "Charlie showed love, peace, and humility in his life. We must follow his example. We must follow what the Bible teaches. That way, we can meet him in heaven."

This testimony time was followed by prayer, Bible reading, and music. The choir sang in English *I Know the Master of the Wind*. Miguel told the family that Charlie would "cry peacefully" when Miguel sang this for him, particularly with the words "He can calm the storm, make the sun shine again."

Far into the night the testimonies, preaching and singing continued, until finally Miguel sent everyone to bed around 2 a.m. The final service would be in a few hours, and everyone needed to rest.

THE FUNERAL

Throughout Wednesday, ministry trucks fanned out to pick up those living in faraway villages. The pickups are specially fitted with metal bars to allow passengers a measure of safety, as 25 people often stand packed together for a trip. Many people walked for hours and came from as far away as Tegucigalpa, four hours by car. The dozen women in the kitchen served up scrambled eggs, refried beans, rice and tortillas for those travelling long distances.

The service, scheduled for 2:30, in typical Honduran custom, began closer to 3:30 for the 250 who had come. Dave prayed an opening prayer, Nilsa read Charlie's favorite chapter, John 17, a couple of pastors preached and led the congregation in song, and an electric guitar (with apologies to Charlie) accompanied a trio. Felicia read a letter from Charlie to the people of Honduras, which ended with the line, "The church here loves me unconditionally, and that is why I wanted to die and be buried here." Anne-Marie expressed her gratitude to everyone, promising to return soon, and Dave sang a song he wrote called *Last*

Tears. After Antonio spoke and sang, The Ambassadors played and sang, and then Alvin prayed the benediction.

THE BURIAL

Then it was time to follow Charlie's instructions for the trip to the graveside. The casket was transferred to the back of a pickup, and everyone walked beside, behind and in front of the truck as it bounced its way to the middle of the village of Canchias, watched along the way by everyone who had not come up to the Assembly Hall. In "town" the truck stopped to unload its cargo. Three rough-sawn 2x2 poles were placed under the casket, and half-inch nylon cords secured the casket to the poles, in anticipation of the steep hike up the mountain. The length of the poles allowed for as many as 12 men to carry the casket once the steep part of the ascent began.

As Charlie had requested, his burro was positioned in front of the casket as a symbol of humility. Two men guided the burro, six men carried the casket, and the procession began the trip of less than a mile–but definitely uphill all the way. Anne-Marie and Felicia pushed the wheelchairs that held the children living in Karen's Hope, the hospice center named for their mother. The Ambassadors began playing, and the people started singing.

The wheelchairs were forced to stop at the Assembly Hall where any semblance of a road ceased, but everyone else kept going. The barefoot children skipped across the stream, and ran easily along the grassy, rocky, and sometimes muddy, trail. Mothers carried their babies and effortlessly made the hike in flip flops; even the aged walked with apparent ease. The long procession worked its way along the mostly gradual slope of a trail that had been cut and landscaped by Tony Bayles. In places the way was steep and narrow or a small tree would block the progress of the casket and its 12 bearers, but only the burro had to turn back. Everyone else arrived safely at the summit, still singing to honor their friend.

Miguel said a few words, the family sang *In the Light of God,* which was one of Charlie's favorite hymns, and everyone sang *Alleluia.* Charlie's hat, Bible and harmonica were removed from the casket, which had been left open until now, and Ever screwed on the top with its Ambassador logo. The pine box was lowered with ropes. Alvin and the girls each threw in a rock. It was 6 p.m., and darkness was falling. Flashlights lit the final filling of the grave. Alvin later journaled:

> A cool, gentle breeze graced the spot. The sky was overcast, but the lights of the village sparkled below like diamonds. The flowers that had graced the casket were carefully placed on the site–bouquets the girls had brought

from San Pedro Sula, along with large cans of flowers beautifully prepared by the women of the village. In the almost total darkness, everyone who remained just stood quietly.... Someone started to head down, and everyone else followed. I was the last to leave the top. I had a unique vantage point to see the people below snake down the trail with their flashlights glowing. It was a beautiful sight. I walked with Ever...on two occasions, he tenderly hugged me. At one point we turned off our flashlight and turned around to look at the vast darkness behind. The mountainside was filled with hundreds of twinkling stars. I then realized that the stars were lightning bugs, who added their statement to the evening.

Charlie's wishes had been fulfilled, though as Alvin observed, "Charles' vision of being buried on top of Ambassador Mountain took more to pull off than he would have thought. Visions are often more difficult to put into place than the visionary would first imagine, but the men who took the assignment had the heart for it... Heart is the key to the implemented vision... Charles lived, died, and was buried on the rock."

A few days later, staff member Dave Pischel wrote the following poem about the legacy of his friend:

DOWN THE ROAD

He came, and stood beside the road,
all muddy from his strain and toil,
and, weary, with dirty, calloused hands,
pointed further on, and said
with voice, hoarsened by labor long,
and panting, as his breath was gone,
'This is the way, where I have walked
and worked; now I am tired; my time
is nearing; go! continue on,
complete this course, 'ere day is done!'
And down he lay, and died.

That is all he said; a sign
beside the road, to point us on!
O fools would we be so to stop
and build a monument around
this dirty shell! We'll see him hence
with all the others, shining there,
completed, as we too shall be,
should we continue on the road!
But do we stop, and worship here,
we draw a multitude aside,
beside ourselves, to waste away
in twilight, while the perfect day
awaits us down the road.

326

My memorial service is to be a service of Worship and Praise.
A child of God, An Ambassador Serving the Savior has gone home.
~Charlie Smith

60

A Presbyterian's Perspective

Though Alvin stayed in Honduras with Charlie's daughters for the extensive memorial celebrations there, many friends and family in the United States wanted to honor him, also. On Sunday night, November 2, 1997, a service was held at the Presbyterian Church where his wife Karen's services had been held a scant four years earlier. Charlie had acknowledged that this might happen, and had given a few instructions regarding this service also, including how to dress: "Let it be known that for Charlie Smith's Celebration Service, dress is casual–no coats and ties. Don't do it, Brother Jim!"

Charlie put Dave Pischel in charge of the music, asking that instruments be kept minimal and congregational voices primary. In line with this request, Dave brought a video recording of The Ambassadors from Canchias, which played as people gathered for the service.

Charlie asked that his daughters read Scripture and share whatever was in their hearts to share. He requested that Nilsa Pinell pray the main prayer, that Miguel represent the church in Honduras with his words, that his sister, Lorna and I share from our hearts as key supporters of his vision for ministry, and that Heart to Honduras Board Chair Jerry Grubbs or Pastor Dave Rockness of the Presbyterian Church conduct the communion service. He named Mark Shaner to act as representative of the students from his Warner Southern and H.E.A.R.T. days by saying the closing prayer. And all of this was to be followed by a big party in the fellowship hall, knowing that "I, too, will be celebrating with Karen and all of those who have gone before as we rejoice in the presence of our Lord, the King of Kings."

In addition to following the general outline of speakers, the family asked Miriam Rockness, wife of the pastor and dear friend of Karen Smith, to speak that day. Her words summarize the life of Charles Robert Smith:

∞ ∞ ∞

Though Charlie Smith was a familiar presence to many in Lake Wales, he first became part of my life through his wife Karen and their two daughters,

Felicia and Anne-Marie. Charlie's occasional presence was a strong, vital, presence upon us. It might have been a book he was reading, a thought he was contemplating, or a venture in which he wished to enlist us. It became customary to greet him with two questions: "Where have you been?" and "Where are you going?" Increasingly, the answer to both was Honduras.

Just as Karen's coming into our church fellowship brought Charlie into our lives, her short illness–and home going–drew us closer as together we wrestled with the pain and perplexities of our broken world and then witnessed the grace, style, and celebratory spirit with which the family–led by Karen–faced her "transition" from time to Eternity.

As we all know, it was absolutely impossible to spend time with Charlie without being infused with his enthusiasm. He was a man of vision. He had the rare ability to see beyond the here and now–to visualize with the "eyes of faith" what could be, and walk in the light of that faith. His dreams and vision were often frustrated by those of us who could not see what he saw–but he persevered and carried many along with him...and most of us farther than we would have gone without him.

He was a man of passion. He lived life with zest: whether devouring the books of a favorite author, cooking up his famous fare or opening up his home for others to enjoy it. Who can forget gatherings on the screened porch overlooking the water lilies, or playing his beloved tapes of videos for the benefit of others, or, for that matter, playing his harmonica non-stop from his unending repertoire of gospel songs, and playing or teaching the Word? He detested short services! As he said, and I quote, "If we can watch a movie for two hours, which we all do from time to time, and can spend hours upon hours watching football and other sporting events, would you not think we could worship together as the family of God for two hours?"

He was a man of compassion. Compassion was the thread woven through all the ventures and adventures of Charlie's adult life–beginning with the Peace Corps in the '60s followed by Food For The Hungry, H.E.A.R.T, Project Global Village, Mercy Corps and Hand to the Plow.

Nowhere did these qualities come together more concretely or compellingly than in the two tangible ministries which he left behind...The H.E.A.R.T. program at Warner Southern, here in Lake Wales...and Heart to Honduras in Central America, supported by this church–Charlie representing it annually.

Four years ago, I stood at this very place bringing tribute to Karen–wearing a red hat–as did all her Circle sisters as a testimony to the zany, fun-loving side of Karen.

This evening, I don another hat–this time in tribute to Charlie: a testimony to the zany, on-the-edge (over the edge?) side of Charlie–a baseball cap bearing the logo of his mission: a humble donkey–or an "ass" as Charlie would much prefer it to be called, and I quote "as in the theologically correct King James Version!" There is no doubt about it, Charlie was iconoclastic: he loved to push the edges, deliberately disturbing the peace, particularly of those of us whom he suspected to be too comfortable in our church pews. And there is no doubt in my mind that there was a bit of the "naughtiness" in his explanation of words contained in the acrostic of his mission: AMB**ASS**ADORS SERVING THE SAVIOUR.

But beneath the surface of daring and fun contained in this logo was the very heart of Charlie–his vision, his passion, his compassion–based on two precepts: 1) We Christians should be, must be, ambassadors for Jesus, bringing light and love and life to the lost, the hurting, and the hungry–both physically and spiritually, and 2) As ambassadors, we must see ourselves rightly, in our true position: simple donkeys (in the "religiously correct" version!) carrying Jesus.

If Charlie had his way about this "Home Going Celebration," he would have the doors locked, exit only with the pledge of giving one week a year to Honduras...or better yet, one year of one's life (if not one's entire lifetime!). Honduras was the paradigm, to use his term, through which he saw the world–and would wish us to see it!

Yet, true to the quiddity of Charlie's heart, and perhaps his lasting legacy to us all, was something more basic than any given place: the challenge inspired by his very presence that we, like he, would examine our own hearts, indeed, our posture before God and our fellow man, and ask our Maker and Savior: "What would you have me to do?" Then go forth–and do it.

It is hard to imagine this world without Charlie. It was hard for Charlie to imagine leaving this world. There was so much he loved and wanted to still go do. He admired Karen's gracious acceptance of her death, confessing, "I'm not like her. I am fighting the idea." And yet, he came at the very last to the point where he could say, "Ready," even though it wasn't his idea.

Charlie came into the world a recipient of a rich heritage of family and faith. He leaves the world with a rich legacy: his family and faith, the fruit of which will follow.

329

A FINAL WORD FROM CHARLIE

If in some mystical way Charlie could have attended his own funeral service, the eloquent words of Miriam Rockness would have caused him to shift uncomfortably in his pew, as he never sought the praise of man. But later in life, when the fruit of his vision began to lift the poor man out of his miry clay and the rich man out of his empty day, the praise of man began to seek out Charlie.

Often we are in the presence of greatness and fail to recognize it. One Sunday afternoon, Charlie and I were sitting on the front porch of the Martha House. It was a few months before Charlie started using a portable oxygen tank. He was looking to his right, gazing up toward a mountain range, and said, "Jimmy, I want you to go with me to climb *The Mountain of Those Who Have Gone Before.*" It was Charlie's original name for *Ambassador Mountain* that has now been climbed by thousands of visitors to Canchias, but was just another part of the backdrop of mountains that day.

The shelter on top of what came to be known as Ambassador Mountain marks the spot where Charlie was buried. It overlooks the village of Canchias, causing Miguel to remark, "Charlie is still our Overseer."

330

Charlie, scouting for a burial place

Charlie asked me to bring my camera, but he never gave the reason for the camera or the climb. The mountain was about a 15 minute walk from the Martha House. It was covered with pines trees, undergrowth, weeds and rocks. As Charlie began to climb, his breathing became heavy. He never made it to the top. I was confused about the reason for the climb, but knew Charlie well enough to know that another possible vision just might be brewing in his mind. Charlie would always mull over his visions before sharing them. He didn't tell me he was scouting for a burial spot for himself.

I remember taking pictures of pine trees and sagebrush on this dismal mountain. As we paused in the middle of the climb, I was fascinated by a strange-looking insect on the bark of a pine tree that resembled a praying mantis, bright as snow beneath a glaring sun. I exclaimed, "Charlie, come and look at this weird insect." Charlie came and looked at the bug, and then turned and looked once again up at the top of the mountain, deep in thought.

After Charlie died, I came across the pictures I took with him on that day. I was taking pictures of a bug while he was scaling the heights of a mountain in search of a resting place for his body as a memorial for His Lord. I know I was unaware of Charlie's purpose on the mountain, but life is swiftly passing by, and so many people are looking down at bugs when, like Charlie, they need to be gazing upward at eternal things.

Those were some of my final days with Charlie, and I learned a valuable lesson from them. I learned that all finality has a measure of eternity in it.

A few weeks before Charlie died, he wrote some final words to all who would heed them. They are prophetic, seeming even to predict the tragic falling of the Twin Towers on September 11, 2001. These words are a warning and a clarion call to heed the teachings of Charlie's friend "The Word."

∞ ∞ ∞

There is one final message I want to leave with you. It is our Lord's final command to us, His followers, to go into all the world and make disciples. That is our commission–our Great Commission.

The church has neglected this command. Like the early believers in Jerusalem, we have become content to stay at home. It took persecution to scatter them throughout the world with the gospel. I hope it will not take the same kind of persecution to get us out of the pews and into the lives of the poor, the lame, the blind, and the lost.

Follow the money trail. If a congregation spends more on herself than on making disciples, then something is wrong. Priorities must be reexamined and set straight.

But it's not just money, it's our hearts the Lord wants–broken hearts for a world that has turned its back on God, the Word that was before the beginning.

However, before you can go out into the world, you must first know the commands of Jesus and commit your life to putting them into practice. This message is to the church: stop "preaching" and start teaching the Word of God– in particular, Jesus' commands. Do this in your homes with your children, and at church, starting with the youngest all the way up to the oldest member of the Body. Do it from the pulpit. When these teachings become the center of your lives, you will find peace and joy. Let nothing hinder you from doing this.

Many have asked what will happen to Heart to Honduras when I am no longer present to lead it. My hope and prayer is that this Kingdom work with its implications for the church and mission will be taken throughout the world and on to completion. Don't let up! Redouble your efforts! Give sacrificially! This is very important for the advancement of God's Kingdom on earth.

This mission is even more important for the church in the developed world than for the church in Honduras. The church in the United States has incorporated so much of the world that she has become blind and unattractive to those wanting true commitment to something that can give their lives significance and purpose. The church is not providing what should be part of her very nature. Moreover, she is so dependent on the world that when the "towers fall," when

Wall Street crumbles and the shelves of the grocery stores are empty, she will be in danger of dying along with the rest of the world.

The rapid technological changes that have occurred in the developed world during this century have induced us to trade a way of life that is sustainable for one that is dependent. High-speed transportation, television, computers and other dramatic technological and social changes have reoriented our way of thinking and living so that we have become dependent on agribusiness for food, technologically based urban businesses for employment, and an impersonal way of life that results in the disintegration of family and loss of community. This change in lifestyle has far-reaching implications for the future of our families, communities and cities. Any breakdown in the complex systems that support this way of life could be disastrous. We are no longer able to adapt to a more sustainable way of life that would increase our ability to survive should change come.

The message to the church today is: stop building monuments and platforms for "star" preachers. Cut your dependence on the world. Teach your children about a loving God who cares for them. The signs of the time abound. It is imperative that we read the signs and respond in life-giving, life-sustaining ways.

A model is developing in Canchias, Honduras. Learn from it. Learn from what is being done to help the poorest of the poor out of their poverty and into a way of life that is free from fear and unnecessary suffering. Learn how this is being done at basic, fundamental levels, then replicate it in the States.

But above all, as is being done in Honduras, make disciples of Jesus, teaching them to put into practice all that He commanded us. Then send them out into the world to preach the message of repentance and forgiveness.

Would that I could be there with you to help. But in a way, I am with you, and in you, because I am in Christ Jesus, and He is with you, and in you. He is your strength, your source of every good thing. Follow Him!

Charlie

EPILOGUE

After Charlie was welcomed home on October 20, 1997 by "The Word," as he so fondly referred to his Lord, the ministry continued to move forward. Heart to Honduras was a well-oiled machine with her vital parts in place.

There was an immediate sadness among the people in the Yure River basin, a sensing of a vacuum, a fear that life would leave the organization as it had left their beloved Charlie. But just as H.E.A.R.T. had continued its mission under new leadership when Charlie moved on, so would the ministry in Honduras. If Heart to Honduras was a train moving rapidly down the tracks, all that was needed was a new "conductor" to harness the momentum of this powerful vision.

The leadership of the ministry had been given ample warning that new personnel would be needed. Charlie had recommended the implementation of a Leadership Team composed of Dave and Candy Pischel, Monty and Kelly Harrington, and Rick Dike to continue the holistic vision so dear to Charlie's heart. Dave would be the chairman of this leadership team, and he would work closely with Miguel Pinell in Honduras.

In terms of structure, logistics, staff leadership, facilitating North American teams, and continuing ministries and programs, Miguel and his committed team in Honduras rarely missed a beat. Jerry Grubbs continued sharing his set of administrative and managerial skills as chairman of the board, meaning support for the stateside staff was not a problem.

Charlie was an extraordinary person, a powerful visionary, a good leader and a fairly good manager. He was a gentle and kind leader, and this is why staff members were loyal to him. A woman who had been to Honduras under his leadership remarked, "Charlie Smith was the most gentle person I have ever met." His presence, kindness and visionary skills were sorely missed, but as leadership specialist Andrew Ward states, in evolving organizations, you have the Creator, the Accelerator and the Sustainer.

The role of the Creator is to envision and birth the organization from scratch. He or she breathes life into the organization, sets the heroic mission, instills a sense of urgency and maintains focus. The Accelerator translates the heroic mission set by the Creator into systems and routines to enable the organization to grow without bursting at the seams. The Sustainer leads the ministry into a steadier state of maturity.[49] Charlie was the Creator of the vision, and now it was time for the Accelerator and Sustainer.

---

[49] Andrew Ward, *The Leadership Lifecycle: Matching Leaders to Evolving Organizations*

The new organizational framework worked well for a while. Dave and his team worked diligently to follow Charlie's passion and dream, but soon, relational fissures began to seep into the team approach, and Miguel requested a new leadership arrangement. During 1998, the board conducted an intensive search for a new leader. They did not have to look far. An excellent prospect with a passion for missions was sitting right in front of them on the board. His name was Gordon Garrett.

At the 1998 fall board meeting, Gordon was unanimously chosen to be the president of Heart to Honduras. Under Gordon's leadership, the ministry expanded even beyond the plans Charlie had left behind. With the building finished, the School of Discipleship began training young people for ministry, and as of this printing has more than 200 graduates of its discipleship program. By 2013, a Sister Church program had paired 43 North American churches with Honduran congregations. Calling themselves *Brazos Abiertos Para Amar y Restaurar* (Open Arms to Love and Restore), the pastors' fellowship of the 50 Honduran congregations in the association has been empowered to train the pastors and manage the local congregations.

North American teams, which now number well over 50 each year (68 in 2012), have built scores of homes for widows, single mothers, and other families in need. Gordon appointed a stateside health care coordinator, and medical team visits number nearly a dozen annually. Land has been purchased on a beautiful lake near Santa Elena and a youth camp has been located there that ministers to hundreds of local young people each year, in addition to hosting summer youth campers from North America. Because of its location near a main highway, the camp is also the location to which the offices are being moved from their long-time site in San Isidro.

The staff in Honduras numbers around 30, and the full-time staff in the United States is six, with two more serving part-time. Mindful of the aging of original North American staff members, Gordon dedicated himself to seeking out young people and fanning into flame their spark of interest in missions. Some of these have lowered the average age of the staff serving in the stateside office, others are serving in Honduras. Under his tenure, the board has added new members, some of them international, and he has released the staff in Honduras to take more responsibility for their areas of the ministry.

Under Charlie's tenure, the bookkeeper and graphic artist worked out of the Florida office. The other two staff members, Rick Dike and I, worked out of our homes in Ohio and Alabama respectively. When Gordon became president, he was living in Denver, which put the staff at great distances from each other. The increasing number of teams began to put a huge strain on the feasibility of this arrangement, and Gordon began to look for a solution.

335

Three years into his term, Gordon initiated the relocation of the stateside offices from Florida. He found an opportunity to obtain office space on the former Ohio Soldiers and Sailors Orphanage property in Xenia, Ohio, which was in the process of becoming a ministries campus. This Midwest site was more centrally located for the majority of the ministry's supporting churches, and it provided much more space than the cramped quarters in Florida.

In 2002, the Garretts and the Ushers moved to Ohio. The new office was within reasonable driving distance for Rick, and a bookkeeper from the area, Pam Cook, was found to replace Candy when the Pischels elected not to move. Dave continued to serve as graphic artist for several years, designing the newsletters from his Florida home.

In addition to the ongoing growth of Heart to Honduras, the seeds Charlie planted through H.E.A.R.T. continue to bear fruit. Perhaps one of the greatest accomplishments of Charlie's life was the planting of seeds in the lives of young people who now have gone all over the world to create holistic ministries. Three original H.E.A.R.T. students today are examples:

Steve Coder is now president of Hand to the Plow, with a ministry focusing primarily on Haiti. Steve said Charlie's class in anthropology changed his life from wanting to climb the corporate ladder to being a missionary.

Phil Murphy, now serving as president of the H.E.A.R.T. program after a career as a missionary in Haiti, recalled Charlie's impact on his life:

> Charlie lives on through [my wife] Lonnie, [our children] Michelle and David, and myself. I think Charlie comes to my mind almost every day. Sometimes his wisdom and words spur me on, and other times his antics and style bring a smile to my face. Lonnie and I think about him and Karen all the time; and we have told thousands of people about them. We feel blessed to have had Jesus models like Charlie and Karen to pattern our lives after. We love and miss them so much.

Mark Shaner is student pastor and missions pastor at Eastside Church of God in Anderson, Indiana, and has led more than 65 mission teams overseas. He was instrumental in opening the door for the Church of God to birth a church in Chelyabinsk, Russia. He wrote of the H.E.A.R.T. seed Charlie planted at Warner Southern University and in his own life:

> Today over 900 missionaries have been trained and equipped out of H.E.A.R.T. and sent to 90 different countries in the world because of one man who had a dream. Charlie was a man of passion. He was a dreamer, a visionary. He could

see what others could never see. Charlie was used by God to define my life. I never will forget Charlie saying, "Mark, you may never bring revival to America, but you may raise the kids that do." It was his way of coaching me to make my family a very high priority. Now [that I have] four incredible kids who love Jesus and His Church, and have a heart for missions, I say thanks! No words could ever express the debt I owe this man and his family.

One huge change that occurred since Charlie's heavenly graduation was the resignation of Miguel Pinell in 2010. In the beginning, Charlie was the visionary and Miguel was the implementer of the vision. It was an incredible partnership that God used to bring about this vision. Since resigning as national director, Miguel and his wife Nilsa have started a new ministry called *Wings of Mercy*, which seeks to continue many of Charlie's ministry concepts in the country of Honduras.

One can hardly imagine how the loss of two parents in the prime of their lives will affect the children. When Charlie passed away, his daughters Felicia and Anne-Marie began to question many things in their lives regarding vocation, relationships, family, friendships, theological beliefs and values, and each has responded to the challenge in her own unique way. Felicia and her husband Lyle Graybeal continue to live in the Denver area, where she serves as the pastor of an Episcopal church.

Anne-Marie relocated to Indianapolis and owns her own company, to which she attached her childhood nickname, calling it *Annie O's Events*. She is an event planner, which allows her to carry out her parents' love of parties that celebrate life and bring people together around food. Anne-Marie and her husband, Marty Dezelan, have adopted a teenager whom they met as a fourth grader. At that young age, he was concerned that changing schools due to family circumstances was going to be detrimental to his desire to go to college. They admired his determination to do well in his education, and are helping him prepare for that goal.

The School of Discipleship assembly and dining hall in 2010.
This centerpiece of Charlie's vision now brings students from
all over Central America and serves as a gathering place
for unity services and discipleship training events
for area churches and for mission teams.

In the spring of 1997, when Charlie's physical condition began to deteriorate rapidly, many people wondered if Heart to Honduras would survive without his leadership. Those at H.E.A.R.T. had asked the same question in 1983 when Charlie tendered his resignation. But there were two factors that concerned people failed to realize.

First of all, H.E.A.R.T. and Heart to Honduras were not Charlie's visions. He would have been the first to say that they came from God. Secondly, because they came from God, Charlie's visions had staying power. They were well thought out with the basic needs of man in mind. And because of these two factors, both H.E.A.R.T. and Heart to Honduras are presently on track to accomplish two of Charlie's greatest desires: to feed the poor and to make disciples.

The Winter 2012 Heart to Honduras newsletter announced their newly formed partnership with H.E.A.R.T., bringing full circle these two products of Charlie's heart. A team of students from the Hunger Education And Resource Training institute went to Honduras to "learn first-hand the ups and downs of cross-cultural ministry," meeting with village leaders and with HTH leadership. The newsletter said, "This is the first step in a mutually beneficial relationship as we endeavor to serve the needy together." How pleased Charlie must be with this cooperative venture!

That first student team was led by Phil Murphy, a member of Charlie's first H.E.A.R.T. team in Florida. After a moving experience as Phil finally had the opportunity to visit Charlie's grave to mourn his passing and celebrate his impact, one of the students on the team wrote a poem about Charlie's "footprint left in silence." Her words effectively summed up the goal I had when I set out to write this book–that others would be encouraged to follow their call because they have read how Charlie followed God's call on his life.

Some would say it is too bad Charlie did not see the dedication of the school built by Bill DeJong's team in Canchias, or the first graduating class of students from the School of Discipleship. But he did see them both. He saw the school when Bill and the 11 men, none of whom had ever experienced a setting like this, sat in a circle on the Martha House porch in April 1997 listening to Charlie's vision and his encouragement to cast their own vision on the dirt road just across from Simeon's house down in the village. And he saw the Discipleship School as he watched the Assembly Hall building take shape from his chair on the Martha House porch and envisioned all the people who would gather there to eat and fellowship and learn.

He saw when no one else could see, and now every visitor to that place can see the fruition of the vision that continues to expand under those who have taken over the leadership, and those who have been encouraged to follow their own vision.

First group of students who studied at the
School of Discipleship in 1999 and 2000.

Why Charlie Smith's life was cut short, we will never know this side of eternity. But one thing we do know is that Charlie still lives on through thousands of people. His army of volunteers moved from being a platoon to a company to a squadron to a regiment, as more than 7,000 people have made visits to Honduras. In each of them, the vision lives on.

He lives in the hearts of his daughters. He lives in the seeds he planted. He lives in the visions he cast. He lives in students he taught. He lives in the poor he loved. He lives in the words he wrote. And the words etched on his graveside plaque affirm this living presence, as spoken by The Word he loved so much: "Because I live, you shall live also."

Silent Footprints

I never met or thought of you,
I never saw or spoke with you,
I never prayed or cared for you,
I never helped or worried about you.

Yet somehow through your life gone by,
You touched my own and made my soul sigh
As I watched your friends tell you goodbye
And saw them so openly cry.

You taught me to love unconditionally,
And to live this life for Christ freely.
You taught me the importance of my legacy,
For others who will follow me.

So thank you for your faithful witness,
Thank you for your bold kindness,
Thank you for your constant perseverance,
Thank you for your footprint left in silence.

~Susanna Fahner, 2012 H.E.A.R.T.

Charlie Smith
Ambassador who Served the Savior
July 26, 1938 ~ October 20, 1997
Son of Myrtle and Frellsen
Husband of Karen Stone Smith
Father of Felicia and Anne-Marie
He was a disciple of Jesus
He loved the poor
He loved the church
He loved his family
"I am the resurrection and the life.
He who believes in me will live, even though
he dies; and whoever lives and believes in me will never die."
Do you believe this?
* Jesus *

**The plaque on Charlie's grave features a burro and an
inscription in English and Spanish**

MINISTRY INFORMATION

To learn more about current information on programs and ministry, visit:

Heart to Honduras – www.hth.org

H.E.A.R.T. – www.heartvillage.org

Prayer Plan Missions – www.ppmissions.org

Proceeds from the sale of this book will be divided among Heart to Honduras, H.E.A.R.T., and Prayer Plan Missions. The latter is a ministry formed by the author in 2010 to work in the Comayagua Department of Honduras, with its center in the village of Chagüitillos.

Contact author Jim Usher at **jeusher@yahoo.com.**

ACKNOWLEDGEMENTS

Biographies, even those written by close friends, of necessity entail a lot of research. Because Charlie was a writer, I had access to far more material than could be included in this book, but I still needed information that only family members and colleagues from his various endeavors could provide for me. It is impossible to list everyone here, but to each person who told me their Charlie stories or shared a photograph or provided a date, I am grateful.

As the years of work on this book multiplied, I often found myself experiencing a bit of frustration. Then a little beep on my iPhone would signal the arrival of an email from Charlie's youngest sister, Lorna. She would be sending me some sought-after information with an added note of encouragement to stay the course. More than once, she and her husband Jon opened their home to me as they shared family lore and photographs. Without the support of this couple in resources and wisdom, Charlie's visions probably would never have materialized, and thus there would have been no biography. Thanks, Lorna and Jon, from me, and from Charlie, too.

High on the list of those to whom I'm indebted would be Charlie's two amazing daughters, Felicia and Anne-Marie. Without the love letters and Charlie's 15-page personal diary that Felicia had, I would have never been able to write the *Summer of Love* and *Chantilly Lace* chapters. Felicia, I will always remember the night we sat on your living room floor with hundreds of FAXes, photos, and papers, searching for friends, folks, figures and faces.

Charlie's younger daughter, Anne-Marie, was as honest as Abe Lincoln and as brutal as a demanding professor when it came to editing this book about her father. Her suggestions helped me eliminate, in her words, the "cheesy" stuff. Anne-Marie, I felt you had read the draft with a bucket of red ink in one hand and a three inch brush in the other, but all that you recommended made the book more readable. And I am grateful for the hours you spent combing through the family slides which enhance this tribute to your father. Your input had a tremendous impact on the final product.

Charlie's twin sister Marie and younger brother Alvin also made significant contributions. Marie had the best knowledge of Charlie's growing-up years. Marie, you were so kind to host me, feed me, and send your husband Dave with me to copy some of your prized family photos. Alvin, Hurricane Katrina interrupted our first planned visit, but you were kind to let me stay in your home when things settled down, and the entire family joins me in our debt to you for your documentation of Charlie's last days.

344

Charlie's paternal aunt, Florine Martin, shared her five-page historical account of the Smith and Carver families, which is rich in anecdotes, special dates and important events that made that part of this book a delight to write. Thank you, Florine, for the bed, the good southern cooking and your gracious hospitality when I came to Ruston, Louisiana to interview Charlie's childhood friends.

Dr. Juanita Leonard served as chairman of my dissertation committee and guided me through my 2009 dissertation, titled *Biography as Mission: The Life of Charlie Smith: Founder and Visionary of Heart to Honduras.* Dr. Leonard, you were such an encouragement to me in the research project that became the seed for this book. Words cannot express what your assurance meant to me. I want to thank Dr. Barry Callen and Dr. Jerry Grubbs for serving on the committee as well. You were very busy men who took time to help this struggling doctoral student.

Three people in Lake Wales, Florida extended hospitality during my visits to interview Charlie's professional colleagues at Warner Southern. Max and Jayne Linton let me stay in their guest house for several days. I had the run of their kitchen and enjoyed the wonderful meal Max cooked especially for me. Dr. Bill Rigel let me stay in the college guest house on a subsequent trip.

Midway through the writing, my brother Tommy and his wife Stefanie allowed Carol Lynne and me to stay at their home, where we had access to their back patio on the 10th fairway of a PGA championship golf course, and to their secret little sand bar on the Chattahoochee River. What a wonderful, quiet week we spent there working on the book. As the project was drawing to a close, my wife and I gratefully used a retirement gift from a ministry friend. Patty Ernst had given us three days at a mountain resort in Tennessee, and we were blessed to be able to review a nearly final copy of the book in a relaxed setting.

The final format of this book was shaped in large measure by three young professionals. Editors Heidi Newman and Ria Megnin were able to see the manuscript with the unprejudiced eyes of relative strangers to Charlie's story. Heidi and Ria, your insights were invaluable. Graphic artist Hanna Minges' skill at turning photos of varying quality, even those we only had on newsprint, into usable digital versions made it possible to illustrate his story in a way that I feel would please this man who loved taking pictures. And, Hanna, your translation of our various brainstorms for titles and photos created a cover beyond my dreams.

And lastly, I am indebted beyond superlatives to describe what my wife Carol Lynne has invested in time, wise suggestions, needed encouragement and support in this six-year project. She put aside her own book editing project to work on mine. This was a great sacrifice, because the project is a collection of letters her parents wrote while courting during World War II, and some of her parents' family and friends have since died and will never share in this memory.

345

Carol Lynne, you are the best friend I have ever had. I am grateful for your support.

In addition to those of you who read the drafts and made suggestions, there are about 40 other people who contributed photos, granted interviews, and gave encouragement. I would love to publicly thank you, but space limits my doing so. You know who you are, and I hope you found many of your memories preserved in this book. You were an important part of Charlie's life, and I thank you so much for sharing your anecdotes with me. They enriched this tale of an amazing man who strove his whole life to follow God's call. We can all thank God for his example and be challenged to do the same.

JIM USHER